EFFICACIOUS LOVE

Its Meaning and Function in the Theology of Juan Luis Segundo

Theresa Lowe Ching, R.S.M.

UNIVERSITY
PRESS OF
AMERICA

Lanham • New York • London

Copyright © 1989 by

University Press of America,® Inc.

4720 Boston Way
Lanham, MD 20706

3 Henrietta Street
London WC2E 8LU England

Printed in the United States of America

British Cataloging in Publication Information Available

Library of Congress Cataloging-in-Publication Data

Ching, Theresa Lowe, 1934–
Efficacious love : its meaning and function in the theology of
Juan Luis Segundo / Theresa Lowe Ching.
p.   cm.
Originally presented as the author's thesis (doctoral—University of
St. Michael's College)
Includes bibliographical references.
1. Liberation theology—History of doctrines—20th century.   2. Love—
Religious aspects—Christianity—History of doctrines—20th century.
3. Catholic Church—Doctrines—History—20th century.   4. Segundo,
Juan Luis.   I. Title.
BT83.57C465   1989   230'.2'092—dc20   89–36838 CIP

ISBN 0–8191–7561–7 (alk. paper)

In memory of my mother and father

Acknowledgments

This book was originally written as a doctoral thesis which was presented to the Faculty of the University of St. Michael's College, Toronto, Canada. The thesis was directed by Professor Roger Haight, S.J. I am deeply grateful to him for his untiring guidance and encouragement throughout the course of my doctoral studies. I also wish to thank in particular Professor Walter Principe, C.S.B. and other members of the Faculty, the students and librarians of St. Michael's College and the Toronto School of Theology who have given me significant help and support at various times. For assistance in the technical preparation of the manuscript, I extend sincere appreciation to the Very Reverend Paul Zilonka, C.P., Reverend Kenneth Mock Yen, Gladstone and Maisie Chang, and Matsam Ltd. of Kingston, Jamaica, West Indies. Finally, I would like to express my gratitude to my religious community, the Sisters of Mercy of Jamaica, Province of Cincinnati, to the Sisters of St. Joseph of Toronto and to my family and friends. Without their support and encouragement this book would not have been possible.

Table of Contents

Foreword

Juan Luis Segundo is well known in the world of Christian theology. Few theologians have not read some portion of his work. For three decades his prolific writings have touched on all the major aspects of Christian thought. Working in Montevideo, Uruguay, he is usually regarded as a liberation theologian, for he participated in the genesis of that movement in Latin America in the early 1960s. But no label can quite contain his thinking and he often hesitates to accept the designation.

Most readers of Segundo would agree that his thought is both profound and complex. He uses no single method to develop a theme. Sometimes he comments in a highly interpretive way on classic texts to recreate their meaning for a new context. At other times he uses basic concepts and distinctions to build a constructive argument. His writing is meditative when he subjects an idea to an extended phenomenological analysis. He is always in dialogue with some other thinker or responding to a concrete problem. Segundo is eclectic; he borrows ideas from a whole range of figures often discordant among themselves but leaves behind their systems to integrate the ideas into his own framework for his own ends. He also draws upon categories from a host of widely diverse disciplines such as physics, sociology, the sociology of knowledge, evolution theory, linguistics, literature, and philosophy. He picks up fundamental ideas and distinctions and uses them analogously to structure his theological understanding. A dialectical thread runs through Segundo's thinking in the sense that he revels in reversals. Like Jesus' parables Segundo turns many of the accepted conclusions of theology on their head. Christianity is universally relevant, but everyone is not called to be a Christian; Jesus is God means God is Jesus; yes, grace is synergistic; yes, human beings do contruct the kingdom of God.

Segundo's interpretation of Christianity depicts it as an active and creative, one might even say aggressive, force in the world. The idea of a passive Christianity is for him a contradiction of terms: God's salvific grace frees freedom for construction of the world. The church has a God-given role in the history of the human race. Its mission is to faithfully preserve, place before society, and implement God's values within the human community. But this requires a creative reinterpretation of the Christian message in each age, and it will go against the grain of both society and the church itself. For the church cannot do this by mere speech. The church should represent the vanguard of humanity always holding before the eyes of nations the ideals which God wills human beings to create and which will constitute the final reality of the end-time.

In his latest writing in christology Segundo has interpreted the meaning of Jesus and Paul's understanding of Jesus by applying what he calls a hermeneutical key to New Testament writings. A key consists of a theme, a subject matter, or distinct topic that most adquately holds together that which is to be interpreted. Thus the selection of the right key unlocks and opens up a coherence of meaning in a set of wide ranging data or a complex text. A political key more than any other shows the deep consistency in the life, teaching, and mission of Jesus. Paul himself in his Letter to the Romans reinterprets Jesus in an anthropological key, so that Segndo's interpretation of Paul generates an anthropology of salvation.

Theresa Lowe Ching has discovered a hermeneutical key for understanding the whole complex theology of Juan Luis Segundo. The key is contained in the phrase "efficacious love". The idea of efficacious love does not remove the complexity of Segundo's theology or gloss over its meditative depth. Rather Professor Lowe Ching uses it to reach into that complexity, go behind it, and then underneath it to uncover a unifying theme. She then raises it to the surface, explains it, and allows it to illumine the diverse elements of Segundo's thought so that they appear as parts of an integral whole. Her book postulates and then demonstates that efficacious love is one of the principles that holds the whole work of Segundo together in a dynamic unity.

With this book Professor Lowe Ching has provided a concise, accurate introduction to the theology of Juan Luis Segundo. It is comprehensive in its brevity. After presenting Segundo in terms of the historical development of his work, she explains the main influences on his thought, the principal categories and distinctions that distinguish his language, and the elements of method that structures the genesis of his theology. She draws from the whole corpus of his writing and by comparative analysis is able to shed light on many of Segundo's basic distinctions that befuddle many. No one has done a better job of clarifying the fundamental categories that recur again and again in Segundo's thinking.

Beyond re-presenting Segundo's theology, Lowe Ching has also provided a coherent and plausible interpretation of it. In each successive chapter she builds the argument that the theme of efficacious love holds the various dimensions of Segundo's theology together. Its commanding influence is reflected in his appropriation of his sources and in the structure of his method. Finally, the very core of Christian salvation becomes illumined on the personal and social-historical levels in the light of efficacious love: salvation consists in human co-operation with God's impulse toward creative love in history whose effects will in the end constitute ultimate reality.

Not only students of liberation theology and readers of Juan Luis Segundo will be grateful for this book. The work of Segundo transcends Latin America and relates to the essence of Christianity in a universal way. All those interested in the meaning of Christianity itself will find Professor Lowe Ching's unlocking of the thought of Segundo both challenging and edifying. Segundo's theology has an inner logic that makes sense, and Theresa Lowe Ching explains why.

Roger Haight, S.J.
Manila
January 15, 1989

Introduction

Juan Luis Segundo is one of the most formidable representatives of the Latin American liberation theological movement. Not only is he a most prolific writer,[1] but his works also evidence a firm grasp of the major theological issues that confront Christianity in Latin America.[2] Like his Latin American colleagues, Segundo is searching for a reinterpretation of the Christian message that will more adequately respond to the Latin American situation of massive poverty and oppression.[3] A thorough investigation of Segundo's theology can thus yield important insights not only for a deeper understanding of the Latin American liberation theological movement in general, but also for the development of contemporary theology as a whole. The reality of suffering, oppression and injustice pervades the entire world. Theology must confront this problem in order to be relevant to the present.

Segundo's theology is clearly influenced by the Enlightenment critique of religion.[4] This is true of liberation theology in general which Matthew Lamb has described as the "religious correlate" of the Marxist inspired critical theory of the Frankfurt School.[5] The latter arose in sympathy with the "victims of history" which resulted from the failure of "pure reason" to create a more human society. It, therefore, aims to retrieve the positive elements of the Enlightenment through the negation of its negative elements. In a similar vein, liberation theology is thus suspicious of "pure religion" which is unaware of its concrete historical implications and relegates salvation to the life beyond. Its goal is to discover the genuine aspects of the Christian faith as manifested in action that is both transforming and liberating.

In his effort to retrieve an understanding of Christianity that is more true to its nature as a historical revelation, Segundo probes beneath the inherited and a-historical concept of Christianity as a "religion".[6] In order to do this, he employs a theological method described by him as the *hermeneutic circle*.[7] His method stresses the need for a suspicious attitude towards the ideological deformation of reality and of theology itself in particular. His hermeneutic circle, therefore, interweaves this twofold suspicion with two basic "preconditions", namely, significant questions that demand a change of attitudes towards the most essential aspects of human life in society, and reinterpretation of scripture in response to these questions.[8] The model of theology that he thus develops is centered on *praxis,* historical action with social and ethical implications.[9]

What this model entails for the major Latin American theologians, including Segundo, is lucidly explained by Matthew Lamb who names it the "critical praxis correlation model."[10] The method interprets the Christian message as an indissoluble unity of theory and praxis, more fundamentally

1

mediated through praxis than through theory. It rejects an identification of Christianity with either the "sacred" or the "secular" sphere and opts for the distinction in unity of these two aspects of reality. Thus, according to this model, an interpretation of the Christian message, a theory that is truly critical, is at the same time a praxis that is genuinely liberative and transforming of reality. Unlike the "critical theoretic model" which places the emphasis on theory and regards praxis as the goal of theory, this model, with its stress on praxis, further claims that "praxis itself as action or performance grounds the activity itself of theory: *Praxis in not only the goal but also the foundation of theory.*"[11] This model, therefore, maintains that the question of "truth is directly related to human performance, both individually and collectively considered."[12] Conversion of consciousness and change of social structures are thus concomitant. Both are required by the challenge of the Christian tradition understood as concretely embodied in a praxis that is dynamic and on-going.[13]

In Segundo's theology, the notion of *efficacious love* is equivalent to that of historical praxis. It specifies what is perhaps his most basic concern, namely, human salvation in history through the exercise of freedom. It is the concrete expression of that freedom. Just as is generally the case in liberation theology, Segundo's view of efficacious love throws the whole emphasis of his theology on historical praxis, that praxis which releases the transforming potential of the Christian message. The notion of efficacious love, therefore, assumes a key position and becomes, as it were, a *centering concern*[14] or unifying principle in Segundo's theology. Thus it warrants further study. This book will attempt an investigation of the meaning and function of this most central concept, the notion of efficacious love in the theology of Juan Luis Segundo.

To date, the theological works on Juan Luis Segundo have dealt with the question of efficacious love more or less as an important aspect of his theology but not with the thematic focus that I intend to pursue in this book. Hennelly's *Theologies in Conflict*[15] is a careful exposition of the methodology and basic elements of the theology of Juan Luis Segundo. Through the analysis of key texts, he endeavours to present Segundo's thought from within the development of the Latin American liberation theological movement and as the open process it purports to be. Hennelly thus refrains from systematizing Segundo's thought and aims at promoting dialogue between Latin American theologians and their North American colleagues. His ultimate goal is to contribute towards the eventual formulation of a North American theology of liberation that would retrieve the most basic insight of the American vision. He, therefore, highlights the links between Segundo's thought and the contemporary theological issues that have special significance in the North American context. Hennelly identifies a challenge from Latin American theologians to the entire theological enterprise. The challenge, comparable to the dymythologization project of Bultmann, in his view, is that of the deideologization of Western theology. He predicts a similar impact on the theological world.

Of the doctoral dissertations written on Segundo's works, perhaps the most faithful reflection of his theology, taken on its own terms, is Gerald Persha's

"Juan Luis Segundo: A Study Concerning the Relationship Between the Particularity of the Church and the Universality of Her Mission".[16] His intention is to demonstrate the inner coherence of Segundo's thought in terms of its historial development. His method is a chronological exposition of key texts ordered around his chosen theme. Concurring with Roger Haight's claim in his review of Segundo's *The Liberation of Theology*,[17] Persha identifies the main concern of Segundo to be the freedom of the human person in history.[18] He emphasizes the existentialist influence of Nicolas Berdyaev as the most dominant in the development of Segundo's thought. Of special significance for this book is his criticism of Segundo's stress on love's search for efficacy in history to the point of neglecting the power of love that can also be present in suffering caused by confrontation with sinful structures.

Anthony Tambasco's dissertation, "The Contribution of Juan Luis Segundo to the Hermeneutical Question of the Relationship of the Bible to Christian Ethics",[19] is more interpretative and attempts to examine Segundo's method of doing ethics through the use of scripture. He locates and evaluates Segundo's position within the framework of four contemporary models of ethical method. Assessing Segundo's own use of his hermeneutic circle, Tambasco concludes that Marxist analysis is the guiding principle of Segundo's use of scripture for doing ethics according to the liberal model of Walter Rauschenbusch.[20]

Stanley David Slade, in his dissertation, "The Theological Method of Juan Luis Segundo",[21] uses as a frame of reference David Kelsey's adaptation of Toulmin's proposal for evaluating "informal arguments" in terms of "data", "warrant" and "backing". With this he focusses on Segundo's use of scripture specifically as related to the latter's own employment and development of his hermeneutic circle in his five-volume work, *A Theology for Artisans of a New Humanity* [22] and the explication of his method in *The Liberation of Theology*.[23] He identifies and discusses as Segundo's main sources, the major Documents of Vatican II, Teilhard de Chardin's evolutionary theory, and Marxist "hermeneutic of suspicion" and "praxis". He concludes that Segundo grounds his synthesis on an "essentially Teilhardian base" and faults him for being too dependent on Teilhard's "pilot of history" and Marx's *"homo faber"*. Thus, he contends, Segundo overemphasizes human accomplishment in history contrary to biblical evidence. It is significant for the focus of this book that one of Slade's main difficulties with Segundo's theology centres on the ambiguity that he finds in the author's lack of defining the content of faith and specifically what he intends by efficacious love.

In line with Slade's critique mentioned above, Edward Schillebeeckx has drawn attention to the lack of clarity in the Latin American liberation theologians' identification of God's universal offer of salvation with the specific *option for the poor*, the concrete embodiment of their understanding of faith praxis.[24] According to Schillebeeckx, the future development of that liberation theology hinges on the clarification of that very point.[25]

This book will then be an attempt to clarify the meaning and function of the notion of efficacious love, the term most consistently used by Segundo to express the reality of faith praxis. As the review of literature given above indicates, there is still scope and need for this particular focus.

The structure of the book will be as follows: Chapter one will begin with a brief summary of the historical and cultural context of Juan Luis Segundo. This will be followed by an overview of his life and the major influences that have fashioned his thought. A review of his works will indicate that the major issues of liberation theology were already present in his works even prior to its official genesis at Medellín.[26] It will be of interest to note how Segundo's thought developed through the deepening of insights acquired in his early years.

Chapter two will endeavour to clarify the content that Segundo gives to the notion of efficacious love. Close attention will be paid to the scriptural foundation for his understanding of the notion. It will, then, be seen how the meaning of efficacious love acquires fuller dimensions, personal, social and cosmic under the three major influences that fashioned his thought. These influences are the existentialist philosophy of Nicolas Berdyaev, Marxist thought, and the evolutionary theory of Teilhard de Chardin.

In Chapter three the way in which the notion of efficacious love functions in Segundo's theological method will be examined. The place Segundo gives to efficacous love within the inner structure of his theological enterprise will be noted, as well as the extent to which the notion actually illumines and unifies the major categories of thought and sources that he employs.

Chapters four and five will attempt to explain ways in which the notion of efficacious love permeates Segundo's reinterpretation of the Christian message and, hence, the content of Christian doctrine. Chapter four will consider the subjective aspect of efficacious love. It will examine the relationship of efficacious love to personal salvation in reference to the existential realities of grace, freedom, faith, cultic worship, human action and Jesus Christ as personal Saviour.

The objective aspect of salvation will be explored in Chapter five. The effects of efficacious love in history will be examined in terms of the universal meaning given in Jesus Christ, its continued embodiment in the Church as the "sign" of the Christ mystery, and its presence as the determining factor in the humanization of the world.

The sixth and last chapter, will assess how well the notion of efficacious love is able to focus and integrate the major elements of Segundo's theology. I will advance some critical reflections and note the challenges that Segundo offers to the theological enterprise in general. Finally, questions that might prove fruitful for further exploration will be raised.

The overall hypothesis on which this book lies is as follows: The notion of efficacious love is the centering concern of Segundo's theology. It functions as the source from which his theological questions arise and the goal towards which his reinterpretation of the Christian message aims. It also serves to verify an authentic approach to God, involving not only personal conversion but concomitantly the transformation of reality.

In order to be as faithful as possible to the intent of Segundo, my approach will be mainly positive, allowing insights and conclusions to emerge from the analysis of key texts that are directly related to the specific theme of efficacious love. I will bear in mind the historical development of Segundo's thought although I do not intend a chronological presentation of his works.

A substantial number of books and articles written by Segundo are available only in the original Spanish. Direct references drawn from Spanish texts are my own translations. The footnotes will indicate my use of English translations. My attempt to employ inclusive language does not reflect Segundo's general tendency, especially in his earlier writings. I intend to consult the entire corpus of Segundo's works up to and including his Christology, *Jesus of Nazareth Yesterday and Today.* [27]

Notes

1. See accompanying bibliography, *Primary Sources.*

2. See esp. Juan Luis Segundo, *La cristiandad ¿Una Utopia? I: Los hechos* (Mimeográfica "Luz", 1964).

3. According to Roger Haight, this is the most urgent problem that poses the question of the meaning of historical existence today. See his *Alternative Vision: An Introduction to Liberation Theology* (New York/Mahwah: Paulist press, 1985), passim.

4. Cf. esp. Juan Luis Segundo, *Our Idea of God,* translated by John Drury (Maryknoll, New York: Orbis Books, 1973), p. 14.

5. Matthew Lamb, *Solidarity with Victims* (New York: Crossroad, 1982), pp. 28-60.

6. Cf. Juan Luis Segundo, *Etapes precristianas de la fe: Evolutión de la idea de Dios en el Antiguo Testamento* (Montevideo: Cursos de Complementación Cristiana, 1962; *Los Sacramentos hoy* (Buenos Aires: Carlos Lohlé, 1971). English translation, *The Sacraments Today* (Maryknoll, New York: Orbis Book, 1974).

7. Juan Luis Segundo, *The Liberation of Theology* (Maryknoll, New York: Orbis Books, 1976), pp. 7-38.

8. *Ibid.,* pp. 8-9.

9. Cf. Juan Luis Segundo, *The Humanist Christology of Paul,* trans. by John Drury (New York/London: Orbis Books/Sheed and Ward, 1986), p. 223, note 251; Gustavo Gutiérrez, *A Theology of Liberation: History, Politics and Salvation,* translated by Sister Caridad Inda and John Eagleson (Maryknoll, New York: Orbis Book, 1973), 3-19, esp. 6-11.

10. Matthew Lamb, "The Theory-Praxis Relationship in Contemporary Christian Theologies", *Catholic Theological Society of America Proceedings,* XXXI (1976), p. 154.

11. *Ibid.,* p. 171. Cf. esp. Jon Sobrino, "El conocimiento teológico en la teología Europea y Latinoamericana", *Estudios Centroamericanos,* V, no. 30 (1975), pp. 434-37; Raul Vidales, "Methodological Issues in Liberation

Theology", in *Frontiers of Theology in Latin America,* edited by Rosino Gibellini (Maryknoll, New York: Orbis Books, 1979), pp. 43-53.

12. *Ibid.,* p. 151. Cf. esp. Juan Luis Segundo, *The Sacraments Today,* pp. 53-59.

13. *Ibid.,* p. 177. Cf. esp. Juan Luis Segundo, *The Community Called Church,* translated by John Drury (Maryknoll, New York: Orbis Books, 1973).

14. This is the expression used by Roger Haight to describe a central methodological focus which, he maintains, is necessary for a theology to be "unified, coherent and relevant." See his *Alternative Vision,* p. 53.

15. Alfred Hennelly, *Theologies in Conflict: The Challenge of Juan Luis Segundo* (Maryknoll, New York: Orbis Books, 1979).

16. Gerald Justin Persha, "Juan Luis Segundo: A Study Concerning the Relationship Between the Particularity of the Church and the Universality of Her Mission", Ph.D. Dissertation, University of Ottawa, 1979.

17. Persha, "Juan Luis Segundo", p. 260. Cf. Roger Haight, "Book Reviews ... Juan Luis Segundo's *Liberation of Theology", Emmanuel,* LXXXIII, no. 12, pp. 605-10.

18. Judith Ann Merkle develops this insight by using "freedom" as the focussing metaphor of her dissertation, "The Fundamental Ethics of Juan Luis Segundo", Ph.D. Dissertation, University of St. Michael's College, Toronto, 1985. Using as a frame of reference the basic principles established by James Gustafson for determining a sound fundamental ethics, she argues that Segundo has consistently and coherently constructed such an ethics. The principles set down by Gustafson are: (a) the under-standing and interpretation of God; (b) the interpretation of the meaning of human experience; (c) the understanding of persons as moral agents and their actions; (d) the description of their manner of making moral decisions and judgments.

19. Anthony Joseph Tambasco, "The Contribution of Juan Luis Segundo to the Hermeneutical Question of the Relationship of the Bible to Christian Ethics", Ph.D. Dissertation, Union Theological Seminary in the City of New York, 1981. Published under the title, *The Bible for Ethics* (Washington D.C: University Press of America, 1981).

20. Cf. T. Howland Sanks, "Liberation Theology and the Social Gospel: Variations on a Theme", *Theological Studies,* XLI (December 1980), 668-82. From an analysis of the works of key representatives of the Latin American liberation theological movement, including Segundo, and those of Walter Rauschenbusch as the most significant representative of the Social Gospel movement, Sanks discovers several points of similarities and differences between the two movements.

21. Stanley David Slade, "The Theological Method of Juan Luis Segundo", Ph. D. Dissertation, Fuller Theological Seminary, 1979.

22. Juan Luis Segundo, *Theology for Artisans of a New Humanity,* 5 vols., translated by John Drury (Maryknoll, New York: Orbis Books, 1973 -74).

23. Juan Luis Segundo, *The Liberation of Theology,* translated by John Drury (Maryknoll, New York: Orbis Books, 1976).

24. Cf. Juan Luis Segundo, *The Historical Jesus of the Synoptics,* trans.

by John Drury (New York/Melbourne/London: Orbis Books/Dove Communications/Sheed and Ward, 1985), pp. 86-103; Gustavo Gutiérrez, "Revelación de anuncio de Dios en la história", in *La Fuerza histórica de los pobres: Selección de trabajos* (Lima, Peru: Centro de Estudios y Publicaciones, 1979), p. 19; Segundo Galilea, "Liberation Theology and the New Tasks Facing Christians", in *Frontiers of Theology in Latin America,* edited by R. Gibellini, translated by John Drury (Maryknoll, New York: Orbis Books, 1979), p. 178; Roberto Oliveros, *Liberación y teología: Génesis y crecimiento de una reflexión* (1966-1977) (Lima, Peru: Centro de Estudios y Publicaciones, 1977), pp. 214-16.

25. E. Schillebeeckx, "Liberation Theology Between Medellín and Puebla", *Theology Digest,* XXVIII (Spring 1980), p. 6.

26. The reference here is to the endorsement of the language and method of liberation theology by the Latin American Conference of Bishops which was held at Medellín, Columbia in 1968. Drawing mostly from the document *Gaudium et Spes,* the Conference sought to adapt the teachings of the Vatican Council II to the specific Latin American context.

27. Juan Luis Segundo, *El Hombre de hoy ante Jesus de Nazaret,* 3 vols. (Madrid: Cristiandad, 1982). English trans., *Jesus of Nazareth Yesterday and Today,* 5 vols., trans. by John Drury (New York: Orbis Books, 1985-88). Segundo has subsequently published another work, *Theology and the Church,* translated by John W. Diercksmeier (Minneapolis/Chicago/New York/London: The Seabury Press, 1985). It is a commentary on the *The Instruction on Certain Aspects of the Theology of Liberation*issued by the Sacred Congregation on Faith and Doctrine (Vatican City, 1984). An Excursus entitled "The Beginning of Faith: The History of a Small Idea" (pp. 73-85) will be referred to in this work.

Chapter One

Juan Luis Segundo:
His Context and His Works

The life and works of Juan Luis Segundo, as of any other person, cannot be adequately understood outside of the historical and cultural heritage which fashioned him. Hence, before proceeding to the main objective of this chapter which seeks to introduce the man through an overview of his life and works and to illustrate the way in which his thought developed over the years, it will be necessary to consider first the context within which he has lived and worked.

Geographically, the context to be considered here includes the entire region of Central and South America and those islands in the Caribbean which were, until recently, part of the external empire of Iberia. It consists of the twenty countries known as Latin America today. Segundo himself has chosen this wider context as the point of reference for his theological reflections. This is because he sees the destiny of the entire region as intertwined and, hence, requiring collaboration beyond narrow nationalistic borders. Yet, this is not to say that he is unconcerned about his own native country of Uruguay.[1] In relating to the region as a whole Segundo is emphasizing the specific perspective, that of the "periphery", which is common to all of the Latin American countries.

1. The Historical and Cultural Context

Latin America awakened to a consciousness of its own peculiar dignity and responsibility as a region of "independent" nations at the same time that it began to recognize its dependency status within the global socio-economic, political and cultural structure. Unequal distribution of wealth and power and cultural domination were identified as the root causes of the massive poverty and suffering that years of "development" had intensified rather that alleviated.[2] Thus a different perspective, one from the periphery began to challenge established theories[3] that created and maintained dominance at the "centres".[4]

The reality and implications of the dominant perspective can be amply demonstrated by even a cursory glance at the histories that have been written. A classic example is Hubert Herring's *History of Latin America*[5] which portrays in ironic eloquence the "unholy yoking of wealth and bitter poverty"[6] that typifies to a greater or less extent the twenty republics whose variety of natural

9

resources, peoples and individual histories defies an easy synthesis.[7]

With unimpassioned "objectivity", Herring recounts the familiar story of the Iberian conquest, colonization and domination that is the common heritage of Latin America.[8] Within the framework of significant influences at work in Europe and in America, he weaves together the facts of the heroic exploits of conquistadores;[9] the establishment of the *encomienda* and *repartimiento* system;[10] the appointment of *cabildos, audiencias* and viceroys;[11] the transfer of Iberian culture;[12] and the Church's granting of the *real patronato de las Indias* to the sovereignty of Spain.[13]

Detailed analyses of the above reveal not only the contribution but also the abuses and human costs. However, what is most significant here is Herring's evaluation. Of the former he writes:

> Spain gave all she had to the colonies: as a mother transmits life, Spain passed on governmental patterns, social and economic fashions and cultural gifts as well. Spanish America was favoured by being born in the golden days of her mother country's greatness, when Spain was alive with religious fervor and the flowering genius of painters, writers, sculptors and architects.[14]

And regarding the latter he explains:

> In relating these ugly events, we remind ourselves that the Spaniard simply added his part to the cruelty of early industrial enterprise, amply shared by the English, the French, and the German. To Spain's credit there was protest from brave statesmen and churchmen, who never tired of demanding with Padre Montesino, "are these not men?"[15]

Thus, in his view, Spanish America was fashioned from "the bone and blood and muscle of sixteenth century Spain"[16] with all that implies, and in that context, even the most heinous of human cruelty was *understandable*.

The wars of Independence followed in the wake of the French Revolution and the American War of Independence. Aided by internal trouble in Spain, Portugal and France, the colonial creole oligarchy threw off foreign rule between 1804 and 1824,[17] but as Herring's recounting of the subsequent history of the individual nations shows, the problems of domination and poverty persisted, albeit in different forms.

Writing as he did in the nineteen sixties, Herring envisioned "development" as the only solution[18] despite the failures of the "Alliance for Progress".[19] He was optimistic that the United States, realizing that its destiny was irreparably linked to the southern republics, would endeavour to foster "just and friendly relations" to the benefit of all.[20] However, the more recent establishment of national security states with their records of repression, violence and inhuman suffering has shattered the optimism with which Herring ends his *History* and given credibility to another perspective.[21]

It is thus the "cry of the poor" and the anguish of the oppressed that has prompted the rejection of the history of Latin America written by "white, western, bourgeois hand."[22] The view from the "reverse of history", as Gutiérrez calls it, names the problems differently and reflects solidarity with native ancestors and anger at their violation and exploitation.[23] Latin Americans have identified their primary problem as that of the non-person, created by destruction of native culture and the imposition of an alien civilization; having no personal identity; lacking in self-determination; and manipulated by the economic and political megamachinery of a capitalist world system.[24]

This different perspective has called into question the adequacy of the Church's response in the Latin American situation. Again, a re-reading of the history of the Church can easily uncover the devastating effects of the identification of Christianity with Iberian civilization and the close alliance that existed for too long between the Church and the State in Latin America.[25] This, of course, does not discount the contribution that the Church has made. Authors generally point out this contribution but subtle prejudices can be detected in their generally impartial and scholarly account. For example, J.L. Mecham writes of the natives:

> Given their undeveloped, primitive minds, and their bewilderment on being thrust suddenly into a social state into which they could not adapt themselves for hundreds of years, what could be expected of the missionaries? The catholic Church with its imagery and cere-monials was best adapted to appeal to the savages, and realizing this, the friars quite naturally made good use of pomp and display. If the result was a veneer of Christianity, that at least was an achievement. The missionaries were deserving of more credit for what they accomplished than condemnation for what they failed to do. And, as for the whites, those of European origin, and the castes, their religious shallowness must have been the result of the failure of the clergy to distunguish between their mentality and that of the Indians. [26]

Latin Americans now reject this judgment while accepting Mecham's account of the failure of the Church in witnessing to a Christianity unattached to power and wealth and fostering a faith effectively responsive to the realities of their situation.[27] Latin American Christians are, therefore, deliberately assuming a different perspective as a renewed vision begins to take hold.[28]

Vatican Council II marks the awakening of the Catholic Church to the reality of the modern world. The modest desire of John XXIII for *aggiornamento* in the life and doctrine of a Church, defensively static for too long in a post-Reformation posture, was unexpectedly changed into an aspiration for the transformation of the entire world in the unprecedented call from the Council floor that brought into being the Constitution, *Gaudium et Spes*.[29] As "perhaps the most characteristic achievement of an essentially 'pastoral' Council",[30] this Constitution advocates sensitivity to the *signs of the times* amidst the rapid changes that mark the modern era. Acknowledging the advance of science and technology and the contribution of the human sciences, it advises collaborative use of the latter in the light of the Gospel. To promote the dignity and integrity of the human person as inherently social, *Gaudium et*

Spes thus presents a synthesis of the social teachings of the Church from the *Rerum Novarum* of Leo XIII through *Mater et Magistra* and *Pacem in Terris* of John XXIII in relationship to contemporary socio-economic, political and cultural issues.[31]

Granted the situation of Latin America briefly reviewed above, it was this constitution that was the most influential in the renewal attempts that launched a period of optimism in a Church in deep crisis.[32] With rapid change as one of the most significant signs of the times in Latin America, the epochal Episcopl Conference at Medellín in 1968 thus focussed on *The Church in the Present Day Transformation of Latin America in the Light of the Council*,[33] bringing authoritative approval to public statements that were already made by groups of laity, priests and bishops. As Gutiérrez notes, the process that led to Medellín and its aftermath can only be properly understood in terms of those related texts that, in his opinion, are clearer and more in tune with the concrete commitments of Christians and "less neutralized by the system."[34] However Medellín was the official clarion call for a distinctive Latin American Christian response, starting from a concrete analysis of the *realidad* and employing a methodology initiated by *Gaudium et Spes*. A different perspective, one based upon a clear option for the poor, opened the way for the transformation of the dominant concept of "integral development", appropriated from *Populorum Progressio* of Paul VI, into a definite, though still hesitant language of *liberation*.[35] At that moment, the Latin American liberation theological movement formally came into being.

Chief among the pioneers of that movement was Juan Luis Segundo, a native of Uruguay, born in Montevideo in 1925.[36] The following brief consideration of his life and works is intended to serve as an introduction to the man through his works and to indicate in a general way the development of his theology. This development will be seen to be primarily one of deepening insights and principles established in his early years by approaching them from different angles and thus expanding the parameters of their application.

2. The Man and His Works

When in 1964 at a meeting in Petropolis, Brazil, theological reflections on the social and cultural realities of Latin America got on the way and stimulated the series of conferences that were to culminate at Medellín, Segundo had already completed his training as a Jesuit priest and theologian. He was then involved in leading groups of university students in Montevideo to reflect more deeply on the implications of their Christian faith.

This focus on the social sciences comprises an important aspect of Segundo's intellectual development as a liberation theologian.[37] He had become convinced that European theology's main reliance on philosophy, the traditional "handmaid" of theology, was no longer adequate to mediate the truth that was presently hidden in the heart of his oppressed continent. Social analysis was now necessary to get at the real causes of the poverty and oppression visible everywhere in Latin America.[38] Henceforth, a turn to the social and the concrete aspects of human existence would mark his theological reflections.

Segundo's philosophical studies in the early years of his priestly formation at the Jesuit Faculty of San Miguel near Buenos Aires, Argentina, beginning in 1941, aroused his interest in Existentialism. Indeed, it was the subject of his earliest publication in 1948.[39] His concern then was with human existence in its fulness and the need for the complementarity of philosophical and poetic language to capture both the intellectual and affective dimensions of that existence which he claimed to be ultimately grounded in the Divine. Existentialism thus provided the philosophical underpinning for an understanding of human existence starting from the concrete situation of the subject. By stressing the affective base of the "existential contact" that characterizes human interpersonal existence, Segundo was able to overcome the individualistic tendency of Existentialism and to interpret human existence as inherently social.

Segundo's theological studies took him to the Jesuit Faculty of Saint Albert in Louvain where he came under the influence of three persons in particular. Leopold Malevez, a professor of theology, impressed upon him the real possibility of grace being in the non-Christian. A study of the second Council of Orange subsequently convinced him that the supernatural dimension of any good act depends on it being in the service of others. These insights would become a basis for Segundo's most fundamental theological presupposition and would thus enter significantly into his reinterpretation of Christian doctrines.[40]

From another professor of theology, Gustavo Lambert, Segundo learned to appreciate and to stress the progressive understanding of God as revealed in the development of the Old Testament tradition and its culmination in the revelation of the New Testament. These ideas were to be developed by Segundo and made applicable to the Latin American context in a work published in 1962.[41] This pedagogical aspect of God's dealing with human beings remained another major insight as Segundo sought to relate the Christian message to concrete and changing historical situations. His emphasis would be on the continued revelation of the Spirit leading to fuller truth in tune with the signs of the times. Hence, a dynamic thrust would also become characteristic of his theology.

Rudolf Bultmann was the third major influence of that period. He provided Segundo with an existentialist interpretation of scripture which stresses the primacy of interpretation over narrative. He gave Segundo the basis for a method, the hermeneutic circle, that would become the formalization of the method that was being developed by the Latin American liberation theologians. Perhaps, most important of all, Bultmann's project of demythologization was to inspire a parallel in Segundo's own project of deideologization in which Marxist social analysis would play an important role and enable Segundo to go beyond Bultmann's mainly individualistic concerns.[42]

Following his ordination to the priesthood in 1955, Segundo pursued doctoral studies at the University of Paris. Berdyaev's concept of the person became his focus.[43] Here he encountered again and delved more deeply into what is, perhaps, the most dominant and lasting influence of his student days.

Berdyeav had integrated into his philosophy insights drawn from Heidegger, Hegel, Kant, Boehme and Russian Marxism, a unique blend of East and West, of mysticism and rationality. From him Segundo accepted the assertion of the primacy of liberty over being and a redefinition of God and concomitantly of the human person as freedom. This would make Segundo's major concern the freedom of the human being in history, and give to his entire theological enterprise a decisive liberative thrust. The freedom that Berdyaev stresses, however, and Segundo with him, is a freedom in tension with the determination of nature. Freedom is limited and must be realized in the struggle to creatively direct and use the instruments of nature. This would consequently lead Segundo to place, perhaps, an even greater stress on the concrete embodiment and eventual verification of that feedom, namely, on love that must likewise attend to the instruments of nature in order to be *efficacious*.

Even before he published his doctoral dissertation in 1963, Segundo became interested in Teilhard de Chardin. Teilhard strengthened his interest in the value of history in a way that Berdyaev, from his point in time, could not have done.[44] Teilhard's evolutionary view of history as the development of human consciousness would eventually provide Segundo with an important "key" to interpret Christianity. Within an evolutionary perspective which is at once dynamic and transformative, Segundo would grapple with the concrete implications of historical liberation, and the liberation of theology itself in service of that liberation.

Thus, under the major influences of his early years Segundo appropriated insights which he would continue to deepen and expand by applying them to the various areas of his theological reflection. A review of Segundo's major works will illustrate this development. In particualar we will note how Segundo's consistent emphasis on the social, concrete and dynamic draws out important dimensions of Christian self-understanding and occasions some important shifts in his reinterpretation of traditional Christian symbols.

The social and practical turn of Segundo's thought was already apparent in his earliest theological work which centred on the function of the Church[45] as the corporate, social embodiment of Christianity in history. In it, Segundo uses a method which was to become the classic definition of Latin American liberation theology, that is, critical reflection on historical praxis in the light of faith.[46] From a sociological analysis of Christian response in the Rio Plata region, he raises questions regarding the obvious ineffectiveness of the two distinct and mutually exclusive pastoral approaches operative there. He also exposes the inadequacy of their theological underpinnings in view of the authentic meaning of Christianity, described by him as the "religion of true love". Segundo, then, argues for a more creative involement of the Church in the national life of the Rio Plata region on the basis of the fundamental claim of Christianity, that the sacred is immersed in human existence. Thus he redefines the Church as missioned to serve the rest of humanity in its task of making *real* love the foremost criterion to direct a pluralistic world toward growing interdependence and solidarity.

In a subsequent work on the Christian image of humanity,[47] Segundo addresses the question of authentic Christian living from the point of view of personal existence. This he did in dialogue with Marxism and Existentialism, currents of European thought that were having a great impact in Latin America at that time. Marxism posed the post-Enlightenment critique of religion, which, to Segundo, was quite justified in the Latin American context due to a misunderstanding of Christianity. Segundo stresses, in response to Marxism, the revolutionary and distinctive turn of Christianity away from religious rites to concrete, historical, transformative tasks. Existentialism proposed the ideal of human self-creation through liberty. Segundo accepts the redefinition of the human person as freedom but stresses love of neighbour as the concrete embodiment of that freedom. Thus Segundo corrects the individualistic tendency of Existentialism with the Christian emphasis on the social character of human existence.

Segundo returned to his focus on the Church in a second doctoral dissertation[48] that, together with his thesis on Berdyaev, was to qualify him for a state doctorate. Under the direction of Paul Ricoeur, he considered whether or not the social embodiment of Christianity in the model of Christendom could be the ideal form of Christianity in any historical period. In this work, the *mass* and *minority* tension which he had already recognized as underlying the two different pastoral approaches of either fostering mass membership or heroic minority commitment in the Rio Plata region became explicit operative as a "hermeneutical principle". That is, he used it as a key to reinterpret the Church in view of the new social and historical reality of Latin America and in the light of the Christian message. Segundo uncovers the scriptual basis of this tension in the "flesh - Spirit", "world - hour" images as presented by Paul and John respectively. Thus Segundo draws from scripture the basic "principles" to illumine the historical and sociological "facts" which he unearthed in his analysis of the Latin American experience of Christianity.

Despite his conclusion that Christendom was basically a distortion of authentic Christianity, Segundo affirms the positive role of institutions as a necessary means of raising the quality of life and self-understanding in the majority of human beings. Thus Segundo recognizes the need for social institutions and for the Church itself, as a community of believers, to embody the gift of God's love, his grace, and to act as possible counterforces to the structural sinful situation that the Medellín Conference had cited as being characteristic of Latin America.[49] This, it seems, indicates that the theological ground of Segundo's emphasis on the social aspect of human existence is, indeed, the reality of universal grace which itself implies the fundamental equality and solidarity of all humanity.

This becomes evident in Segundo's attempt at a reinterpretation of the major themes of Christian theology in a five-volume work, *A Theology for Artisans of a New Humanity*.[50] This work is comprised of the summaries of lectures and discussions which Segundo developed while he was director of the Peter Faber Centre, in Montevideo, a position which he held from 1965 to its closure in 1975. The five volumes consist of a reinterpretation of the major themes of Christian theology. A development can be discerned in the sequence of these works as well as in the gradual expansion of the application of the insight that grace needs to be socially and concretely embodied in order to be able to make the appropriate impact on structures in need of transformation.

Segundo's starting point is, significantly, a recapitulation and further elaboration of his reflections on the Church[51] which, as we have seen, was his primary focus up until then. What becomes clearer in this volume is the theological grounding of Segundo's mainly functional understanding of the Church on the revelation of grace as universally at work in humanity. The Church, understood as a particular community of faith and sacraments, is meant to effectively embody and communicate the knowledge of that grace, of God's unconditional love to all of humanity.

Segundo's subsequent reinterpretation of the symbol of grace[52] itself is, then, a companion volume to his ecclesiology. In it he makes the significant move from an emphasis on the individual appropriation of grace to its social implications for the creation of a new humanity.

The focus on the social, concrete and dynamic reality of grace becomes more pronounced in Segundo's reinterpretation of the Christian concept of God.[53] For him, the Trinity is a *society* of persons, revealed as being involved in *history* and defined by *liberty,* freely choosing to be committed to the creation of humanity. Human existence thus drawn into solidarity with the Trinity is suffused with love, with grace that is everywhere and is meant in turn to unite all human beings into the one people of God.

The explicit celebration of God's love gratutitously and effectively at work in human existence, as symbolized in the sacrametns,[54] became Segundo's next area of doctrinal focus. His reinterpretation is marked by its functional view of the sacraments, intended to fashion and challenge the community of faith. Thus the sacraments are the signs *par excellence* of social grace, given within the community for its effective, concrete transformation.

In the final volume,[55] Segundo addresses the existential reality of sin as primarily a social structure. He explains it within the evolutionary context which had become for him the "key" to interpret Christianity. Hence, this "synthesis" of Segundo's doctrinal reinterpretation culminates, as it were, in a direct confrontation between grace and social sin. Segundo affirms the triumph of grace over sin in Jesus Christ and consequently the eventual transformation of the structures of an oppressive, sinful society through the power of love.

An explicit articulation of the method that Segundo was consciously attempting to develop emerges in subsequent publications. In *De la sociedad a la teología*[56] Segundo discusses the need for the development of a liberation theology from within the Latin American context, too long dominated by an imposed Western Christian thought. He examines not only the practical costs of a basically inauthentic pastoral approach but also the anti-intellectualism and false concept of salvation from which theology itself needs to be freed in order to be relevant to the Latin American context.

The need for a liberative method for extricating pastoral practice from ineffective means of evangelization was reiterated and further elaborated in Segundo's exposure of the *hidden motives* of Latin American pastoral action.[57] Through an analysis of the social context of the Church he identifies the root cause as a basic attitude of fear which is diametrically opposed to the confidence of Christian maturity.

An even more explict focus on methodology is present in Segundo's explication of the theme of masses and minorities[58] that was already playing a hermeneutical function in his theology. In effect, it forms the basis of what would be more fully and explicitly developed as his major methodological contribution to the Latin American liberation theological movement, *The Liberation of Theology*.[59] This work can be regarded as a culmination of Segundo's theological reflections up until then.

It is significant, therefore, that in the structure of Segundo's three-volume Christology[60] which appeared seven years later there is a kind of reversal in the development that we have so far observed in the order of Segundo's theological publications. It is a movement which starts from the analysis of the Latin American reality in relationship to the pastoral practice of the Church in the Rio Plata region. It then proceeds to doctrinal reinterpretation and ends in an explicit articulation of method.

The first volume[61] is a methodological work which explains the basic principles on which Segundo's theology has been grounded. Hence, key concepts are clarified in terms of the dominant categories of *faith* and *ideology*. The second volume[62] then examines the doctrine of Jesus Christ, starting with its scriptural foundation in the Synoptics and in Paul. It traces the development of Christology in the context of specific historical moments and the establishment of Chalcedon as the measuring rod of orthodoxy. It is significant to note that it is within the framework of Christian spirituality, concrete Christian life, that Segundo advances a critique of the traditional Christology. Using Paul as the paradigm of the authentic creation of Christology, Segundo eventually proposes an outline for the development of a Christology from within the Latin American context. Hence, his final volume[63] ends where he had begun his theological reflections, that is, with an analysis of the socio-economic, political situation of Latin America, now compounded with the crisis of an ecological destruction of the culture. Thus Segundo's Christology presents us with a view of the development of his theology in reverse. This has the advantage of providing a vision of the whole while specific parts are being explained.

What the content of this work evidences is the continued deepening of Segundo's theological reflections through dialogue with major contemporary authors and social scientific desciplines. Of significance is a more explicit dialogue with Marxism in which he stresses the "realism" of the Marxian dialectic and the turn towards the concrete transformation of the structures of society. A bolder use of scripture is also brought to bear upon the specific Latin American problematic in order to point in the direction of creating the

Christology which the Latin American liberation theological movement desperately needs for its continued growth.[64]

Numerous articles, published mostly in *Dialogo de Perspectivas*, parallel these major publications and could be used as an index of Segundo's developing theology.

Ever since the epochal meeting in Petropolis at which Segundo delivered a paper on the social problems of Latin America, he has continued to be a significant presence at other Latin American and international conferences on liberation theology. Of special importance are the meeting in Santiago, Chile in 1966 where Segundo reflected upon the historical dimension of salvation in Latin America in conjunction with Gustavo Gutiérrez and others;[65] the meeting at El Escorial in Spain in 1972 at which Segundo delivered two papers;[66] and, finally, the conference on method in Mexico City in 1975 where, again, Segundo was a leading participant, presenting the paper "Condicionamientos actuales de la reflexión teológica en latinoamerica."[67]

The issue of the relationship of Latin American liberation theology and other theologies has led to international conferences to provide a forum for dialogue and further development of the movement. Segundo has been an active participant since the initial conference at Detroit, Michigan in 1975.[68]

Segundo has lectured widely and has taught at several universities in the United States, Canada and Europe. These include Harvard Divinity School, Jesuit School of Theology in Chicago, the Divinity School of the University of Chicago, the McCormick Theological Seminary, Jesuit Faculty of Theology in Madrid and Regis College in Toronto.

Presently, Segundo continues his work of lecturing and directing the discussions of committed groups of Christians in Montevideo. But, perhaps, most important of all, Segundo continues to reflect upon the crucial questions that confront Christians in our contemporary world.

We turn now to an examination of the theme of efficacious love as a centering principle of Segundo's theology. The objective is to eventually determine how well the notion of efficacious love is capable of drawing together the many insights which Segundo has integrated into his theology and developed throughout his writings. It is obvious from the above that any clarification of this central notion in Segundo's theology cannot but enrich the Latin American liberation theological movement and, indeed, the entire theological enterprise inasmuch as that movement makes its impact felt.

Notes

1. See Juan Luis Segundo, "Hipótesis sobre la situatión del Uruguay: algunas possibilidades de investigación", in Juan Luis Segundo, Pedro Olmos, Dionisio J. Garmendia et al., *Uruguay 67: Una interpretación,* vol. I (Montevideo: Editorial Alfa, 1967), pp. 11-32.

2. Cf. Fernando Henriques Cardoso & Enzo Faletto, *Dependency and Development in Latin America,* translated by Marjorie Mattingly Urqudi (Berkeley: University of California Press, 1979).

3. Cf. W.W. Rostow, *The Stages of Economic Growth* (Cambridge: Cambridge University Press, 1960), Chapters 2, 6, 8-10; Alex Inkeles , "The Modernization of Man" in Myron Weiner, ed., *Mordernization: The Dynamics of Growth* (New York: Basic Books, 1966), 138-50.

4. Cf. Raul Prebisch, *Economic Development of Latin America and its Principal Problems* (New York: United Nations, 1950), 1-7; 49-59.

5. Hubert Herring, *A History of Latin America from the Beginning to the Present,* 3rd. ed. (New York: Alfred A. Koff, 1968).

6. *Ibid.,* p. 886.

7. Cf *Ibid.* Herring's *History* is listed as the "best comprehensive history" of Latin America in H. Blakemore, *Latin America* (London: Oxford University Press, 1966), p. 119.

8. *Ibid.,* pp. 119-233. This period lasted from 1492-1810.

9. *Ibid.,* pp. 119-149. The well known story of the conquest of the Aztec Empire of Mexico by Hernan Cortes and the Incas Empire of Peru by Francisco Pizarro has the character of an "epic" according to Blakemore, p. 33.

10. *Ibid.,* pp. 184-89.

11. *Ibid.,* pp. 156-60.

12. *Ibid.,* pp. 204-12.

13. *Ibid.,* pp. 167-83. Cf. J. Lloyd Mecham, *Church and State in Latin America* (Chapel Hill: The University of North Carolina Press, 1934, 1966).

14. *Ibid.,* p. 204.

15. *Ibid.,* p. 188.

16. *Ibid.,* p. 87.

17. *Ibid.,* pp. 253-81.

18. *Ibid.,* p. 890.

19. *Ibid.,* pp. 939-47.

20. *Ibid.,* p. 947.

21. Cf. José Comblin, *The Church and the National Security State* (New York: Orbis Books, 1979); Penny Lernoux, "The Long Path to Puebla" in *Puebla and Beyond,* edited by John Eagleson and Philip Scharper (New York: Orbis Books, 1979), pp. 3-27.

22. Cf. Gustavo Gutiérrez, "Revelación de Annuncio de Dios" in *La Fuerza histórica de los pobres: Selección de trabajos* (Lima, Peru: Centro de Estudios y

Publicaciones, 1979), p. 36.

23. Cf. Enrique Dussell, *Histoty and Theology of Liberation: A Latin American Perspective*, trans. John Drury (New York: Orbis Books, 1976), esp. pp. 78-109.

24. Cf. Segundo Galilea, "Liberation Theology and the New Tasks Facing Christians" in Rosino Gibellini, ed., *Frontiers of Theology in Latin America* (New York: Orbis Books, 1979), p. 172; José Miguez Bonino, *Doing Theology in a Revolutionary Situation* (Philadelphia: Fortress Press, 1975), pp. 30-31.

25. Cf. Mecham, *Church and State in Latin America*, esp. pp. 3-37.

26. *Ibid.*, p. 42.

27. Cf. *Ibid.*, pp. 422-23.

28. Cf. Enrique Dussell, *History of the Church in Latin America*, trans. Alan Neely (Grand Rapids, Michigan: William B. Eerdmans Publishing Co., 1981), esp. pp. 137-239.

29. Walter M. Abbot, ed., *The Documents of Vatican II* (U.S.A: Western Publishing Co., Inc., 1966), p. 184.

30. *Ibid.*, p. 183.

31. Cf. *Ibid.*, pp. 185-97; *Guadium et Spes*, esp. nos. 53-82

32. Mecham, *Church and State in Latin America*, p. 423.

33. Documents of the Medellín Conference. *The Church in the Present-day Transformation of Latin America in the Light of the Council*, 2 vols., English trans. (Washington D.C: Latin American Division, United States Catholic Conference, 1970).

34. Gustavo Gutiérrez, *A Theology of Liberation: History, Politics and Salvation* (New York: Orbis Books, 1973), pp. 107-19.

35. Cf. Galilea, "Liberation Theology and the New Tasks Facing Christians", pp. 164-66. In tracing the development of the language of "liberation", however, Enrique Dussell finds its roots in the writings of Bartolomé de las Casas, the renowned defender of the Indians against Spanish avarice, cruelty and oppression. Following Las Casas, he maintains, is a tradition of liberative praxis evidenced in prominent missionaries of the early colonial period, fighters for Latin American Independence, and more recently, political liberators. In accord with this point of view, the language of "liberation" is understood as a counterfoil of the language of "oppression" and the genesis of liberation theology in Latin America is linked with the rise of the theory of "Dependency". See Enrique Dussell, "Historical and Philosophical Presupposition of Latin American Theology", in *Frontiers of Theology in Latin American Theology*, pp. 185f. Cf. Dussell, *History of the Church*, p. 201; Gutiérrez, *Theology of Liberation*, pp. 83-86; Hugo Assmann, *Theology for a Nomad Church* , trans. Paul Burns (New York: Orbis Books, 1975), pp. 37f.

36. The biographical data reported here are taken, for the most part, from Gerald Justin Persha, "Juan Luis Segundo: A Study Concerning the Relationship Between the Particularity of the Church and the Universality of Her Mission", Ph.D. Dissertation, University of Ottawa, 1979, pp. 40-51. Persha obtained most of his information from an extended interview with Segundo.

37. The earliest articles published by Segundo were directly related to the socio-economic and political situation of Latin America. See especially "Dianóstico Político de América Latina", *Mensage,* II (1962), 656-61; "Los caminos del desarrollo político latinoamericano", *Mensage,* II (1963), 701-707; "La variable política", *Revista Interamericana de Ciencias Sociales,* no. 2 (1963), 1-32.

38. Cf. Segundo, *The Liberation of Theology,* pp. 47-68. Segundo argues that there is need for collaboration between theology and sociology but that there is presently no sociological approach adequate for that task. See also Juan Luis Segundo, "Teología y ciencias sociales", in *Fe cristiana y cambio social en América Latina: El encuentro de El Escorial, 1972* (Salamanca: Sígueme, 1973), pp. 285-95.

39. Juan Luis Segundo, *Existentialismo, filosofía: Ensayo de Síntesis* (Buenos Aires: Espasa-Calpe, 1948).

40. See Chapter III, p. 50 for a fuller explanation of this basic theological presupposition of liberation theology.

41. Juan Luis Segundo, *Etapes precristianas de la fe: Evolución de la idea de Dios en el Antiguo Testamento* (Montevideo: Cursos de Complementación Cristiana, 1962).

42. See esp. Chapter II, pp. 36f.

43. Juan Luis Segundo, *Berdiaeff: Une Réflexion chrétienne sur la personne* (Paris: Montaigne, 1963).

44. Segundo, *Berdiaeff,* p. 408.

45. Juan Luis Segundo, *Función de las Iglesia en la realidad rioplatense* (Montevideo: Barreiro y Ramos, 1962).

46. See Gutiérrez, *Theology of Liberation,* p. 6.

47. Juan Luis Segundo, *Concepción cristiana del hombre* (Montevideo: Mimeográfica "Luz", 1964).

48. Juan Luis Segundo, , *La cristiandad, ¿una utopia?* I: *Los Hechos* and II *Los principios* (Montevideo: Mimeográfica "Luz", 1964).

49. Documents of the Medellín Conference, *Peace,* no. 1.

50. Juan Luis Segundo, *Teología abierta para el laico adulto,* 5 vols. (Buenos Aires: Carlos Lohlé, 1968-72). English trans. *A Theology for Artisans of a New Humanity* (New York: Orbis Books, 1973-74).

51. Juan Luis Segundo, *Esa comunidad llamada Iglesia* (Buenos Aires: Carlos Lohlé, 1968). English trans., *The Community Called Church,* translated by John Drury (Maryknoll, New York: Orbis Books, 1973).

52. Juan Luis Segundo, *Gracia y condición humana* (Buenos Aires: Carlos Lohlé, 1968). English trans., *Grace and the Human Condition,* translated by John Drury (Maryknoll, New York: Orbis Books, 1973).

53. Juan Luis Segundo, *Nuestra idea de Dios* (Buenos Aires: Carlos Lohlé, 1970). English trans., *Our Idea of God,* translated by John Drury (Maryknoll, New York: Orbis Books, 1973).

54. Juan Luis Segundo, *Los sacramentos hoy* (Buenos Aires: Carlos Lohlé, 1971). English trans., *The Sacraments Today,* translated by John Drury (Maryknoll, New York: Orbis Books, 1974).

55. Juan Luis Segundo, *Evolución y culpa* (Buenos Aires: Carlos Lohlé, 1972). English trans., *Evolution and Guilt,* translated by John Drury (Maryknoll, New York: Orbis Books, 1974).

56. Juan Luis Segundo, *De la sociedad a la teología* (Buenos Aires: Carlos Lohlé, 1970).

57. Juan Luis Segundo, *Acción pastoral latinoamericano: Sus motivos ocultos* (Bunoes Aires: Busqueda, 1972). English trans., *The Hidden Motives of Pastoral Action,* trans. by John Drury (New York: Orbis Books, 1978).

58. Juan Luis Segundo, *Masas y minores en la dialética divina de la liberación* (Buenos Aires: La Aurora, 1973).

59. Juan Luis Segundo, *Liberación de la teología* (Bunoes Aires: Carlos Lohlé, 1975). English trans., *The Liberation of Theology,* translated by John Drury (New York: Orbis Books, 1976).

60. Juan Luis Segundo, *El hombre de hoy ante Jesus de Nazaret,* 3 vols. (Madrid: Cristiandad, 1982). English translation *Jesus of Nazareth Yesterday and Today,* 5 vols. Translated by John Drury (New York: Orbis Books, 1984-88).

61. Juan Luis Segundo, *El hombre de hoy ante Jesus de Nazaret,* vol. I: *Fe e ideología* (Madrid: Cristiandad, 1982). English translation, *Faith and Ideologies,* translated by John Drury (New York/Melbourne/London: Orbis Books/Dove Communications/Sheed and Ward, 1984).

62. Juan Luis Segundo, *El hombre de hoy ante Jesus de Nazaret,* vol. II/1: *Historia y actualidad: Sinópticos y Pablo* (Madrid: Cristiandad, 1982). English trans., Part I: *The Historical Jesus of the Synoptics,* translated by John Drury (New York/Melbourne/London: Orbis Books/Dove Communications/Sheed and Ward, 1985); Part II: *The Humanist Christology of Paul,* trans. by John Drury (New York/London: Orbis Books/Sheed and Ward, 1986).

63. Juan Luis Segundo, *El hombre de hoy ante Jesus de Nazaret,* vol. II/2: *Historia y actualidad: Las cristologías en la espiritualidad* (Madrid: Cristiandad, 1982). English trans., Part III: *The Christ of the Ignatian Exercises,* trans. by John Drury (New York: Orbis Books, 1987); Part IV: *An Evolutionary Approach to Jesus of Nazareth,* trans. by John Drury (New York: Orbis Books, 1988).

64. Segundo, *The Historical Jesus of the Synoptics,* p. 15. Cf. Hugo Assmann, "The Power of Christ in History", in *Frontiers of Theology in Latin America,* edited by Rosino Gibellini, translated by John Drury (Maryknoll, New York: Orbis Books, 1979), pp. 133-50.

65. See Juan Luis Segundo, "Intellecto y salvación", in Gutiérrez, Gustavo et al. *Salvación y construcción del mundo* (Barcelona: Editorial Nova Terra, 1967), pp. 67-90.

66. Juan Luis Segundo, "Las elites latinoamericanas: Problemática humana y cristiana ante el cambio social" and "Teología y ciencias sociales" in *Fe cristiana y cambio social,* pp. 203-12; 285-95.

67. Juan Luis Segundo, "Condicionamientos actuales de la reflexión teológica en latinoamérica" in *Liberación y cautiverio: Debates en torno al método de la*

teología en America Latina (Mexico City: Comité Organizador, 1975), pp. 91-101. See also his evaluation of the Conference, *ibid.*, pp. 561-63.

68. See "Statement by Juan Luis Segundo" in *Theology in the Americas*, ed. by Sergio Torres and John Eagleson (New York: Orbis Books, 1976), pp. 280-83. Other international conferences held subsequently include: "Ecumenical Dialogue of Third World Theologians," Dar es Salaam, 1976 (proceedings published in *The Emergent Gospel*, edited by Sergio Torres and Virginia Fabella. New York: Orbis Books, 1978); "Pan African Conference of Third World Theologians", Accra, 1977 (papers published in *African Theology en Route*, edited by Kofi Appian-Kubi and Sergio Torres. Maryknoll, New York: Orbis Books, 1979); "International Ecumenical Congress of Theology", Sao Paulo, Brazil, 1980 (proceedings published in *The Challenge of Basic Christian Communities*, edited by Sergio Torres and John Eagleson, translated by John Drury. New York: Orbis Books, 1981); "Ecumencial Association of Third World Theologians. International Conference", New Delhi, 1981 (proceedings published in *Irruption of the Third World: Challenge to Theology*, edited by Virginia Fabella and Sergio Torres. New York: Orbis Books, 1983); "Ecumencial Association of Third World Theologians. International Conference", Geneva, Switzerland, 1983 (papers published in *Doing Theology in a Divided World*, edited by Virginia Fabella and Sergio Torres. Maryknoll, New York: Orbis Books, 1985).

Chapter Two

The Meaning of Efficacious Love in the Theology of Juan Luis Segundo

Efficacious love is the Christian question *par excellence.* This Segundo claims, while indicating that "true and efficacious love is a complex reality", its efficacy being subject to ambiguities and oversimplifications.[1] An initial clarification of the meaning of efficacious love will, therefore, be attempted in this chapter, with the assumption that a more adequate understanding can only emerge as the notion is subsequently seen to function significantly in the theological reflections of our author.

The meaning of efficacious love as the most fundamental value of Christian experience will be drawn, first of all, from its biblical roots. Subsequently it will be seen how the notion emerges from scripture to take on fuller dimensions under three major influences. The existentialist philosopphy of Nicolas Berdyaev surfaces the personal aspect of efficacious love and throws the emphasis on its capacity to create persons in freedom. Marxist thought draws out the social implications of that love that is efficacious only in so far as it concretely transforms the structures of society. Finally, the evolutionary theory of Teilhard de Chardin develops the cosmic extent of efficacious love and unfolds its dynamic movement towards the ultimate reconciliation of the universe in Christ. This discussion will consider each of these aspects of efficacious love in turn.

1. The Scriptural Basis

Scripture is normative for the interpretation of Christian experience. It is the primary source to which the theologian must constantly revert with the questions that arise in changing, historical circumstances. Scripture, however, does not provide ready-made solutions to contemporary problems. Rather it is a process whereby one learns how to respond to concrete situations in the light of faith, that is, with the mentality of Jesus of Nazareth.[2] Segundo's use of scripture will be seen to be mostly in accord with this understanding of it, although he does not intend to disregard the exigencies of historical, biblical criticism.[3] The scriptural sources on which Segundo primarily relies are John and Paul, the biblical writers who, for him, first consciously reflected on human existence and the new dimensions introduced by Christianity in historical contexts other than the earliest, most spontaneous Christian community. Their letters thus provide Segundo with "the first phenomenology of Christian existence"[4] and, hence, with the paradigm for subsequent theological reflections in changing, historical situations.

It is important, then, to establish the scriptural basis for Segundo's use of the term "efficacious love" and the meaning that is revealed in that context. We shall proceed by considering the two terms of the notion of efficacious love, namely the reality of love, and the efficacy of love. Segundo unfolds how love, as free self-gift, defines the very nature of God. The revelation of this love, from the very beginning, draws human beings into a relationship that is creative and transforming of both self and others. But human love is also conditioned by life's situations. The need for efficacy comes, then, only with the novel revelation of an incarnated Love.

(a) The reality of love

Segundo's understanding of what comprises true love is rooted in the revelation of God as Love as recorded in John's writings (cf. 1 Jn. 4:8, 16). This is the "definition" of God which reveals the only valid image of the Christian God. It comes from the very interior of the life of God in the person of the Incarnate Son (Jn. 1:18).[5]

Segundo argues that it is John's experience of the concrete love of Jesus of Nazareth that led to that definition. Hence, he claims that the meaning of the love of God must be sought in terms of human language. This he describes as follows:

> To love in our language . . . signifies to give, yes, but to give in that limited measure that we are, to draw from ourselves and our flesh the being that we offer to the loved one, in other words, to give ourselves. And it is also to receive, to receive gratuitously something which we cannot in any way achieve by ourselves, something which, nevertheless, fulfils us and affects us at the deepest level of our being. And to live by loving is to live depending upon the other, suffering the suffering of the other, feeling the joys of the other, to be eminently vulnerable.[6]

Here, we notice the total gift of self which love implies as well as the reciprocity, the creation of person and solidarity with the beloved. If God is, indeed, love, as revealed in human experience, he must, then, be a love disclosive of all of that.

It is, therefore, in accord with that human experience of love that John draws attention to God's infinite self-gift (1 Jn. 3:16). It is a gift of self that not only includes self-sacrifice and full immersion into human history and a vulnerable condition, but more, the very sharing of the divine life (1 Jn. 3:9; 1 Jn. 3:1). God gives what he is most essentially and intimately, viz., Love. This love of God is the source of all genuine love in human beings. God gives limited human beings the capacity to give of themselves, to love truly, in spite of their inherent poverty. This gift opens up a totally new horizon to human existence. "We know (experientially)", Segundo asserts with John, "that we have passed from death to life because we can love one another (1 Jn. 3:14)."[7] Thus he draws into focus the divine origin of human love. "Provided that it is a matter of true love," Segundo maintains, "though minimal or most insignificant in terms of its power or object, it testifies empirically, according to John, to a divine force."[8]

But God is not only the source of all true love, he is also its object, and concretely so. The basis for this lies in the commandment which links love of God and love of neighbour (Mt. 22:39), and even more significantly, makes the latter the point of emphasis. Segundo argues, then, for an identification of love of God and love of neighbour inasmuch as the reality of God's love demands visible expression in human life. It is a matter of loving "not in word nor in speech, but truly in deeds (1 Jn. 3:18)."[9]

The requirement of this concreteness, for Segundo, flows from the danger of self-deceit that lurks in love that purports to be directed to God as its object. It is thus that Segundo interprets the radical assertion of John: "If anyone says that he loves God and does not love his brother he is a liar. Because how could he who does not love his brother whom he sees, love God whom he does not see?" (1 Jn. 4:20). This indicates the realism, indeed, the "materialism" of Christian love.[10]

But, even more significantly, the solidarity that obtains between human beings and God makes God the object of whatever love is directed at the neighbour. *"All love loves God"*, Segundo declares. By this he stresses that the object of all authentic love is as divine as its origin.[11] The identification of God and neighbour is not, then, a matter of an intention to love God in the neighbour. It is based upon the union with the beloved, which belongs to the very dynamic of love. The entire New Testament concurs with John in making such a claim (cf. Rom. 13:8; James 1:26; 1 Peter 1:22-25; 4:8-11; esp. Acts 9:5).[12]

The importance of this identification of love of God and love of neighbour is further disclosed in the central position which Mt. 25:31-46 assumes in Segundo's reflections. Its significance lies in the fact that in that scene the specific human acts of love or egotism towards others assume a "religious" connotation in being made to determine the eternal destiny of persons. This is so because the object of those actions is God himself. The divine, limitless love of God himself is thus intimately linked with the individual destinies of human beings. Segundo, therefore, concludes:

> This image allows us to appreciate the supreme realism of that love of God which is the decisive criterion of salvation and which is "materialized" in bread, in water, in friendship, in all the dynamisms of the world, since all are susceptible of changing for weal or for woe the existence of other human beings.[13]

What we have seen so far is an understanding of efficacious love as the only true love that is grounded in God and returns to God through love of neighbour. It is free, personal, real, concrete, creative and self-giving love which effectively transforms the other. It is verified in deeds. As such, it becomes the very criterion of salvation in being the norm by which one judges where, indeed, God is actually in union with human beings.

In effect, this understanding of true love is basically in continuity with the Old Testament revelation of God's love. Where the novelty of Christianity enters in, according to Segundo, is in throwing the emphasis on the efficacious aspect of genuine love. What he means by this, we will now endeavour to explore.

(b) The efficacy of love

Segundo argues that an evolutionary development of God's image in the Old Testament prepared the way for the "revolutionary" disclosure of the New Testament. That is the possibility of a personal intimacy with God which creates an indissoluble union between God and humanity.[14] On the basis of this new intimacy, the utter seriousness of God's love is manifested. Jesus, in becoming human, reveals God in complete solidarity with humanity. Simultaneously, he manifests the possibility of the mature, filial collaboration of humanity in the divine-human task of humanization. The implications of the Incarnation thus specify what it means for love to be "efficacious".

Segundo finds in Paul and John a scriptural basis for affirming a basic tension of opposite yet complementary forces, which he identifies as structuring human existence in all its dimensions.[15] These forces represent, on the one hand, passivity and death; and on the other, creativity, activity and life. Segundo's examination of how these forces are to be interpreted in the light of Christianity uncovers what the efficacy of love entails.

Segundo's extensive treatment of the "flesh-Spirit" tension in Paul[16] draws out the implications of the exercise of filial relationship as the novel revelation of Christianity. It entails an attitude which is meant to replace the "religious" attitudes of "dependence, fear and reverence" that appropriately characterize a creature before a transcendent creator. Hence, Segundo argues, the power of the Spirit is given for the responsible directing of the universe towards its total transformation in Christ, in the face of the pervading, persistent structure of sin.[17] Over against this, the flesh signifies the "carnal" attitude of submission to the forces of nature, an attitude which is, then, virtually a denial of the novelty introduced by Jesus Christ (cf. Gal. 3:3). This attitude, he insists, renders Christ's redemption useless (Gal. 5:2).[18]

These carnal attitudes are represented in these three antitheses of Paul, viz., faith vs works (Gal 3:6-14); promise vs contract (Gal 3:15-19); and liberty vs slavery (Gal 4:1-11). Segundo finds in the last the key to understanding the previous two. Hence, the intimacy of mature filial relationship, the liberty of sons and daughters, is meant to supercede the slavish reliance upon mediations, the fear of leaving behind familiar supports and calculable means. The carnal attitude is, then, basically a substitution of law for the grace of Christ.[19]

What Segundo is, indeed, rejecting in the above is the claim of anything created, laws, rites, even morality, to have efficacy in itself. The consequence would be the unacceptable obligation to subordinate personal liberty to a thing in order to reach God.

Nevertheless, Segundo still maintains that there is an "indirect efficacy" in all things, which must be taken into account if Christian liberty is not to be transformed into a new slavery (cf. Gal. 5:13).[20] The point he is making is that instruments must be used in accordance with their nature, but under the direction of the Spirit. With this new attitude, the created universe comes under human jurisdiction, as Paul claims: "All are yours; and you are Christ's; and Christ is God's" (1 Cor. 3:22f.). This is a basic assertion which Segundo will recall repeatedly.

The implications of the above for Segundo's understanding of efficacious love is obvious. Love, to be effective, must be the mature exercise of liberty in the use and direction of appropriate means. It carries the responsibility of knowing available mechanisms in order to use them creatively.

Segundo identifies a parallel to the Pauline "flesh-Spirit" tension in John's "world-hour" image. He explains John's use of the term "world" in its negative sense as referring to a "collective, massive, impersonal force." It is opposed to the "hour" of Christ's redemptive irruption into human existence. John thus represents this world as a structured, closed totality that resists all penetration from without (cf. Jn. 2:16). Its values and desires are identical with the objects of nature (1 Jn. 2:16). It comprises, then, a closed circle of inauthentic, systematized values, a structured determinism that rejects all novelty and is incapable of the "crisis" necessary to break that circle. In such a portrayal of John's concept of this world, Segundo is uncovering the enslaving determinism of instruments that are not directed by personal liberty. Hence, the "hour" of Jesus, which John opposes to the "world", is primarily the triumph of truth and liberty, the glorification that is achieved in the total self-emptying of Jesus. It is simultaneously the judgment of the world (Jn. 12:31f.).[21]

Segundo notes that this victory of Christ is not according to the categories of the world, for although the Word uses means that pertain to its structure, he maintains his liberty towards what he desires to save and transform, even though death is the price of this liberty (Jn. 10:36). Similarly, a full human life entails living the hour within the structure of this world. This implies hope for the insertion of the light into the mechanism of the world, the indispensable requirement of efficacy. Nevertheless, an element of ambiguity persists. As Segundo puts it:

> Even though liberty bursts into the world from outside the vicious circle of the world, the only place where it can work itself out is the world. The *hour* in which liberty and persevering love find fulfilment must take place in the world. For the world is nothing else but the community of mankind, and it also constitutes the very object of liberty. To give into the world and its mechanisms is to oppose Christ; but by the same token, to love the world and give one's life for it is to follow the pathway of God himself. "God loved the world so much that he gave his only Son" to save it from itself by injecting

a higher liberty into its mechanistic routine.[22]

As with Segundo's analysis of the Pauline "flesh", so in this interpretation of the Johannine "world", it is clear that the efficacy of love can be interpreted as directly related to the mechanisms of nature, intended here primarily in its social, systematized dimensions. Love, as the concrete expression of liberty, must be the absolute value that creatively directs the instruments which its efficacy necessarily demands. It thus gives to nature meaning and profundity, effecting, indeed, a "new creation." In that consists the victory of Christ's self-sacrificing love. The term "efficacious love", therefore, reveals the very tension which characterizes human existence. For the value of gratuitous love is inevitably linked with the requirement of efficacy in accord with the concrete human situation.

In summary, then, Segundo emphasizes the efficacy of love as the novel stress of Christianity. By this he intends not only the fact that love must be concrete in order to be real and authentic, but even more, that it must be expressed according to the exigencies of human existence. It must use the instruments available, knowing their mechanistic determinisms in order to direct them in the interest of humanization, through the exercise of freedom. Hence, human limitations are implied both in the receiving and giving of love. But this is, indeed, the condition of its efficacy.

As can be seen from the above, Segundo's use of scripture is not an arbitrary selection of proof texts to be taken in their literal sense. Rather, he is seeking to retrieve from scripture hitherto neglected elements in order to respond to questions that arise in the experience and critical analysis of concrete, historical situations. Adequate interpretation of the Christian message, in his view, must then include insights drawn not only from philosophy, traditionally used to mediate past truth, but, perhaps, even more from the social sciences which are necessary to mediate the truth of present realities.[23] It is, therefore, imperative to consider the other major influences mentioned above as formative of his thought. These will not only illumine Segundo's exegesis of specific scriptural passages, but will also deepen the understanding of efficacious love thus far explicated. We turn now to Segundo's use of existentialist philosophy and, in particular, that of Nicolas Berdyaev as it relates to the development of this notion.

2. The Existentialist Philosophy of Nicolas Berdyaev

As mentioned above, the existentialist philosophy of Nicolas Berdyaev has a decisive influence on Segundo's theological reflections.[24] In view of this, it is reasonable to expect that Segundo's understanding of the notion of efficacious love will assume added dimensions as it is considered in direct relationship to aspects of that philosophy. Hence, in what follows we will examine that assumption in accord with these three aspects of human existence which Segundo explores: (a) human existence as existential plenitude; (b) human existence as characterized by the union of person with God; and (c) human existence and objective reality. In considering these three points Segundo brings to the surface the rootedness of human existence in the Divine Love. Participation in that love creates and transforms persons. However, the union of love by which human existence is meant to be characterized implies a mutual self-gift of God and human beings. Therefore, it requires free, personal response. But since human freedom is limited and conditioned by external reality, human response of love will always be in accord with the concrete conditions of human existence. We shall see how Segundo argues these points, beginning with the first.

(a) Human existence as existential plenitude

An initial statement of Segundo's basic understanding of existentialism appears in his earliest publication, *Existentialismo*. It is significant that in it he stresses the necessity of grasping human existence in its total reality, in its existential plenitude.[25] This implies, firstly, that human existence is oriented towards "existential contact" with others; secondly, that there is a complementarity of the cognitive and affective dimensions of that contact such that existential knowledge is subordinated to, yet necessary for, existential meaning; and thirdly, that ultimately, human existence is grounded in the absolute existence of God.

In reference to the first, Segundo defines human existence as a "self-construction through love." He argues this on the basis of human finitude which calls for complementarity and fulfilment through contact with others. As Segundo puts it, "Love is, then, what through the means of existential contact allows one to *project* oneself indefinitely, to construct oneself."[26] Likewise, it is through love that others around us acquire their meaning and become part of our existential plenitude. Accordingly, in this very orientation, the social dimension of human existence emerges as an important aspect of that existence.

In explaining the second point, viz., that the cognitive dimension of that existential contact, as the necessary complement of the affective dimension, is at once subject to and subordinated to existential meaning, Segundo places the emphasis on the "affective existential contact" as the "fundamental act" of existence. It can be practically expressed in the need "not to explain life but to communicate it." Hence the immediate objective of this existential reality is to open up new horizons, to fashion a fuller existence.[27] Here, the creative and transformative power of love is disclosed as a primary value.

It is in the exposition of the third point, that human existence is ultimately grounded in the absolute existence of God, however, that the understanding of the experience of love as a moment of existential plenitude is brought out most fully. Human existence is seen to be immersed in infinite Existence, in the superabundant love of the Absolute. As Segundo puts it:

> Through him we participate in each one of our loves, since we love something of his in every moment of existential plenitude. Is our yearning not for existence without limit? And could that existence

without limit be an abstraction? What we love in reality, if we know
how to express it well, is an Existence without limits, a person
existing in himself, in an Absolute *You*.[28]

In this way, human life is being gradually filled with the plenitude of God, the
gift of his love, of his superabundance.

Such insights from existentialist philosophy support Segundo's biblical
interpretation of love as creative and transformative of human existence. But
most of all, they indicate that the Johannine definition of God as love which
emerges from the inner reality of God's own life, means, for Segundo, the
superabundance of life that is at the very depth of all forms of created existence.
This will remain a basic given throughout his theological reflections.

(b) Human existence as union of person with God

To explore further the implications of the union of love between God and
the human person as established above, Segundo draws from Berdyaev the
notion of *theandrism*. This is the application of the characteristics of the
hypostatic union in Jesus Christ to the union of God and the human being.
These characteristics are: the distinction of the divine and the human;
interiority, i.e., the union without loss of distinction; and reciprocity, mutual
self-giving. The last implies the synthesis of the former two. As Berdyaev puts
it: "For God, the human person is an *end*, a friend, from whom He awaits love
and creative achievement. For the human being, God is the *end*, the object of
love. He is the one in whose name a person accomplishes creative acts."[29]

Segundo emphasizes that this does not signify mutual dependence but
rather the relating of one to the other as *end*, not as means, the strange need of
love not to monopolize but to give. Although Berdyaev does speak of a mutual
"need" of God and the human person as revealed in spiritual experience,
Segundo is aware of the inexactness of the term. "Indeed," he comments, "the
need of love in its profound sense, that is, as it takes the beloved as an end,
intends that the beloved's very self be realized."[30]

Now, since, for Berdyaev, God is primarily liberty, the gift of himself
which love entails is a gift of liberty to the human person. This gift then
becomes the inner law of liberty and of creation, the "deification" of the human
being. Transposed to the level of nature, reciprocity consists in God bestowing
on the human person the "*natural* conditions of liberty." In turn, the human
person relates to God "in consecrating to him a new creation, a new situation of
being, a work of liberty, absolute novelty by which humanity gives to God what
God himself cannot give to himself."[31] This reciprocity of love and co-creation
God can only await as a free human response.

Such a free and reciprocal relationship between God and humanity
portrays, for Berdyaev, a different image of God from the static, unmoved, self-
sufficient God of Greek philosophy. It implies not imperfection, but the perfect
freedom with which God loves, a liberty which indicates the sacrifice and
tragedy of love as coming not from insufficiency but from plenitude and
superabundance.[32]

This understanding of love as reciprocal thus clarifies what Segundo
intends in his interpretation of God's love starting from human experience rather

than from the static image of Greek philosophy.[33] For him, love is free because it flows from absolute liberty and is, in turn, authentic only as it expresses that liberty. It is creative of the person who, in response, co-creates the universe with God because God chooses to be in need of human collaboration. Efficacious love is seen here to be liberty in action, the divine, creative force of the universe.

But that which becomes even clearer in reference to Berdyaev's existentialist philosophy, is what Segundo means by God's self-gift making the human person a sharer in divinity. The Eastern theme of *theosis* grounds this affirmation, making of the union of God and humanity the closest imaginable, one that intensifies rather than obliterates differences. An understanding of God as object of all love, and consequently of love of God being identified with love of neighbour, is thus in accordance with the very dynamic of this union.

(c) Human existence and objective reality

However, where Berdyaev's influence is, perhaps, most decisive in Segundo's understanding of love is precisely in regard to its need to be efficacious, to be concretized in reality. This relates to the very core of Berdyaev's prophetic philosophy, described by Segundo as the revolt of the subterranean human being against the necessity of the objectified world. The latter is experienced as exterior constraint as soon as the personal is suppressed. Berdyaev argues for the primacy of liberty over being and, hence, a directing of nature by liberty to serve the construction of persons, though according to the structures of nature itself. As Segundo expresses it, "the destination written in the essence of being is to be the instrument of personal love."[34] In accord with this, Berdyaev also focusses on the need for love to be concrete. "Absolute love", he says, "is always a love of the individual and of the concrete. It is always love of the person... because one cannot love what is general and abstract."[35] And with this emphasis Segundo concurs.

Such an understanding of love's efficacy reinforces the valuation of human life and of the created universe. This indicates a strict application of the incarnational principle as evidenced in Segundo's exegesis of the Pauline "flesh-Spirit" and Johannine "world-hour" tension.[36] Segundo thus insists repeatedly that visible transformation must accompany and verify the presence of authentic love. He also demands that love use efficaciously the mechanisms of nature, its only available instruments, to personalize and liberate the universe in the face of an inherent tendency toward impersonalization and servitude.

To summarize, the existentialist philosophy of Nicolas Berdyaev, in particular, is a major influence in Segundo's understanding of the notion of efficacious love. Love defines the structure of human existence as inherently social, interpersonal and grounded in the infinite plenitude of Divine Life. It implies reciprocity in the relationship between God and the human person. This reciprocity indicates God's free self-gift to humanity, in effect, a sharing of divine liberty which makes possible a free response of love. It invites human beings to be co-creators of persons. But in doing this, love must be "efficacious", must respect and use nature for the realization of concrete persons and projects of love. Efficacious love is, then, the authentic exercise of liberty in the construction of the universe.

3. Marxist Thought

Segundo has noted the influence of Russian Marxism on Berdyaev. He has also admitted Marxist influence on his own thought and that of Latin American theologians in general. This influence he explains partly in terms of the decisive impact of Marxist thought, albeit recognized as diversely interpreted, on Western social thought. "After Marx", he writes, "our way of conceiving and posing the problems of society will never be the same again."[37] But apart from this, on a more practical level, Segundo holds that the objective of Marxism which subordinates atheism to the construction of a just society coincides with Christianity's which subordinates the sabbath to humanity.[38] Hence, although Segundo does not explicitly speak of efficacious love in relationship to Marxism, his dialogue with aspects of that thought will, nevertheless, expand the parameters within which his understanding of the notion is to be grasped.

A clear and concise statement of Segundo's interpretation of Marxist thought appears in his *Faith and Ideologies* in which he examines Marxism as the most important example of an ideology according to his neutral or positive definition of the term as a structure of means ordered to a goal.[39] He attempts "to salvage the imperishable nucleus of the Marxist ideology insofar as it does relate precisely to faith."[40] He focusses, then, on an analysis of both historical materialism and dialectical materialism. These we will consider in turn.

(a) Historical materialism

Segundo's analysis of Marxist thought takes as its point of departure Marx's objective to *change* rather than to *explain* reality, as stated in the eleventh thesis of Feuerbach.[41] This is particularly significant in view of the fact that response to this Marxist challenge is an important formative element of Segundo's theology, as of the entire Latin American liberation theological enterprise.[42]

On the basis of that stated objective of Marx, Segundo argues that the theory of historical materialism does not necessarily intend a deterministic relationship between the system of ideas (the superstructure) and the actual economic conditions (the material base) which are generally identified as the main elements of that theory. He writes:

> Any immediately deterministic conception of the relationship between structure and superstructure, logically ends up as an "explanation" of what necessarily takes place. For in such a conception, the material base deterministically produces everything essential on the plane of consciousness. But since only the plane of consciousness could, voluntarily and initially, introduce changes in the economic process itself (i.e., in the mode of production), it follows from the above conception that all meaningful change must

remain alien to human will and praxis.[43]

On the contrary, Segundo contends that a more nuanced understanding of Marxist historical materialism surfaces these elements:

1) There is a certain necessary and determining (i.e., causal) relationship between the mode of production and the particular ideology in question.

2) This necessary and determining relationship is not immediate. It is operative in the last instance or ultimately, and hence it is open to a relative autonomy.

3) This necessary and determining relationship does not permit us to value, in the first instance, any ideological element without further ado.[44]

Corresponding to these three elements are three interrelated "levels" or factors which provide the content for Segundo's own interpretation of the concept of historical materialism.

(1) The level of the materials

The first level is that of the "materials". It stresses the fashioning of the ideological superstructure out of the materials of the concrete world. It posits a causal link between the highest degree of abstract and often distorted ideas (the superstructure) with the material base (the structure), more specifically described as the modes of production of an era and the human relations that are generated through the division of labour. Segundo argues that a more faithful reading of Marx demands an interpretation of that structure-superstructure relationship according to changing, historical circumstances. This would entail the evaluation of the means employed to achieve specific ends. However, to speak of desired goals immediately implies the need to refer to Marx's system of values, to his basic humanism.[45] Segundo, therefore, concludes that there is, indeed, a basis in Marx for positing a primary level of dependence of a system of ideas and implied values on the material base.

The implications of Segundo's interpretation of this first level of historical materialism for his understanding of efficacious love is readily apparent. The use of materials, as provided in limited, historical situations, is the condition, *sine qua non* for the realization of any value-inspired project. This necessarily limits the reach of love's efficacy.

(2) The level of the last instance

This level refers to the ultimate determinism which Segundo sees as expressed in this basic assertion of Marx, "the ruling ideas (or ideologies) of every age in history were always the ideas of the ruling classes."[46] However, Segundo argues that Marx's explanation of that insight is inadequate because he was unaware of an important scientific law which explains that precise phenomenon. The law to which Segundo is referring here is the thermodynamic law of *entropy*.[47] Basically it refers to the constant amount of energy in the universe and the tendency of that energy to deteriorate. This explains the passive and simplistic acceptance by the general populace of whatever socio-economic and political structures are imposed by the ruling social group. As a consequence of this lack, Marx also overlooks, in Segundo's view, the contrary tendency to overcome that degradation which science also identifies. That contrary tendency is present in certain elements of the "superstructure". However, these elements have not been allowed to make their impact felt in Marxist thought. The reason, Segundo claims, is the failure to "draw out the logical consequences from the basic intention of historical materialism",[48] as expressed in that classic statement of Marx.

For Segundo, then, a more authentic interpretation of this "last-instance" determinism would be alert to the mechanisms of destruction and passivity inherent in the general population. Such an awareness would utilize the creative, though momentary contributions of superstructural values and ideas. And included in these, is, of course, the absolute value of efficacious love.

(3) The level of the first instance

The level of the first instance indicates, for Segundo, the need for critical evaluation of cultural forms. This need logically arises if there is, indeed, an interconnection between the superstructure and the structure, and if the superstructure does have a specific contribution to make to societal growth. The affirmation of this has been the point of Segundo's entire interpretation of Marx's historical materialism. Hence, ideological critique has become the aspect of Marx's historical materialism that Segundo has incorporated most significantly into his theological method. He writes of the need for this Marxist "suspicion":

> What historical materialism does, to the extent that it avoids relapsing into coarse determinism by ignoring the level of the first instance, is to establish in a richer and more realistic way the often unnoticed relationship between the values one professes and the realizations one accepts. If Marx has been called one of the great "masters of suspicion", it is precisely because he showed that human beings committed to certain values allow themselves to be convinced that the existing cultural forms do in fact represent those values; that they spend their days in the face of realities which belie those values without even noticing it; that their own experience of sustaining values is infiltrated by the distorting influence of their adaptation to a reality whose forms are totally opposed to their values.[49]

The Marxist notion of historical materialism, therefore, provides a theory capable of uncovering the authentic face of reality, necessary for the exercise of efficacious love. It is significant that Segundo's interpretation is guided by Marx's objective to transform rather than to explain reality. This dovetails with his insistence that love that is efficacious truly transforms persons and the structures of society. It is also significant that Segundo accepts the conditioning of the materials of the world in the realization of values, but insists on a relative autonomy on the level of the superstructure. It is obvious from this that love must use the instruments available to realize its efficacy. But, perhaps, most significant of all, is Segundo's conclusion that Marxist suspicion is an important consequence of historical materialism. In this is based the notion of *ideological critique* which will play a pivotal role in Segundo's theological method. It suggests that the efficacy of love will demand such a critique of reality in order to arrive at an authentic response in any given historical situation.

(b) Dialectical materialism

Segundo affirms the centrality of the dialectical method in Marxist thought. The key issue which he attempts to address in his explication of that term is the specific characteristic which distinguishes the Marxist dialectic from that of Hegel, viz., its *realism*.

Following Lukácks, Segundo indicates that dialectic relates parts to a whole specifically in terms of a totality "fashioned by a *human project*." Thus he stresses that it is to the realm of human *history* that dialectic applies. However, he indicates that "it is not just a knowledge of history, it is part of history, giving direction to the latter and making it."[50] By this he intends to emphasize the fact that it is not a matter of viewing the events of history as elements which eventually comprise a total process. Rather, he claims, it is the reciprocal interaction and change of elements which is crucial for dialectics. The basis of that claim is Engels' representation of the dialectical laws of Hegel,[51] and particularly the second which is "the law of the interpenetration of opposites." In the application of this law to the area of human projects, Segundo contends, "the 'dialectical' method takes on much greater realism and precision."[52] This is what Segundo attempts to do in order to get at the real intent of the Marxist dialectic.

Assuming that there are obstacles in every human project, Segundo points out that true opposition is not located in persons or things generally, but rather in the "intentions" or "projects" of persons. Hence, it is not conflict as such which comprises a dialectic. On the contrary, the latter involves a critical point beyond which an intention loses its objective and becomes counter-productive. As a result, a dialectic is to be understood as opening up possibilities towards transformative praxis. It is not a matter of contemplating the mechanical unfolding of historical events.[53]

It is not surprising, then, that Segundo will look for the determining characteristic of the Marxist dialectic precisely in its intent to put the Hegelian dialectic on its feet. The shift that he emphasizes is, therefore, that from "idealism" to "realism". The terms of the Marxist dialectic, he claims, are "real human beings" on whom the movement and development of the dialectic will depend. "No one and no thing *behind* it", no "cunning of reason" will be responsible for that.[54] Thus "real movement and real changing of the world" mark the Marxian dialectic. "What cognition now finds before it", Segundo writes,

is a realist hypothesis: the world is the way it is because a real
someone is interested in it being that way. And once philosophy (or
cognition) is applied to the praxis of changing that objective world,
dialectic shows us how that *practical* process is set in motion.[55]

It is to be noted, however, that such an understanding of dialectic does not
immediately account for Marx's option to struggle on the side of the proletariat.
This option is rather implied by the dialectic as a pre-dialectical commitment,
that is, an option "to change the world by establishing values."[56] Hence,
Segundo's interpretation of Marxist dialectic, as was the case with his
explication of historical materialism, reverts to the humanism of Marx as a
decisive factor that must be taken into account.

As can be seen from the above, Segundo stresses in particular two facets of
the Marxist dialectic. Firstly, the interaction of the terms of the dialectic as
involving mutual transformation; and secondly, the concrete, historical reality
of the terms involved in the dialectical movement. He draws out a third factor,
namely, the direction of the movement by a prior option of specific values as the
logical implication of the dialectic. These three emphases are consistent with
the fundamental objective of Marx, to change rather than to explain the world.

Interpreted in the light of the above, the notion of efficacious love itself
underlies the dialectical nature of all human historical response in which *real*
transformation is effected. The stress on mutual interaction of the terms of the
dialectic, again suggests the conditioning of love by the reality it seeks to
transform and a consequent need for love to be sensitive to specific historical
conditions. The realism of the dialectic implies a love that is no other than the
Johannine love which is primarily of deeds, not of words. Finally, the pre-
dialectical option of values is indicative of Segundo's conviction that the value
of love must guide the instruments it uses in its movement to efficaciously
create a new world.

4. The Evolutionary Theory of Teilhard de Chardin

The synthesis of Teilhard de Chardin represents a timely response to the
problematic of modern atheism and its allure of promethean control over human
destiny. The prelude to all this was the new humanism, born of a sense of
responsibility for history and for the earth. The question of human liberty
captured philosophical attention and the construction of a better world became
the goal of human endeavour. In the face of this challenge, in some respects
shared both by Berdyaev and by Marx, Teilhard brought back the novel
emphasis of Christianity, viz., the identification of religion and human
responsibility for the building up of the earth. The shift from an immobilist
vision to an evolutionary thrust, the specific contribution of Teilhard to the
Second Vatican Council, launched Catholic Christianity into the modern era.[57]

Thus Teilhard de Chardin has provided Segundo with a "key" for
interpreting the Christian message with relevance for the contemporary world.
Because Segundo's reinterpretation of the major symbols of Christianity will be

specifically within this evolutionary framework, basic insights drawn from Teilhard will recur throughout his writings. Hence, the concern is to see what further light such insights will throw on Segundo's understanding of the notion of efficacious love. But first, it will be necessary to consider his discussion of Teilhard's evolutionary theory.

(a) Teilhard's evolutionary theory

The aspects of Teilhard's evolutionary theory which Segundo presents, relate specifically to Christianity as the culmination of the rise of consciousness that marks the human threshold. Hence, he points to the principle of analogy as the most basic given of that theory. Through the application of that principle, Segundo explains, Teilhard is able to remove the theory of evolution from the specialized field of paleontology and to convert it into a "system of images, concepts and symbols of value applicable to humanity and to the universe."[58] What legitimizes the use of this principle is a "powerful desire for coherence" which Teilhard claims is at the depth of humanity.[59]

It is in accord with that basic supposition that Segundo interprets Teilhard's understanding of Christianity as "an indispensable and definitive factor" of universal evolution. Christianity adds to humanity's consciousness of itself, God's revelation of the mystery of the human person who is revealed in Jesus to be structured by love. Hence, Christianity, for Teilhard, is a "phenomenon of universal breadth which signifies the *appearance,* in the interior of the human structure, of a new vital order."[60] This new vital order is that of a Christified universe, structured by the same principle which governed the life of Christ, that of love. This, according to Teilhard, is not "only a secondary effect added to the creative process, but the operative factor and the fundamental dynamism."[61]

As a "new vital order", Christianity, in Teilhard's view, marks a "threshold", or a critical point of evolution. A threshold is characterized by two, almost contradictory, aspects. On the one hand, it registers, in terms of a *quantitative* increase, a change that it imperceptible; on the other hand, it is a *qualitative* breakthrough to a new world. The former refers to the fact that, from the perspective of a lower cycle, there is no way of grasping what will become clearly visible at the following level. The reason is that there is no perceptible change in quantity to make that possible. This, Segundo holds, is what is meant by Teilhard's basic claim that "the mystery of each cycle of the world is in the following cycle."[62] In other words, not everything that is presently at work in the universe is immediately verifiable.

The second aspect that characterizes the threshold, the *qualitative* change, is empirically unverifiable because it does not denote a *quantitative* increase. It is the breakthrough to a new level of existence. It is the capacity to act in a new way, to perceive reality from a different standpoint. Teilhard's interpretation of Christianity as a new threshold thus signifies an "empowering" of humanity to assume the responsibility of mature filial cooperation with God for the direction of the universe. Teilhard's image of "piloting" as a substitute for "drifting" expresses this well:

> Up to now human beings have lived apart from each other, scattered around the world and closed in upon themselves. They have been like passengers who accidently met in the hold of a ship, not even suspecting the ship's motion. Clustered together on earth, they found nothing better to do than to fight or amuse themselves. Now, by chance, or better, as a natural result of organization, our eyes are beginning to open. The most daring among us have climbed to the bridge. They have seen the ship that carries us all. They have glimpsed the ship's prow cutting the waves. They have noticed that a boiler keeps the ship going and a rudder keeps it on course. And, most important of all, they have seen clouds floating above and caught the scent of distant islands on the horizon. It is no longer agitation down in the hold, just drifting along; the time has come to pilot the ship. It is inevitable that a different humanity must emerge from this vision.[63]

Segundo's repeated use of this image suggests that he shares Teilhard's conviction that the "great human task" is, indeed, the "direction of history", though he may not entirely agree with the latter's optimism regarding the manner of its achievement.[64]

Segundo is careful to note the great disproportion between the quantitative and the qualitative in the universe. This is evidenced in the comparatively small number of human beings, who have a qualitatively greater capacity for creativity, *vis-à-vis* the abundance of organic life. He contends that the thrust of evolution, as indicated by Teilhard, is, indeed, in the direction of qualitative change. It is the achievement of greater complexity, of higher syntheses, which entails the sacrifice of immediate satisfactions such as belong to the lower levels of the evolutionary process. Nevertheless, there is a quantitative dominance of the contrary force. Both movements are simultaneously at work, the one towards simpler forms, to the quantitative, to *entropy*, the other towards the more complex, to the qualitative, to *neg*-entropy. Applied to the process of humanization, the tension of forces is represented in what Segundo, following Paul, calls the "law of members" over against the realization of self, of personalization.

Segundo insists that the process of humanization is not realized in suppressing the quantitative. Rather, it is achieved by utilizing its law according to its own effectiveness. The concern to hold together in creative tension these two basic characteristics of evolution, viz., the quantitative and the qualitative, entropy and negentropy will remain with Segundo. How this tension influences his notion of efficacious love itself we shall now see.

(b) Evolutionary theory and efficacious love

The notion of efficacious love captures the unity in tension of love as ideally expressed in the free, unconditional gift of self, in total gratuity, and love needing to be concretely expressed and effectively creative of the other. We will discuss the implications of each of these two aspects of efficacious love in turn.

(1) The gratuity of love

Segundo links the possibility of gratuity in human love to the evolutionary force of negentropy. Like the latter, gratuity moves against the grain; it is capable of making immediate sacrifices for more mediate benefits. It is the *qualitative* breakthrough over against *quantitative* proliferation. As Segundo puts it, it is a "minority affair without being an elitist one." He writes:

> It is a minority affair because it wells up from the entropy-ridden base that continues to dominate quantitatively even on the human level. It is not elitist because the love which thus comes to light is at the service of negentropy in the universe. It structures the universe for syntheses that are richer, more human, more redemptive.[65]

In accord with this position, Segundo envisions, with Teilhard, the proposed ideal of free, unconditional love fashioning the Christian synthesis towards greater complexity and concentration, towards a veritable "synthesis of centres."[66]

In focussing on the gratuity of love, Segundo thus makes liberty the hallmark of the Christian synthesis. In this way, he is able to assert the value of the person as defined by liberty over against the statistical law of numbers. This renders unacceptable the instrumentalization of the person to which every simplistic synthesis tends. Hence, in the process of personalization a "synthesis of absolutes" is created.[67]

Human liberty, expressed in love and in the unity of persons in love, is, therefore, released in Christianity for the continued progress of humanity. The question of the precise moments when a new synthesis can be achieved remains a crucial one.[68] This we shall see in Segundo's argument for a truly *efficacious* love.

(2) The efficacy of love

Segundo argues that it is possible to apply the terms of the final judgment as represented in Matthew 25:31-46 to every stage of human evolution. He maintains, "the measuring rod is real, effective love described by Matthew in terms of its content closest to home: food for the hungry, water for the thirsty and so forth." However, what this means will differ in accordance with specific situations because evolution is not uniform. Segundo claims that there are situations which "due to stagnation or regression, are situations in which love must be particularistic, exclusivistic, violent, and solidly based on instinct if it is to be efficacious."[69] Segundo supports this claim by appealing to the type of morality advocated by Jesus (cf. Mk 7:18-27). This morality, he argues, is not an a-temporal application of pre-determined judgments of good and evil, but rather the consideration of ethical values inhering in human projects. In other words, it is the concrete realization of specific values in given circumstances that determine the moral quality of human actions. Thus he can conclude that "efficacious love is the only demand imposed by Jesus for all times."[70]

To stress the efficacy that love requires, however, is not to lose sight of the challenge that Jesus offers in advocating love of enemies as the special mark of the Christian (cf. Lk. 6:27-36). This and similar passages Segundo interprets as Jesus' call to "another kind of *efficaciousness* that is possible for love. It is a form of efficacy that we tend to spurn in our normal, everyday lives, that is, the *risky adventure of gratuitous,* of grace-full living."[71]

Segundo, therefore, calls attention to three possible interpretations of the Gospel's requirement of efficacious love: (1) an identification of the Gospel message with free, unconditional love, that is, non-resistance to evil at all times, a virtual rejection of evolution; (2) making the gratuitous aspect of love subject to the more decisive requirement of love to be *efficacious*; and (3) a unity in tension of the previous two interpretations. This last position affirms that the only criterion of divine judgment is love that is efficaciously in touch with reality, while simultaneously accepting the challenge of unconditional love in opening up "new vistas of efficaciousness."[72] Segundo supports the third position.

To cultivate a gratuitous way of responding to the Christian message, finally, is the task of a whole lifetime in which the entire person is structured psychically by every transformative action. Tension does exist, then, in one who accepts that the efficacy of love can be present in situations of violence and yet is psychically unable to participate in that efficacy because of a determination to live love unconditionally. "If this tension is truly lived and overcome", Segundo concludes, "then Christians who are deeply Christian will shoulder the task of efficacious love when new conditions decide the issue: i.e., whether stimulus for active solidarity should be physical, economic or moral."[73]

Efficacious love is, then, not the love that avoids harming others at all costs but rather the love that furthers the progress of evolution by affirming authentic human existence in all its forms and structures. It is love that will be sensitive to the precise moments when a positive thrust can turn into destruction by going beyond the bounds of its real usefulness.[74]

In summary, then, within the evolutionary framework of Teilhard de Chardin, efficacious love is, for Segundo, the measuring rod of what the Christian message demands at every stage of human development. It makes clear that for love to be efficacious it must respect the rhythm of history, of individual and societal growth.

Most of all, an evolutionary outlook affirms the real possibility of the Christian authentically appropriating the new attitudes introduced by Jesus of Nazareth, specifically the challenge of loving one's enemies. These new attitudes point to a love that is efficacious precisely by being free and unconditional. Far from suggesting a static norm, they are the end point of an effort which is creative and sensitive to the occasions in human life when new and richer syntheses can be brought about only by this free gift of self.

Finally, an evolutionary understanding of Christianity explains more fully the extraordinary nature of living gratuitously, that is, beyond the confines of strict reciprocity. It is extraordinary, not because few achieve it, but rather because love's triumph in the process of evolution is always qualitative. It is love at the service of negentropy, structuring the universe for "richer, more human, more redemptive" syntheses.

5. Reflections and Conclusion

As can be seen from the above, these major influences on Segundo interpenetrate and interact with scripture in his understanding of efficacious love. Each functions on a different level, on the personal, social, and cosmic level, in drawing out fuller dimensions of Segundo's understanding of the notion of efficacious love. If, then, scripture remains, for Segundo, the decisive point of reference for his notion of efficacious love, his use of the other disciplines is eclectic, each on its own terms providing insights to deepen and expand his understanding and explication. These insights witness to the richness and unity of human existence, which Segundo is able to incorporate into the meaning of efficacious love.

In evaluating these influences, we must credit Berdyaev for providing Segundo with an open system of thought, capable of undergirding a basic liberative thrust and of capturing and coherently structuring the practical and social turn of his theology as expressed in the notion of efficacious love. It is to be noted, however, that Berdyaev had already initiated a dialogue between Christianity and Marxism, albeit Russian Marxism, which Segundo would further. Hence, the method of dialectic with its turn to the concrete and the realistic, is what, Segundo argues, marks Berdyaev's system. Segundo incorporates Marxist "ideological suspicion" into his own theological method as we shall see more clearly in the following chapter. In respect to both aspects of Marxist thought, the *efficacy* of love is what is emphasized and, for Segundo, this correlates with the novel stress of Christianity. But, perhaps, most important of all is the synthesis of science and faith that Teilhard achieved, thus providing the basic presupposition for Segundo's theology and, indeed, for Latin American liberation theology in general. It is the unity of history with, nonetheless, sacred and secular dimensions. Apart from this, the dynamism of Teilhard's evolutionary theory will advance the objective of Segundo's theological effort to shift theology from an immobilist to an evolutionary framework. Teilhard, then, makes possible the real insertion of the Christian message into the historical, scientific world. This Berdyaev's philosophy of the spirit could not have provided in its own time.

It is not surprising, then, that the clearest statement of Segundo's understanding of efficacious love is formulated in evolutionary terms. "The most efficacious love," he says, "is not a love that avoids occasions of harming others; it is a love that moves evolution forward and leads it toward more human forms and structures of life".[75] This statement captures both the major concern of Berdyaev, the liberation of the human person in history, and that of Marx, the need to transform, not to explain the world. These are the objectives that Segundo himself pursues. And the dynamic power that moves humanity to achieve those goals is that of efficacious love. This notion links in creative tension the divine ideal of free, unconditional, "gratuitous" love with the historical demand for that love to be concretely "efficacious". Thus the notion of efficacious love captures the Teilhardian synthesis of heaven and earth, tempered with Marxist realism and the concrete consequences of Berdyaev's concept of liberty as definitive of both God and the human person.

Segundo, therefore, defines efficacious love as the free gift of God's very self, manifested most fully in the complete self-emptying of Jesus on the cross. Efficacious love is an expression of the existential plenitude of the life of God which overflows into the creation of human life, substantially transforming that life and making it, in turn, capable of giving life. But God is not only the origin, he is also the object of efficacious love. Love of neighbour is, then, the concrete embodiment of love of God, identified with it, and necessary for any knowledge of God. In this concrete form, efficacious love becomes the very way to union with God, to salvation.

Love's efficacy is the novel stress of Christianity. This efficacy means a real insertion of love into human life according to the exigencies of that life. Efficacious love is, then, the authentic expression of freedom. It is the mutual self-gift of God and humanity. It draws human beings into the closest intimacy with God and engages them in the divine-human task of co-creating the universe.

Efficacious love transforms not only persons but also structures. Since it is conditioned by the instruments it must employ for its realization, it must understand the nature of these instruments and critically direct their use in the service of humanization. Efficacious love is limited by the amount of energy available. Nevertheless, it is the positive vector of evolution, in constant struggle against the forces of destruction that beset human existence. As such efficacious love makes possible even richer syntheses as humanity progresses on the way to maturation. Love that is most efficacious is, then, the love that moves the evolution of humanity towards its fullest realization.

In the following chapter, we shall consider how the concept of efficacious love functions in the theological method of Juan Luis Segundo. This will, it is hoped, uncover deeper dimensions of Segundo's understanding of this most central notion.

Notes

1. Juan Luis Segundo, *The Sacraments Today,* translated by John Drury (New York: Orbis Books, 1974), p. 58.

2. See especially, Juan Luis Segundo, *Etapes precristianas de la fe: Evolución de la idea de Dios en el Antiguo Testamento* (Montevideo: Cursos de complementación cristiana, 1962), pp. 9-11; *The Liberation of Theology,* translated by John Drury (Maryknoll, New York: Orbis Books, 1976), pp. 111-12.

3. Segundo, *The Historical Jesus of the Synoptics,* pp. 45-70.

4. Segundo, *Concepción cristiana del hombre,* p. 8. Segundo burrows this phrase from R. Bultmann.

5. Segundo, *Función de la Iglesia,* p. 32. Cf. *Concepción cristiana del hombre,* pp. 8-10.

6. *Ibid.* Cf. *Concepción cristiana del hombre,* p. 10.

7. Segundo, *Función de la Iglesia,* p. 33. Cf. *Concepción cristiana del hombre,* p. 10.

8. Segundo, *La cristiandad, ¿una Utopia?* II, p. 70.

9. *Ibid.,* p.71.

10. *Ibid.* Cf. *Función de la Iglesia,* p. 34.

11. *Ibid.,* p. 72

12. *Ibid.,* p. 73. Cf. *Concepción cristiana del hombre,* p. 12; *Función de la Iglesia,* p. 34

13. *Ibid.,* p. 74.

14. Juan Luis Segundo, *¿Qué es un cristiano?* (Montevideo: Mosca Hnos. S.A. Editores, 1971). This work is a reprinting of *Etapes precristianas de la fe: Evolución de la idea de Dios en el Antiguo Testamento* and a complementary publication *Concepción cristiana del hombre.*

15. See Chapter III, pp. 51-66 for a fuller discussion of this tension of opposite forces.

16. *La cristiandad, ¿una utopia?* II, pp. 1-45, 75-95.

17. *Ibid.,* pp. 8-21.

18. *Ibid.,* pp. 25-31. This conflict of attitudes was the real issue at stake in Paul's controversy with the Judaisers, according to Segundo. Cf. *The Humanist Christology of Paul,* pp. 13-41.

19. *Ibid.,* pp 31-37. Cf. *The Humanist Christology of Paul,* pp. 42-58.

20. *Ibid.,* p. 37.

21. *Ibid.,* pp. 51-57.

22. Segundo, *Grace and the Human Condition,* p. 81

23. Segundo, *The Liberation of Theology,* pp. 39-66.

24. See Chapter I, pp. 13f.

25. Cf. Segundo, *Existentialismo,* p. 22.

26. *Ibid.,* p. 21

27. *Ibid.,* pp. 42-57.

28. *Ibid.,* p. 83.

29. Nicolas Berdyaev, *De la destination de l'homme. Essai d'ethique paradoxale* (Paris: "Je Sers", 1935), p. 319, cited in *Berdiaeff,* p. 127.

30. Segundo, *Berdiaeff,* p. 127.

31. *Ibid.,* p. 128.

32. *Ibid.,* p. 133.

33. Cf. above pp. 24-29. In *The Liberation of Theology,* pp. 46f., Segundo argues that the adoption of this image by the popular mind was not due so much to the influence of the Greek philosphy itself, as to the need to justify a societal structure in which the success of some was founded on the suffering of others. The triumph of impassibility and self-sufficiency was thus divinized.

34. Segundo, *Berdiaeff,* p. 209.

35. Berdyaev, *De la destination,* p. 244, cited in Segundo, *Berdiaeff,* p. 209.

36. Segundo, *La cristiandad, ¿una utopia?* II. Segundo clearly states the following: "So here, in the person and work of Jesus, the Son, we have the second constitutive element of human history: God with us. In these words, the language which God uses in speaking to us acquires its totally definitive realism through the Word, the divine Word turned into an historical person. It is a language that is infinitely committed and involved, and thus it bestows decisive and absolute value on man's commitment in history." *Our Idea of God,* p. 28.

37. Segundo, *The Liberation of Theology,* p. 35.

38. *Ibid.,* p. 133.

39. See Chapter III, pp. 54f. for a fuller explanation of this term.

40. Segundo, *Faith and Ideologies,* p. 179.

41. Segundo, *The Liberation of Theology,* p. 13. Cf. *Faith and Ideologies,* p. 195, where Segundo argues that this statement is not confined to the youthful Marx.

42. Cf. Jon Sobrino, "El conocimiento teológico en la teología Europea y latinoamericana", *Estudios Centroamericanos,* XXX (1975), pp. 429-34; José Miguez Bonino, *Christians and Marxists: The Mutual Challenge to Revolution* (Grand Rapids, Michigan: Eerdsmans, 1976); José Miranda, *Marx and the Bible: A Critique of the Philosophy of Oppression,* translated by John Engleson (Maryknoll, New York: Orbis Books, 1976).

43. Segundo, *Faith and Ideologies, p. 182.*

44. *Ibid.,* pp. 180-82.

45. *Ibid.,* p. 188.

46. *Ibid.,* p. 189.

47. See Chapter III, pp. 61f. for a more detailed explanation of this term.

48. Segundo, *Faith and Ideologies,* p. 193.

49. *Ibid.,* p. 194.

50. *Ibid.,* p. 204.

51. These are "The law of the transformation of quantity into quality and *vice versa;* the law of the interpenetration of opposites; the law of the negation of the negation." Frederick Engels, *Dialectics of Nature,* English translation (New York: International Publishers, 1940), p. 26, cited in *Ibid.,* p. 207.

52. Segundo, *Faith and Ideologies,* p. 211.

53. *Ibid.,* p. 216.

54. *Ibid.*, p. 234.

55. *Ibid.*

56. *Ibid.*, p. 235.

57. Segundo, *Grace and the Human Condition*, pp. 82-86.

58. Segundo, *De la sociedad a la teología*, p. 155.

59. *Ibid.*, p. 156.

60. Teilhard de Chardin, *Le Christianisme dans le monde* (unedited, 1933) cited in Emile Rideau, *The Thought of Teilhard de Chardin*, trans. by René Hague (New York/Evanston: Harper and Row, 1967), p. 534, & cited in *De la sociedad a la teología*, p. 157.

61. Teilhard de Chardin, *Introduction au Christianisme* (unedited, 1942), cited in Rideau, *The Thought of Teilhard de Chardin*, p. 370.

62. Teilhard de Chardin, *Genèse d'une pensée* (Paris, 1918), cited in *De la sociedad a la teología*, p. 161.

63. Juan Luis Segundo, *A Community Called Church*, translated by John Drury (New York: Orbis Books, 1973), p. 121. Cf. *De la sociedad a la teología*, p. 163; *An Evolutionary Approach to Jesus of Nazareth*, pp. 21f. This image is taken from P. Teilhard de Chardin, *L'activation de l'energie* (Ed. du Seuil, Paris, 1963), p. 80.

64. See Segundo, *An Evolutionary Approach to Jesus of Nazareth*, pp. 21-31.

65. Segundo, *Evolution and Guilt*, p. 113.

66. Segundo, *De la sociedad a la teología*, p. 170.

67. See *Ibid.*

68. *Ibid.*, p. 118.

69. Segundo, *Evolution and Guilt*, p. 118.

70. *Ibid.*, p. 120.

71. *Ibid.*

72. *Ibid.*

73. *Ibid.*, p. 121. Cf. Juan Luis Segundo, "Camilo Torres, sacerdocio y violencia", *Víspera*, I, no. 1 (May 1967), 71-75.

74. Segundo, *Evolution and Guilt*, p. 123.

75. *Ibid.*, p. 122.

Chapter Three

The Relationship of Efficacious Love to Theological Method

One of the most basic claims of the Latin American liberation theological movement is that liberation theology is not just another theme. It is rather a whole "*new way* to do theology."[1] But method, as the primary definition of Segundo's theology, is more than a manner of interpreting the Christian faith starting from the perspective of the experience of oppression. It belongs to the inner logic of his theological enterprise. His evolutionary interpretation of Christianity necessarily throws the emphasis on process and development, making the "way" to truth an explicit aspect of truth itself.[2]

Besides, the basic insight of the unity of the universe which informs evolutionary thought will not only be a philosophical basis for the major theological presupposition which Segundo shares with liberation theologians in general, namely, the unity of the history of salvation and secular history,[3] it will also provide an analogical link among all the aspects of human existence which Segundo explores. Hence to interpret that existence in the light of the Christian revelation becomes an ongoing task, disclosing new vistas of God's activities in human life. It requires an ever deeper understanding of all facets of that life as mediated through the use of appropriate scientific tools.

In order to relate the notion of efficacious love to Segundo's theological method, therefore, the following two theses will be developed in an attempt to draw out the methodological concerns implied in the above:

> *Thesis I:* Efficacious love is the fundamental value that binds together and illumines most consistently the categories of thought and the sources out of which Segundo's theology is fashioned.

> *Thesis II:* Efficacious love is the fundamental value that structures Segundo's theological reflection by providing its starting point, its goal and the criterion of its development.

These two theses will uncover both the theoretical and the practical bases of Segundo's theology and disclose the unity in tension of theory and praxis that marks his methodology.[4] The intent of this chapter is to determine how the notion of efficacious love functions in drawing out the significance of the various categories of thought and sources that undergird Segundo's theology and also supports the structure of his method. In short, the following will reveal how central a role the notion of efficacious love plays in the theology of Juan Luis Segundo. Before entering into this discussion, however, it will be necessary to consider first how Segundo establishes the unity of sacred and secular history as the major supposition of Latin American liberation theology, in general, and specifically of his own.

Segundo traces the historical origin of the theology of liberation to the breakdown of the theology marked by the dichotomy between the natural and the supernatural and the relegating of all meaningful human activity to a world beyond.[5] A reinterpretation of the classical notion of grace was the basis of that breakdown. Hence, it will be on that renewed interpretation of grace that Segundo will ground his own theological enterprise.

The theologians whom Segundo credits for the new formulation of the doctrine of grace are Henri de Lubac and, in particular, Karl Rahner. Both of them challenged the suppositions on which the dogmatic assertion of the necessity of grace for salvific human actions was based. These suppositions were centred on the notion of gratuity as implying that what is "free gift" cannot be possessed by all and as presupposing the existence of a "pure nature" prior to the "super-nature" made possible by grace. The arguments against these presuppositions stress the fact that the notion of "gift" does not necessarily imply scarcity and that "pure nature" is merely a "limit concept", that is, it is necessary to keep it in mind as a possibility in order to appreciate the gift as a gift.[6]

In a rare autobiographical excursus,[7] Segundo claims that the notion of the universality of grace had been first communicated to him by Leopold Malevez ten years prior to the second Vatican Council and opened the way for his own "theology of liberation". Malevez had arrived at a novel interpretation of the dogmatic affirmation of the "supernatural" character of the "beginning of faith" by examining the historical context of the arguments surrounding the formulation at the Council of Orange (529 A.D.). He discovered that it was the human "virtues" exhibited by pagans and Christians alike which the Council Fathers referred to as an "evangelical preparation". Hence the conclusion:

> Thus, when the Council of Orange declared that the "beginning of faith" was already supernatural, it was stating that the entire road traveled by the pagans (guided by good will and love) - toward the God who is love and toward the Christian message of that Mystery hidden in love - was already (even though it did not lead to the faith) from God, from freely-given grace, and related to the plane of supernatural efficacy.[8]

In this way, Malevez anticipated Rahner's clear, speculative formulation of this reality in his notion of the *supernatural existential* to designate the inherent, supernatural structure of human existence.[9]

Under the influence of Rahner, the affirmation that there is only one history and that in that history all humanity answers, whether consciously or not, the one divine summons of God, was officially endorsed at the Second Vatican council.[10] The Medellín Conference would finally adopt this affirmation. It is, then, on this "orthodox" foundation that Latin American liberation theology has officially emerged. This unity of history, based upon the universal presence of grace, will remain Segundo's most basic theological presupposition. We turn now to the development of the first thesis proposed above.

1. The Major Categories of Thought and Sources

Segundo has developed his theology through the recurrent use of certain categories of thought and sources. These enable him to uncover the meaning of human existence in its various aspects. Hence, insights drawn from diverse disciplines are subjected to the light of the Christian message and, in turn, elicit faith responses that are more adequate to changing historical moments and contexts. In order to determine how the notion of efficacious love functions in Segundo's understanding and explication of these categories of thought and sources the following thesis will be examined:

> *Thesis I:* Efficacious love is the fundamental value that binds
> together and illumines most consistently the categories of thought
> and the sources out of which Segundo's theology is fashioned.

In the development of this thesis it will be important to note the way in which the value of efficacious love functions as a unifying principle of the various categories of thought and sources. It will also be necessary to specify the connection that exists between the value of efficacious love and each of these terms.

Segundo's theological turn to the human makes of anthropology a privileged *locus theologicus* "the one and only place where God and man encounter each other."[11] The various categories of thought employed by him can then be regarded as fundamentally related to his anthropology, inasmuch as they disclose the meaning of human existence in its many dimensions. The categories of thought are differentiated according to the sources from which they are drawn as follows:

Epistemology:	Ideology-faith
Language analysis:	Digital-iconic
Existentialist philosophy:	Necessity-freedom
Social science:	Mass-minority
Physical science:	Entropy-negentropy
Theology:	Sin-grace.

Nevertheless, because of a basic unity in human existence, an analogical link binds these terms together into a unifying whole.[12] This can be seen in Segundo's consistent use of these terms as anthropological descriptions of human existence seen from different perspectives. The fact that efficacious love is the fundamental value to which Segundo constantly returns in his interpretation of these terms likewise makes that notion a unifying principle of these categories of thought and sources.

On another level, there is a further connecting link among the categories of thought and sources in that all of them are marked by the *mass-minority* dialectic which is designated by Segundo as an important "hermeneutical principle".[13] As used by him the terms refer to the tension of opposite forces which pervade human existence in its various aspects. These forces represent, on the one hand, a "minoritarian" thrust characterized by creativity, complexity, decisive and free activity; and on the other hand, a "mass" inclination to passivity, simplification, immediacy and inertia. The notion of efficacious love, as we have seen, also captures that basic tension.[14] On the one hand, the challenge of the Christian message is to love freely and unconditionally; on the other hand, the demands for historical realism cry out for that love to be "efficacious" according to the requirements of the human situation. However, because the love of God is the definitive force, Segundo claims that efficacious love is essentially minoritarian while still being conditioned by the concrete, mass mechanisms of human existence. If, then, in Segundo's explication of these major categories of thought, his arguments for what comprises authentic human response endorse primarily the terms that are expressive of the minoritarian thrust, without breaking the basic tension, it will be clear that the value of efficacious love is fundamental to Segundo's theological reflections and functions as the unifying principle of his thought. In other words, it will be seen that efficacious love is the fundamental value that illumines Segundo's categories of thought and sources most consistently, and binds them together into a coherently constructed theology.

The specific way in which the value of efficacious love is connected to each of these categories of thought is according to the particular objective of the source from which each one derives. We will clarify this connection in the explication of the terms in the order in which they are listed above.

(a) Epistemology: Ideology-faith

Segundo's analysis of the faith-ideology tension is situated within the cultural context of Western industrial society as inclusive of Latin America. Hence, post-Enlightenment rationality and the dominance of the scientific mentality, coupled with the Marxist critique of a palliative religion, are the underlying challenges which Segundo seeks to meet with a clarification of the terms "faith" and "ideology" by showing their distinction and necessary complementarity. By so doing, Segundo brings into further dialogue Christianity as his primary example of religious faith, and Marxism, the most relevant example of an ideology in our contemporary world. The basic problematic is, indeed, the age-old conflict of "faith" and "reason". Therefore, Segundo's attempt at a resolution of that conflict is fundamental to his entire theological endeavour.

Through a phenomenological analysis of concrete human experience, Segundo attempts to redefine the terms "faith" and "ideology". His objective is to rid the terms of ambiguities and oversimplifications which currently hinder a more effective mediation of the present truth of the human reality.[15] Faith, reductively relegated to the realm of religious piety, has often been rejected as mere "illusion" by a "one-dimensional" scientific mentality.[16] Ideology, negatively identified with rigid systems of thought that are basically distortions of reality, unleashes a veritable verbal terrorism on the ordinary believer. Segundo, therefore, endeavours to neutralize both terms by drawing out their anthropological dimension. Thus he interprets the terms as arising from the very structure of human existence at the level where that existence transcends particular historical and cultural contexts.

Segundo argues that both faith and ideology are necessary dimensions of human existence. Faith determines the basic orientation which orders the realm of values. Ideology structures the systems of means and ends which concretize and make them real. Thus faith, as directly related to values, discloses the meaning achieved in particular human lives only as these values are embodied in ideologies, that is, in specific patterns of behaviour. Faith and ideology are then inextricably linked while still operating on two distinct levels of human experience. Faith pertains to the inner subjective experience of meaning and values. Ideology belongs to the outer objective sphere of concrete action.[17]

Segundo's interpretation of "anthropological faith" is based upon his understanding of the structure of human liberty which, as we shall subsequently see more fully, is influenced by the existentialist philosophy of Berdyaev. It is freedom limited by external reality, a liberty that is gradually lost as it is used. This implies that an option in one direction closes off others. Another consequence of this limited freedom is that it is impossible for a human being to experience all the possibilities of human satisfactions before making significant choices.[18] In accord with this experience of freedom as basically limited, Segundo, therefore, argues that the specific structure of values adopted by each person must be communicated by "referential witnesses", persons who demonstrate in their lives the worthwhileness of following certain paths. Because the datum thus used by a person in such options *transcends* the limits of what can be personally verified, it must, therefore, be "believed" in, be accepted in "faith". Hence, faith on this anthropological level of human experience is revealed to be a kind of knowledge of this "transcendent datum".[19] It is an "indispensable component" of every human life. As we shall subsequently see, "religious faith" is, then, but a particular instance of this more universal human dimension.[20]

Anthropological faith thus serves to structure human existence meaningfully by ordering its complex realm of values and by providing a mechanism whereby persons can effectively assess experiences according to accepted values. This faith hierarchizes values, eventually absolutizing one to which all others are then subordinated and conditioned.

This understanding of faith, derived as it is from the presupposition of human dependence upon others for personal realization, clearly indicates its social dimension. At its base are commitment and trust in others, the indispensable requirement for constructive social interactions and for love to be efficaciously experienced.

The necessity of living this faith according to the exigencies of objective reality poses the question of method and the efficacy of available means. This discloses another dimension of human existence that is radically different from faith. Unlike the latter, which is determined by human judgment, the use of instruments as means has an independent, internal logic that is not subject to human freedom. The instruments of nature follow their own inherent laws, oblivious of human intentions.[22] This, we recall, relates to another basic supposition that Segundo affirms with Berdyaev, that human freedom operates in tension with the objective structure of reality. Reality must, then, be *objectively* known in order to be used effectively. Thus Segundo argues that, apart from faith, a second anthropological dimension, which he calls "ideology", also structures human existence.[23]

Segundo uses the term "ideology" here in a specified way. It applies to a system of efficacy that is attuned to the most scientific and rational possibilities of any given period. Simply described, it is "the system of goals and means that serves as the necessary backdrop for any human option or line of action."[24] As such, it is a positive or neutral term.

Segundo stresses the importance of maintaining in creative tension the two dimensions of faith and ideology.[25] Christian faith's claim to absolute values has, at times, disregarded its need and use of relative ideologies. Likewise, Marxist concentration on scientific instruments has been unaware of the "faith" that determines their orientation towards specific goals. Both, he claims, have failed in principle and in fact in laying claim to having, on the one hand, the total meaning of life, and on the other, a complete image of human life in the world.[26]

However, it is significant for our purposes here to note that Segundo emphasizes the subordination of ideology to faith while he insists upon their necessary complementarity. He writes:

> In principle, *ideology* as I define it here, does not determine the meaning-structure or the value-structure of human life; it is the other way around . . . In other words, a value is never chosen as the dominant one simply because it is *realizable*. On the contrary, human beings will seek out methods that are effective in terms of the values they appreciate most.[27]

In thus making faith the determining factor of creative human response, Segundo is stressing the world of values and meaning without denying the means that must be employed to make that world a concrete reality. Since efficacious love is a value, indeed, the only absolute value which seeks at the same time to be real and effective, a link between "faith and ideology" and "efficacious love" becomes apparent. Efficacious love concretizes both the absolute value to which faith is ultimately directed and the system of efficacy that comprises an ideology in Segundo's positive use of the term.

In sum, on the basis of existential data which disclose the inherent limitation of personal freedom and the consequent social structure of human existence, Segundo establishes an understanding of faith with two essential components, namely, transcendent data and referential witnesses. Hence, faith is an anthropological dimension of every human life which structures meaningfully the values that are appropriated. Alongside faith, a second anthropological dimension of human life, "ideology", relates to the realm of efficacy and structures means and ends. Although distinct, faith and ideology are inextricably and necessarily linked but in such a way that ideology, the realm of science and rationality, is placed at the service of faith and the realization of values. The connection can, then, be made between faith and ideology and efficacious love as the only absolute value which is verified more adequately in "deeds" rather than in "words". This makes of efficacious love the fundamental value which grounds Segundo's anthropological explication of the terms "faith and ideology".

(b) Language analysis : Digital-iconic

The ideology-faith tension finds expression in different types of language. Segundo, following Gregory Bateson,[28] uses the two terms "digital" and "iconic". Digital language indicates information that accumulates through addition, is verifiable, and unaffected by attendant circumstances. It relates to the realm of objective reality and is limited to the purely rational. Iconic language, on the other hand, multiplies information, that is, it refers to the learning of principles to be applied in varying contexts. It is the acquiring of a perspective or a mentality. Iconic language does not, then, provide objective data that can be verified empirically. It can only be validated through its embodiment in its subject. In other words, it is "self-validating". It is the communication of personal witness that intends more than mere words can capture. Hence, iconic language is the more complex, the more creative, the more difficult to master but vital for capturing the fulness of human existence. It is the language of poetry, of art, of values. It is the language of scripture and, as such, must be explored for the proper understanding of the Christian message as particularly embodied in its primary witness, Jesus of Nazareth, the Christian "icon" *par excellence*.[29]

The differentiation of digital and iconic language as used by Segundo draws into view the distinction between the objective and subjective realms of human existence. Each is expressive of a specific aspect of the total human reality and must be judged accordingly. Whereas digital language indicates "facts" that can be verified *objectively*, iconic language affirms or rejects *subjective* impressions and is thus subject to a different kind of verifiability. The criterion of truth for the latter is existential and implies a whole way of living in accord with what is affirmed. Iconic language, therefore, relates to the transcendent data that underlie the judgment, the "wager" of faith. It indicates, then, a "general framework" that is at the basis of every human life and can be expressed thus: *"Given this datum, which I take as true even though I cannot verify it empirically right now, in the end it will be seen that it was better to act thus and so."*[30] This existential reality is not created by language but is rather primarily expressed by it.

Segundo argues for the intermingling of digital and iconic language. Digital language needs the iconic in order to communicate with the world of values, inasmuch as iconic language requires the digital in order to explicitly communicate the understanding of reality that undergirds the realm of meaning. However, it is the iconic that Segundo again stresses in view of the simplistic tendency to regard the digital as more proper to human beings as defined by rationality and, hence, to be promoted exclusively in the cause of human progress. Such a tendency prevents rather than furthers evolution because it is restricted in its view of human existence. It also disregards the energy cost. As Segundo puts it:

> . . . no "idealism" should prompt us to forget that digital language is not a methodology designed to systematically replace every possible form of iconic language. It is equally erroneous to think that historical criticism can replace every manifestation of "faith" in the basic human sense. If that were to happen, then the economy of energy in which human beings are inserted would cause the latter to go backward instead of forward.[31]

In asserting the need for more attention to be paid to iconic language, Segundo is again emphasizing the minoritarian attitudes of complexity and creativity in particular and, above all, the world of values as exemplified in the value of efficacious love. More specifically, efficacious love expresses the existential reality of the truth embodied in the person characterized by self-giving and the objective verification of that truth in effective personal witness which is transformative of others. It is "iconic" language in signifying a specific way of loving and it is "digital" in needing to be effectively concretized in action that expresses the logic of that love.

By way of summary, then, in language analysis, faith parallels the iconic in the iconic-digital tension. The "iconic" is language that evokes the subjective realm of feelings and images, the "digital", the language of objective reality that expresses concrete facts. The latter offers empirical verifiability, the former is validated by experience and is demonstrated only in a personal way of life. Iconic language opens up to the fulness of human existence and, as such, is stressed by Segundo as a deterrent to the ascendancy of one-dimensional rationality in our scientific age. Hence, iconic language, without being separated from digital language, expresses and promotes the minoritarian values of creativity, openness and freedom and particularly that of efficacious love. A specific link is thus revealed between the "iconic-digital" and "efficacious love". Efficacious love must be lived in order to be real. It finds its verification not only in words but more truly in transformative deeds. Efficacious love is, therefore, the underlying value that governs Segundo's anthropological interpretation of the digital-iconic tension.

(c) Existentialist philosophy: Necessity-freedom

The necessity-freedom tension defines the central problematic of Berdyaev's existentialist philosophy, Segundo's main philosophical source, as we recall. Berdyaev's entire philosophical project was initiated by his rejection of an objective world experienced as enslaving. This experience of alienation results from the fact that the values of the person are not being realized by the instruments that are being used. Rather, the instruments follow the course of their inherent mechanism and go contrary to the desires of those who use them. Berdyaev's basic concern is, therefore, centred on the quest for liberty and the realization of persons, as defined by liberty. The context is that of a historical existence which threatens to be an impersonal, deterministic movement. What the necessity-freedom tension reflects, then, is the fundamental opposition between the determinism of the material world and the creative activity of the Spirit, and between the subjection of the person and the liberty and unique destiny of the person.[32]

It is clear that Segundo accepts the problematic of the necessity-freedom tension as posed by Berdyaev as a way of approaching the question of the meaning of human existence.[33] Hence, for Segundo, personal liberty experiences as alienating not only its own "nature", but also the mechanisms of objective reality governed by its own inherent principles. In the face of this determinism, liberty can only be realized in creative activity and personal decision. As such, liberty is "the capacity to bestow meaning and value on elements which, both inside me and outside me (i.e., in both the sensible and the spiritual realm), constitute systems that are independent of my free will."[34]

There is, then, a complementarity between liberty and nature as well as an opposition. Liberty must always be exercised in relationship to "conditions" which not only limit it but also make it possible. As a result, there is the need to recognize the numerous conditioning factors, "determinisms", that exist in personal and societal life. Liberty is never given above and beyond these, it must be created. It is a "*possibility* given and a value to be won by handling an ever increasing number of determinisms."[35]

Now, because Segundo perceives an intimate connection between liberty and grace, as we shall see more fully later on, he draws a parallel between the nature that is graced, that is "super-natural", and that which is under the direction of true liberty as expressed in self-giving love. Hence, it follows that the necessity-freedom tension can eventually be most clearly expressed in terms of the efficacy of love and the contrary movement of egotism. Segundo, therefore, writes:

> Insofar as we allow things to drift instead of imprinting our liberty on the forces at our disposal, we immerse ourselves once again in the natural and the pre-human. We revert to the *natural plane of things*. Realized liberty can only be a gift of self, love. Egotism, even when it is freely chosen by liberty, represents a surrender to the impersonal, the easy way out. To the extent that egotism is introduced into love, the human person is transformed into a thing desired and love is transformed into an appetite. The interpersonal relationship is replaced by a relationship between things.[36]

What the above indicates is the tension of the opposite forces, the easy surrender to the deterministic forces of an impersonal nature *vis-à-vis* the contrary, more difficult, more creative struggle towards personal creation. Despite the fact that the tension can never disappear in authentic human existence, liberty is eventually confronted with the choice between "free, personal, supernatural love" and "natural, pre-human egotism." The one creates liberty and the person, the other destroys them. It is clear that value lies on the side of liberty and love. However, this is not meant to be an absolute either-or choice. What it does suggest is a decided shift from an understanding of authentic Christian existence based upon "integral" nature and conformity to that nature to one based upon freedom and the creative construction of persons through efficacious love. In this way Segundo is able to deepen Berdyaev's initial insight regarding a person being defined by liberty and created through love in the struggle against the impersonality of the enslaving forces of an alienating, objective reality. He does this by drawing out the consequences of the valuation of history based upon the universal presence of God's efficacious love in the universe. With this as his starting point, Segundo is able to project authentic human nature to the future as a possibility revealed and offered in Jesus of Nazareth and, as such, a task to be accomplished.

Thus we have seen that the necessity-freedom tension is a basic philosophical schema which Segundo has taken from Berdyaev and applied to his anthropological description of human existence. It uncovers in that existence the tension of liberty struggling to create persons over against the impersonal forces of objective reality. While still maintaining the inevitable impact of the historical conditions of human nature and of culture on the exercise of liberty, Segundo assigns a primacy of value to liberty and its concretization in efficacious love as the creative, dynamic force of humanization. He is, therefore, able to engineer a significant shift from an interpretation of human authenticity based on adequacy to a given nature or an established culture to one based upon personal and societal construction through the exercise of freedom in efficacious love. This shift will have far-reaching implications for his entire theological enterprise.

In conclusion, efficacious love in relationship to the freedom-necessity tension emerges as the fundamental value that gives meaning to human historical existence. It defines that meaning in terms of the transformative power of love which is free and creative of persons and is at the same time efficacious in taking into account the objective conditionings of that existence.

(d) Social Science: Mass-minority

The "mass-minority" tension itself is a category of thought which, in the language of social science, describes a specifically modern phenomenon. In contemporary thought, both terms are ambiguous and carry negative overtones, the latter even more than the former. Segundo's attempt to clarify these terms, as characteristic of human existence on the socio-political plane, draws upon the analysis of Lenin and Ortega y Gasset as two examples of those posing the problematic of the masses which erupted into contemporary society at the beginning of this century.

Segundo finds in Lenin's analysis of mass consciousness and spontaneity the basis of his definition of the term "mass" as opposed and complementary to the term "minority". The problematic with which Lenin was grappling in his *What Is to Be Done?*[37] as he confronted the task of engineering a Marxist revolution in Russia in 1901, was that of the *mass movement* which had arisen since the time of Marx. For Lenin, that movement posed a new challenge requiring "new" and "more complicated" tasks in theory, politics and organization. The reason is that although Lenin still held on to the factor of economic determinism as part of Marxist analysis, he could no longer expect a spontaneous revolutionary turn in the *consciousness* of the masses. After all, the Marxist expectation of the inevitable demise of Capitalism from its inherent contradictions and the spontaneous activity of the proletariat, created by the industrial revolution, had not been fulfilled.[38]

According to Segundo, Lenin at first seems to have associated revolutionary consciousness with the "bourgeois intellectual class" which had the ability to understand the complexity of the socio-economic system and hence what would ultimately benefit the proletariat. However, closer analysis reveals that what Lenin considered necessary for the emergence of revolutionary consciousness is not membership in a specific class but rather the capacity to resist "mass tendencies". In Lenin's view, therefore, mass spontaneity is guided and conditioned by the line of "least resistance" as suggested by the image of "inertia". The attitude which Lenin applied to workers can be used to describe a general human attitude. As Segundo writes:

> It can be summed up in two terms: *over-simplification* which makes a kopeck and a rouble more important than socialism and politics; and *immediatism*, which places oneself and one's children above future generations . . . the two aspects can be summed up under one head: *over-simplification* both with regard to the means to be used and the stages that must be gone through in seeking a solution.[39]

In the end, Lenin associates the mass mechanisms with every social class. He came to recognize that intellectual and professional training were no guarantee but at best a conditioning for acquiring "the intellectual quality that is crucial for any revolutionary change: i.e., the ability to resist the lure of oversimplification and immediatism in one's conception of the social process."[40]

Segundo's analysis of Ortega y Gasset's *The Revolt of the Masses*[41] emphasizes the similarity between the understanding of the term"masses" as represented there and that of Lenin's, despite diametrically opposed starting points. Ortega, whose aristocratic bent has led to the misunderstanding of his position as being elitist, is critical of the crowd which evidences no respect for the traditional separation between the qualified and the ordinary person. However, as Segundo demonstrates, Ortega's analysis of mass mechanisms bears a close parallel to that of Lenin.

Ortega begins by distinguishing between "masses" and "minorities" in view of professional qualifications. His intent is not to stress distinction according to classes, though, like Lenin, he cannot fully escape that. Ortega's attempt at a redefinition at a deeper level, suggests to Segundo an understanding of the "masses" as those unable to "appreciate the long, complex, and delicate process" that has provided the possibility of satisfying expanded "vital desires." Hence, the masses sacrifice critical future possibilities for present goods. There is present in Ortega's redefinition "a striking coincidence" with the characteristics noted by Lenin, viz., *over-simplification* and *immediatism*.

Besides, in Ortega's analysis, the "physical image of inertia" which emerges is comparable to Lenin's "line of least resistance". Therefore, the definition of "masses" and "minorities" which seems to begin in Ortega with a basis in class distinction ends up by indicating more general human characteristics in his recognition that the most specialized professional in contemporary society, the scientist, is at times the epitome of a mass mentality.[42]

What is significant to note is Segundo's own stress on the presence of *inertia* in the masses. He concludes:

> Thus both Lenin and Ortega find that mass conduct is dominated by *inertia*. Qualitatively speaking, it cannot possibly arrive at the more complex and intermediate solutions that will truly contribute to the solution of social problems. Are they not both saying, by implication at least, that the proportion existing between masses and minorities constitute an inescapable law governing the human world, just as the law of inertia in the strict sense governs the physical universe?[43]

That Segundo is convinced that this is so we will subsequently see. For him, then, both Lenin and Ortega y Gasset have surfaced and described in the terms "mass-minority" a tension inherent in the entire universe and, hence, in all aspects of human existence.

In a further sociological analysis of mass behaviour, Segundo identifies two other characteristics that are descriptive of the masses, namely, uniformity and lack of decision making. Indeed, he argues, the very existence of sociology as a verifiable science is based upon numerical statistics and predictability. On the one hand, that implies uniformity in the majority, not in terms of any specific class but rather in terms of social standing. On the other hand, it indicates the unwillingness of the majority to use their liberty in decision making. They abdicate this task to the minority. Segundo's conclusion is that mass mentality thus defines "the person who, whatever his social position may be, delegates his power of judgment and decision to others in *any given area or aspect* of his existence."[44]

Segundo's emphasis on the fact that masses and minorities do not refer to distinct social classes is significant. But neither is he speaking of distinct groups of people. As he puts it, "*masses and minorities do not exist in any absolute sense*. What we find are 'mass and minority' patterns of conduct on *each and every level of life*."[45] Even more specifically, he intends to affirm mass and minority attitudes as present in every person.[46]

In sum, the attitudes that Segundo associates with the mass-minority tension derive from insights drawn from the social sciences as represented in Lenin and Ortega y Gasset and sociology itself. "Mass" attitudes are characterized by oversimplification, immediacy, uniformity, lack of decision making and passivity. "Minority" attitudes are the exact opposite, viz., complexity, mediacy, creativity, decisiveness, freedom and activity. For Segundo, the minority attitudes are the ones which stimulate human progress but only in collaboration with the energy accumulated in mass patterns of behaviour. Hence, the latter must be constantly elevated to new ways of automatic behaviour.[47]

We have already indicated the way in which efficacious love discloses the meaning of the mass-minority tension.[48] It combines in creative tension the "minority" ideal of gratuitous self-giving and the concrete, realistic embodiment of that love according to the "mass" structures of historical instruments. But, more specifically, it affirms in human existence the value of commitment, of deffered satisfaction and heroic self-sacrifice as opposed to inertia and immediate gratification and as necessary for the building up of a new social reality. Hence, it surfaces the underlying disvalues/values which are inherent in mass-minority lines of conduct and makes clear the direction in which societal construction lies. It is the value-centred response of mutual, liberative self-giving that is concretely and realistically transformative of persons and the structures of society. It can, then, be concluded that the value of efficacious love is at the base of Segundo's anthropological use of the terms "mass-minority".

(e) Physical Science : Entropy-negentropy

Segundo draws from the realm of physical nature the terms "entropy-negentropy" as analogous to the "mass-minority" tension. He uses them anthropologically in order to expand his understanding of human existence. The term "entropy" refers to the tendency of energy to be degraded and dissipated into much simpler forms. In other words, while the "quantity" remains the same, the "quality" deteriorates. This basic law of nature is directly related to two others, namely, the law of the conservation of energy, the fact that the amount of energy in the universe remains constant; and the law of differentiation which establishes that the differences in all beings that exist are due to energy distribution. This latter implies that beings which exhibit a greater concentration of energy in specific areas will evidence deprivation in other areas.[49]

Evolutionary progress implies, then, a movement, contrary to entropy, negentropy which involves more complex, concentrated forms of energy, and a qualitative increase of energy. Applied to matter, the notion of entropy, therefore, refers to the inevitable movement of the quantitative towards simpler forms of synthesis which comprise mere addition of elements. The tension is, then, one of quantity vs quality, two necessary poles in the economy of energy that rules the universe.[50]

This quantitative-qualitative tension cannot be disregarded in the process of humanization. Therefore, although Segundo affirms that it is the qualitative thrust, negentropy, that points in the direction of higher syntheses, he insists that the energy base of human life must never be overlooked. Indeed, just as the possibility of more complex syntheses increases with the numerical increase of opportunities for trial and error, so minority attitudes will produce transformation only through and with the energy of the majority.[51]

It is not surprising, then, that as we have discussed before, although love is the minoritarian attitude *par excellence,* Segundo insists that the novel stress of Christianity is on its efficacy. The efficacy of such love is ever in tune with the amount of energy available at any precise moment in the progress of a people.

Segundo argues against an either-or option and for the necessary complementarity of entropy-negentropy. He is rejecting the Darwinian "survival of the fittest" as the creative impulse of evolution on the one hand, and the Lamarckian stress on "genetic conditioning" on the other.[52] Eventually, Segundo embraces a theory of evolution which places the emphasis on the balance of energy being constantly maintained in a given mechanism through the possibility of trial and error.[53] This interpretation of evolution is translated into an understanding of human "progress" through the combination of the high-energy function of rational critique and the low-energy activity of habitual behaviour. It is understandable, then, that, for Segundo, transformation of society will not be achieved either by a one-sided emphasis on a "prophetic" minority nor on a "messianic" majority.[54] His is the vision of Teilhard,[55] a veritable "synthesis of centres". It is the hope that all will work together for the benefit of all. And this is achievable only through efficacious love.

Efficacious love can then be regarded as the fundamental value which underlies Segundo's anthropological interpretation of the scientific fact of entropy-negentropy. It explains in reference to human existence a phenomenon that is discernible in the objective structure of the universe. Hence, it also discloses the basic unity of that universe as posited by the evolutionary principle of analogy.

To summarize, Segundo deepens his understanding of human existence by drawing from the area of physical science the terms "entropy-negentropy". He interprets them as disclosing on that level the mass-minority tension which pervades human existence. Entropy is the tendency of energy to disintegrate into simpler and more useless forms. Negentropy is the contrary thrust towards greater complexity and higher forms of synthesis. It is the latter which represents the qualitative, forward movement of evolution, but it occurs only in using the quantity of energy available. Segundo adopts the evolutionary theory that best preserves this tension in a functional balance of energy. In this perspective, efficacious love best captures the forward movement of evolution in the creation of the "synthesis of centres", of persons whose unity is preserved and enhanced in differences. Finally, it explains in human terms the struggle between the tendencies towards growth or disintegration that characterizes the entire physical world and human existence as located within that universe.

(f) Theology : Sin-grace

At its deepest level where human existence is open to the divine, the mass-minority tension is interpreted by Segundo with the symbols of "sin" and "grace". He uses the terms "mass-minority" to stress the appeal of the Christian message to attitudes proper to the minority without denying the offer of salvation to the many. This is necessarily so because, as we have seen, Segundo claims that the gratuitous love of God is at the core of the Christian message and is the source of love shown in service of others. And this love is the "minoritarian" attitude *par excellence*.[56]

It is not surprising, then, that in examining the scriptural foundation for the mass-minority tension in the earliest Christian experience, Segundo grounds his discussion on the Pauline notion of grace as the free gift of God's love which enables a person to make a similar gift of self. Therefore, the passages which Segundo also draws from the Synoptics focus on the "extraordinary" nature of the actions made possible by grace.[57] These demonstrate the fact that Christians are called upon to go against the current, to defy the law of statistics, hence, to be "minoritarian" in their attitudes. Where this eventually leads is to the affirmation of a morality that goes beyond the fulfilment of commandments. It conjures up the Pauline image of the Christian as one "liberated from the law in order to carry out the complex demands of truly creative love."[58]

However, Segundo does not intend that such a minoritarian attitude be considered as "elitist". This is shown clearly in his exegesis of the "world-hour", "flesh-Spirit" tension of John and Paul respectively. We have already seen that the "world" and the "flesh" represent not only the deterministic structures of nature and of the law resistant to the redemptive "hour" and "Spirit" but also the instruments by which that redemptive love is incarnated.[59] There, the mass-minority tension is evident.

A further analysis of the first eight chapters of Romans, the basis of Paul's Christology, for Segundo, reveals how that tension functions in the experience of all human beings even though the mechanisms of dehumanization may differ. Segundo argues that Paul's assertion of the enslavement to sin of both pagans and Jews prior to Christ's coming, indicates the same process of dehumanization and alienation. The process does not start with idolatry, as commonly supposed, but rather, with injustice. The latter then leads to rational justifications and the consequent absolutizing of specific instruments (idolatry and the ideological use of the divine). The destruction of personal existence is the end result. Thus pagan "religions" occupy the exact position as the "law" in Judaism. Both can function as rational justifications for injustice and provide the security of divine approval and protection. Both represent "mass" mechanisms which, nevertheless, also provide the instruments necessary for the true worship and service of God.[60]

Where the mass-minority tension becomes even more obvious, however, is in Segundo's reinterpretation of sin within an evolutionary context. Segundo contends that only such an interpretation can resolve the ambiguity that enters in in a simultaneous affirmation and negation of the reality of sin such as is represented in Paul in the experience of the divided human being (Rom. 7: 14-25). In that experience is the basic revelation of sin as the human inability to realize in action the desires of the heart. In other words, sin lies in the gap between intention and performance, in the enslaving subjection of persons to the forces of dehumanization. It is the negation of God's project of creating human beings, which results from yielding to the line of least resistance.[61]

The classical theological language of concupiscence thus provides Segundo with a close parallel to the evolutionary notion of entropy. The characteristics of entropy, we recall, include: (1) an anti-evolutionary thrust; (2) a leaning towards simple and immediate structures; (3) an inclination towards quantitative dominance; and (4) a tendency to be used in a higher qualitative synthesis while still maintaining a quantitative supremacy. From the fact that the last three characteristics are attributed to the concept of concupiscence traditionally understood, Segundo concludes that the first must then be accepted as also applicable. He writes, "the tendency toward sin is the tendency towards the degeneration of energy which, of and by itself, would make all further evolution impossible. Of itself all sin is anti-evolutionary."[62] What is significant here is that Segundo equates the "tendency" towards sin, concupiscence, with sin itself.

Segundo finds the basis for this move in a reinterpretation of original sin through what, he claims, is a more authentic reading of the Pauline passage (Rom. 5: 12-20) which makes the connection between sin and Adam's "fall". There the clear evidence is present that in Christ sin has been overcome both in itself and in its consequences. Segundo argues that if the grace of Christ, as set over against the sin of Adam, destroyed "guilt" without being able to affect its consequences, sin would, indeed, be the stronger force. On the contrary, what Paul asserts is the definitive victory of the grace of Christ.[63]

Within the evolutionary perspective, Segundo maintains that the sin of Adam cannot be conceived as a historical event prior to which the ideal of human existence was already realized in a "paradise". Such a concept of the fall would empty history of all meaning. Human existence would become a matter of merely carrying out a pre-established plan, of passing a "test". Given a history made meaningful by the "redemptive force" of God's love becoming "more and more present in the universe until it becomes a human being" in Christ incarnate,[64] original sin can only refer to the negative force which pervades the universe and which is to be attributed to human consciousness by the evolutionary principle of analogy.[65] Hence, entropy, the tendency to degradation on the level of physical nature, appears as sin on the level of the human where consciousness and deliberation characterize personal action, making guilt a possibility.[66]

Understanding original sin as this negative, structural force that maintains a quantitative victory in history, Segundo likewise interprets the redemption of Christ in an evolutionary perspective as the positive counter force of evolution, and not as a specific historical event. This interpretation stresses the universal presence of grace and the entire process of humanization made possible by it as ordained and culminating in Jesus Christ.[67] In effect, then, the tension that is set up between Adam and Christ signifies the tension between sin and grace as the negative and positive structures of human existence at its deepest level.

For Segundo, sin and grace thus entail a "dialectical" rhythm. By this he means that should either of the two evolutionary poles go beyond a certain point in the relationship of one to the other, its direction becomes reversed and it turns into its opposite.[68] Nevertheless, Segundo maintains that despite the fact that the Christian message recognizes the entire dialectical process it demands functions that are "minoritarian".[69] It is significant to note his reason for such a claim. He writes:

> Only from this vantage point can we appreciate why Christianity applies the word *sin* to all mass lines of conduct even though it realizes that they are and always will be necessary. Only from this vantage point can we understand its deep-rooted emphasis on gratuitousness as an "efficacious" venture in love.[70]

At bottom, then, Segundo's theology is seen to be structured on the notion of the universal presence of grace, of gratuitous love. But it is a love that must take cognizance of the mechanisms in human life that both express and obstruct the transforming activity of that grace. His theology can be seen reductively as grounded on the value of efficacious love.

As specifically connected with the grace-sin tension, efficacious love can then be regarded as a sign of transcendence. It points beyond human experience of love and egotism to locate the ultimate meaning of that experience in the Divine love that sustains and suffuses all of human life by constantly drawing that life out of death.

(g) Summary and conclusion

Human existence is pervaded by a tension of opposite yet complementary forces. In order to penetrate more deeply into the meaning of that existence, Segundo draws categories of thought from different sources and uses them as anthropological descriptions of the various aspects of that existence. The "mass-minority" tension thus emerges as an interpretative principle for understanding the major categories of thought that inform Segundo's theology. The opposing concepts are seen to be inextricably linked, albeit in such a way that the minoritarian aspect of the tension designates the determining, creative, liberative and decisive thrust of human "progress".

Hence, in the context of epistemology, faith structures values to which ideology, as a system of means and ends is ordered; in language analysis, the iconic communicates the world of values and the richness of human existence beyond digital conceptualization; in existentialist philosophy, freedom directs the mechanisms of nature towards the creation of persons in history; in social science, minority thrust towards the mediate and the more complex counters easy and simplistic solutions; in physical science, negentropy is the creative, positive vector of evolution struggling against the degradation of energy and return to the pre-human; and finally, in theology which probes to the deepest level of human existence where it consciously opens up to the transcendent, grace is the transforming love of God that has definitively triumphed over sin in the universe.

It must not be forgotten, however, that, for Segundo, the tension must never be broken and the opposite forces remain as both the limitation and the possibility of what is achieved. Underneath all of these is the tension of efficacious love, the minoritarian attitude *par excellence*, which still needs to be embodied according to the concrete demands of a historical human existence. Hence, the fundamental value of efficacious love is seen to be the controlling factor that illumines and binds together Segundo's major categories of thought and sources.

Besides, a more specific relationship exists between efficacious love and each of these categories of thought and sources. Efficacious love, as the absolute value realized in transformative actions, concretizes the ultimate value of faith which is always in search of more adequate responses to the real. It expresses in the iconic language of existential, subjective commitment a way of life that must also manifest the strict logic of digital reasoning. Efficacious love draws out the practical implications of human existence understood in terms of the tension between free, personal creation and the restrictions of objective reality. It specifies the fundamental value which underlies constructive, social behavioural patterns. Furthermore, it explains in human terms the positive and negative thrust of physical energy that structures the universe. Finally, efficacious love symbolizes the presence of the transcendent in the depths of human life. It is a manifestation of the power of Divine love which permeates and creates the entire universe.

In all of the above, efficacious love has been seen to function as the centering principle that most consistently illumines and binds together Segundo's major categories of thought and sources. These, taken as they are from various disciplines expand and deepen his understanding of human existence as fundamentally and efficaciously grounded on love and, ultimately, on the gratuitous love of God.

Having thus seen how efficacious love functions in reference to the *theoretical* components of Segundo's theological method, we will now turn to the *practical* "hermeneutic base" of his theology.

2. The Structure of Segundo's Theology

As noted in the introduction of this work, Latin American liberation theology can be regarded as a praxis-centred model of theological reflection. It poses questions that arise in historical faith praxis to the Christian message and seeks to draw from the latter fresh insights to illumine and transform dehumanizing historical situations. In Segundo's thought, the notion of efficacious love most consistently describes Segundo's understanding of historical praxis. Hence, in accord with a praxis-centred model of theology the following thesis is proposed for this consideration of the structure of his theology:

> *Thesis II:* Efficacious love is the fundamental value that structures Segundo's theological reflection by providing its starting point, its goal and the criterion of its development.

Before we enter into this discussion, however, it must be noted that the terms "efficacious love" and "option for the oppressed" can be regarded as being mutually implied in each other, although they are not strictly identical. Option for the oppressed is the most radical embodiment of efficacious love. It also captures more accurately the urgent and passionate character of historical praxis in Latin America today.[71] The term"option for the oppressed" will, therefore, be employed as a more precise designation of "efficacious love", in this instance, in our attempt to explain how the notion of efficacious love structures Segundo's theology. This consideration of the thesis stated above will be presented according to two main methodological elements included in it, namely, (a) the starting point and goal: option for the oppressed; and (b) the structure: the hermeneutic circle. It will be of interest to see how the notion of efficacious love functions as the fundamental value that underlies the structure of Segundo's theology. It is the central concern that both initiates historical praxis, as specified in the option for the poor, and also provides the vision towards which that engagement tends, namely, the transformation of society on behalf of the poor. Efficacious love is again the fundamental value that undergirds the commitment to historical faith praxis. Hence, it is the impulse of the movement from one step to another in Segundo's method, in his "hermeneutic circle".

(a) The starting point and goal: option for the oppressed

Efficacious love is the starting point of Segundo's theological reflection. This is so primarily because it best describes what he identifies as "the practical hermeneutic base" of theology, i.e., option for the oppressed.[72] It is that love which is truly *gratuitous* because the oppressed are not ordinarily loved for the sake of the benefits they can return; it is love that takes us beyond the circle of those who are near to place us beside those most in need; and it is love that is *efficacious*, the only true love, because it touches the other in his or her concrete, historical situation, and transforms that person and that situation in accordance with the means at its disposal. Accordingly, a discussion of what Segundo means by "option for the oppressed" will focus on the following elements suggested in the above: (1) its rootedness in the gratuitous love of God; (2) the redefinition of "neighbour"; and (3) the conversion of persons and change of structures.

We shall see how Segundo grounds historical faith praxis in God's own option for the poor. It is an option that is totally gratuitous, based not on personal merit but rather on God's radical rejection of the inhumanity of an oppressive situation. Response to such a love must, then, take the concrete form of love of neighbour as the only valid approach to God himself. Hence, the necessary requirement is conversion by which one assumes God's own sensitivity to the sufferings of the poor and works on their behalf for the restructuring of society.

This presentation will end with a statement on Segundo's position on the necessity and place of this option in theological reflection. We will begin with the first point listed above, namely, the rootedness of option for the oppressed in the gratuitous love of God.

(1) Its rootedness in the gratuitous love of God

Segundo finds a basis for claiming a special option of God for the poor in a biblical tradition that can be traced from the Yahwist image of God as "compassionate love and fidelity" to the "grace and truth" of John's prologue. Hence, Jesus' commission to serve the poor preferentially (Lk. 4:21) is but the concrete consequence of God's absolute, gratuitous love. It is efficacious love expressed in a specifically radical form.

The scriptural exegesis which Segundo employs to explain what exactly God's option for the poor implies centres on the "Q" version of the first beatitude as represented in the Gospel of Luke and on other Lukan material which demonstrates the socio-cultural level on which the evangelist deals with the theme of poverty and riches.

The interpretation of the first beatitude which Segundo adopts is that of Andre Myre[73] who claims that the Kingdom of God is represented there as belonging to the poor by the mere fact of their being poor, and without any reference to their moral state. The preference of God, according to him, flows from the very nature of God who, as compassionate love cannot tolerate the "horror" of the inhuman situation imposed upon the poor.[74] A consideration of the material peculiar to Luke confirms that Luke's interest in the theme of poverty does not flow from any "unconscious prejudice *against* wealth" but is centred on "its *use*". That this is a significant point is demonstrated by the parallel Segundo draws between the parable of Dives and Lazarus and the Lukan beatitude addressed to the poor. The parable is, for him, a clear explanation of the beatitude. The parable represents "two situations", not the interior disposition of two persons. Segundo can then interpret this parable exactly as Myre exegetes the first beatitude of Luke and emphasize the unconditional preference of God for the poor. It is their inhuman condition alone that draws forth the compassionate love of God. Regardless of their personal merit, the poor will take part in the eschatological banquet by reason of the fact that it is theirs by right.[75]

What the above seems to make clear, in summary, is that Segundo's use of the term "option for the poor" points to the socio-cultural reality of poverty.[76] He is insisting that concrete need, not just the religious sentiment of persons or moral purity, is the determining reason for God's preference.[77] And that option must, indeed, be totally gratuitous. This is so, not only because the free gift of self marks the very nature of God, but more because the power for changing that inhuman condition does not lie in that situation but solely in the efficacious love of a gracious God.

(2) The redefinition of neighbour

The option of God for the poor, as explained above, redefines the "neighbour" who is to be the recipient of that efficacious love. According to Segundo, this redefinition is brought about by Jesus' revelation of a shift from obedience to the law as the criterion of judgment to that of love shown to "the least".[78] With this is introduced a new structure of values such as is illustrated in the parable of the Good Samaritan (Lk. 10: 29-37). In it there is a change in the identification of the neighbour whom one is obliged to love. It is not just a matter of turning away the focus from the neighbour one ought to love to the neighbour one concretely loves.

"Neighbour" here does not simply apply to the "other". In Deuteronomy, as the lawyer in the parable would be aware, "neighbour" is a term used in the law to spell out the reciprocal duties attached to family, tribal and national relationships. However, the parable indicates that neighbours cannot be determined ahead of time, they are *created* in the very act of love being shown to others. As Segundo expresses it:

> A heart sensitive to others, a loving heart, finds neighbours wherever it gets a chance to approach a needy person with love. And only those who start from this *pre*-judice in favor of the human being - even though they may be pagans or atheists - understand the law and the will of Jesus' God.[79]

The novel insight which Jesus introduces is what Segundo is stressing here. It is the revelation that the love of God, present in humanity, confers the power to create persons especially where there is the greatest need. Those most deprived of their humanity, the poor and oppressed, therefore, become the main recipients of that love. To opt for the poor in this way is, then, to choose the human with God, to collaborate with Him in the task of creating authentic human beings. It is to make real the creative power of efficacious love.

(3)   Personal conversion and change of structures

If option for the poor is to be lived out concretely, it necessarily entails conflict. This option sets one in opposition to those who are responsible for dehumanizing structures. Hence Jesus' option for the poor is the revelation of God's involvement in a political and religious struggle against the oppressors of his poor, such as many prophets of Israel symbolized. What this means in Jesus' context we will now see.

Because the Israel of Jesus' day was a theocracy, those who held religious authority were also the leaders in the political ordering of the daily life of the people. Therefore, the poor whom Jesus championed against those leaders in that situation were those marginated not only because of economic poverty but also by reason of moral reprobation. This is seen in the identification made between the poor and sinners in Luke 5:30. This is an interpretation which is aimed at hiding and justifying their poverty, i.e., an "ideological" interpretation in the negative sense of the word. It is an abuse of the power that lay in the authority to interpret the law and consists in using that power as an instrument of oppression. This was the root of the conflict in which Jesus was engaged.[80]

In the face of this conflict, conversion becomes a necessary prerequisite for the opponents of Jesus to be able to receive his message of the coming Kingdom. Segundo's exegesis of the parables of Jesus directed at his adversaries demonstrates the requirements of that conversion and the reversal of values that his message demands. On the one hand, those who considered themselves just are revealed to be the real sinners. They are required to leave aside security in the law for a liberative insecurity in opting for the poor. They are called upon to let go of personal privileges and assume responsibility for the oppressed. In that option, they will begin to share the sentiments of God towards the dehumanized and marginated and so become open to his message.[81]

On the other hand, what is demanded of the followers of Jesus is that they be engaged with him in his prophetic mission. Like him, their task is to understand and unmask the ideological structures of oppression in Israel. To that end Jesus instructs them to recognize the "mysteries of the Kingdom". The qualities thus required of the disciples are those of the prophet, viz., "clear-sightedness, heroism and commitment". In following Jesus, they will encounter the painful consequences of their attempt to transform structures. What Jesus asks of his disciples is not conversion, therefore, but that they "open their eyes".[82]

Jesus engages in a similar instruction of the poor multitude, which was designed to make them aware of the good news of the Kingdom. This he does through the use of parables and miracles. The latter were used primarily as *signs* of the Kingdom and Jesus was careful to preserve that sign value.[83] All he required of those poor was that they open their hearts to hear the "good news" of the Kingdom that was theirs by right.[84]

It is clear from the above that Segundo's emphasis is mainly on the need for structural, societal transformation through a reversal of the present order of values.[85] Hence he indicates that a change of mentality is required only of those who create and maintain oppressive structures, before they can even begin to comprehend the message of the coming Kingdom. Segundo, therefore, stresses ideological critique as the main task of his followers. Such a critique would unveil the inhuman situation of the poor and their impotence to change their own situation. Therefore, the stimulus for transformation, according to him, will have to be from outside the oppressed group.[86]

The reason for the claim that the situation alone is the criterion of God's compassionate love is made clearer here. God does not judge those who are not fully human. What he asks of them is to be open to the "good news" of his love which may be too good for them to believe.[87] What is obvious is that the demands of God are seen to be in accord with the exigencies of efficacious love.

In summary, Segundo's theological reflection has as its starting point an option for the oppressed, the most radical expression of efficacious love. This option has its source in the gratuitous love of a compassionate God who is revealed in Jesus to be involved in a politico-religious struggle on behalf of the poor and against the oppressive leaders of Israel. All he asks of the poor is a heart open to accept the "good news" of his Kingdom.

Option for the poor, efficacious love, thus implies a sharing in the mentality of Jesus, a sensitivity and openness to search out and be "neighbour" to those in need. It demands the transformation of structures through a reversal of values and a placing them at the service of the poor and oppressed. This type of conversion becomes the prerequisite for hearing the message of the Gospel.

To follow Jesus in his option for the poor means that the disciple is required to have prophetic qualities and to be able to critique the mechanisms that are used to maintain the *status quo* of oppressive systems. The objective of the option is, then, to overturn such systems and to create situations in which humanity can be restored to those most deprived of it.

Because commitment to the poor is the option of God and hence a sharing in Jesus' mentality, it becomes the very precondition for hearing his message and at the same time the challenge of discipleship. As such, option for the poor, efficacious love *par excellence*, is thus established as both the starting point and the goal of Segundo's liberative theology.

Before proceeding to the next section, it is necessary to consider here the criticism that such a decided option for the poor represents a certain restriction of the Christian message.[88] Segundo's clarification and defence of his position is significant if, indeed, option for the poor, efficacious love, has as central a position in his theological reflection as suggested above.

Segundo claims that option for the poor is a direct consequence of the historical immersion of the Christian message which does not necessarily restrict its universal relevance. Rather, it indicates a commitment to faith that takes seriously the limitations of energy that govern its implementation according to the exigencies of love's efficacy.

The question as formulated within the Latin American context relates to whether or not Christianity can determine the type of contribution required of Christians before they actually become engaged in activity aimed at transforming structures for the benefit of the oppressed.[89] In other words, can option for the oppressed be the implementation of universal Gospel values that are known beforehand? Or must the form of that option be entirely determined by the historical circumstances in which it is lived?

Segundo argues that Christianity does not have a prior contribution to make in terms of the means to be used in a revolutionary process. Indeed, it is in disregarding the economy of energy, that Christianity has historically engaged in idealistic, ineffective forms of social transformation. In so doing it has not paid enough attention to the fact that it is one historical way of responding and not *the* way. Thus, on the level of means the relativity of the option is clear.

On the deeper level of the pre-understanding that guides a specific option, however, Segundo does admit that Christianity can make a positive contribution prior to commitment to a specific revolutionary process. On this level, Segundo maintains, Latin American theologians, in claiming that option for the poor is a prerequisite for hearing the Gospel message, evidence "social realism" and, hence, a rootedness in the Bible. He writes:

> We note the similarity between the pre-biblical criterion and that which the Evangelists and prophets point out: sensitivity of the heart towards the poor. Is it not the criterion which opens to the reading of the Gospel? Is hardness of heart not perchance the insensitivity to injustice, the insensitivity to the situation of the widow, the orphan, the oppressed, which prevents, *at least, the understanding* of the Gospel message, good news *for the poor* and for those who share the hope of the poor?[90]

Briefly, then, Segundo's position on whether or not option for the poor restricts the universality of the Gospel message is the following: On the level of historical means to be used in embodying the Gospel message, it is necessarily particular and relative. However, its universality lies on the deeper level of human experience that prepares for the reception of the Gospel message. Here, option for the oppressed provides both Christians and non-Christians with the type of sensitivity of heart that is the necessary condition for hearing the message of Christ. Hence, option for the oppressed is in exactly the same position as the universal offer of God's gratuitous love in human experience. It prepares the way for faith. It is no wonder, then, that, as we have seen above,[91] option for the oppressed is both rooted in the free love of God and is at the same time the most radical expression of the personal appropriation and embodiment of that love.

Segundo, therefore, concludes that an authentic interpretation of the Christian message must include a revolutionary commitment such as is expressed in the option for the oppressed. It becomes a vital part of a "hermeneutic circle, that is, a unity of interpretation where each one of the elements influences the rest and all together contribute to correct interpretation."[92] The following section will discuss the way in which Segundo constructs his theological method according to such a circle. The point of focus will be the place of the value of efficacious love in this formulation.

(b) The structure: the hermeneutic circle

A formal presentation of Segundo's theological method appears in his book, *The Liberation of Theology*. As has been already noted,[93] it is but the explication of a method which Segundo has employed since his earliest publication. In this section it will be of particular interest to see how the notion of efficacious love and in particular its expression in option for the poor, functions in the structure of this method.

Segundo's use of the term "hermeneutic circle" to describe his theological method is reminiscent of Bultmann's use of it. Yet, Segundo claims that his is a stricter use. The preliminary definition that Segundo offers is as follows: "It is the continuing change in our interpretation of the Bible which is dictated by the continuing changes in our present-day reality, both individual and societal."[94] Basic to this definition is the normativity of scripture in Segundo's theological method as he seeks to interpret present historical situations in the light of the Gospel message. What he is stressing, however, is the changing "reality" that *dictates* biblical interpretation. He is arguing against a theology that traditionally has acknowledged its link to the past and its dependence on the disciplines that have made that past intelligible, while claiming autonomy from the sciences that unlock the meaning of the present. Implicit in this, it seems, is Segundo's judgment of the inadequacy of traditional hermeneutics which has failed to interpret the Christian message in such a way as to make a concrete impact on situations like that of contemporary Latin America. There, the oppression of the poor gives the lie to the central Christian demand of efficacious love and justifies Segundo's attempt at a new interpretation from the perspective of the poor and oppressed.

What Ricoeur designates as a "hermeneutic of suspicion" is, therefore, fundamental to Segundo's theological approach. Concern for the oppressed leads him, as a liberation theologian, to suspect "that anything and everything involving ideas, including theology, is intimately bound up with the existing social situation in at least an unconscious way."[95] Thus it becomes important for Segundo to unearth the "ideas", the ideologies that keep theology captive and faith impotent, unable to authentically inform Christian life. Here the influence of Marxist ideological critique and its bias towards the oppressed victims of society is obvious.

The two preconditions which Segundo establishes for a hermeneutic circle in theology are likewise directly related to the option for the poor, to efficacious love. "The first", he writes, "is that the questions rising out of the present be rich enough, general enough, and basic enough to force us to change our customary conception of life, death, knowledge, society, politics, and the world in general."[96] He argues that such a change, or at the minimum a "pervasive suspicion" regarding those things, is necessary for reaching the "theological level" and for forcing theology back to reality to ask in turn new and significant questions. The close correlation between this first precondition and the "hermeneutical base", that is, option for the oppressed, is obvious.

Intimately linked with the first precondition is the second that is based upon a caveat:

> If theology somehow assumes that it can respond to the new
> questions without changing its customary interpretation of the
> Scriptures, that immediately terminates the hermeneutic circle.
> Moreover, if an interpretation of Scripture does not change along
> with the problems, then the latter will go unanswered; or worse, they
> will receive old, conservative, unserviceable answers.[97]

Again, it is obvious here that the specific questions which Segundo has in mind are those which arise from out of his commitment to the oppressed and, by implication, from his central concern for love to be efficacious. His reinterpretation of scripture gives ample evidence of this.

It can then be concluded from the above that, for Segundo, the objective of a liberative theology is not so much to define content as to provide a method of theologizing in tune with concrete reality. It is to be a theology more "interested in *being liberative* than in *talking about liberation*."[98]

Again, it will be seen that the notion of efficacious love, particularly as lived in option for the oppressed is closely tied into the four "decisive factors" which Segundo identifies in the hermeneutic circle as following from the two preconditions stated above. They are:

> *Firstly* there is our way of experiencing reality, which leads to
> ideological suspicion. *Secondly* there is the application of our
> ideological suspicion to the whole ideological superstructure in
> general and to theology in particular. *Thirdly* there comes a new way

of experiencing theological reality that leads us to exegetical
suspicion, that is, to the suspicion that the prevailing interpretation of
the Bible has not taken important pieces of data into account.
Fourthly we have our new hermeneutic, that is, our new way of
interpreting the fountainhead of our faith (i.e., Scripture) with the
new elements at our disposal.[99]

It can be readily seen that efficacious love as expressed in option for the poor
and discussed above as the starting point of Segundo's theology is identical with
the first step of the hermeneutic circle. It is that radical experience that is
capable of shattering the human bases of faith and of consequently opening up
the way for posing crucial questions to the sources of religious faith.

The second step of the circle, the application of hermeneutic suspicion to
the particular historical situation and to theology itself, likewise indicates option
for the oppressed in the operative assumption which we have noted before, that
the ideological critique will uncover the oppressive structures that theology
itself unconsciously supports.[100] We have already seen the basis of Segundo's
appropriation of this "ideological critique" and its implications for efficacious
love.

The third step, a new experience of theology posed to ask fresh questions of
the Christian sources, leads to the final step, a reinterpretation of scripture
which, as we have also seen, has uncovered specific elements which show
God's own option for the poor and oppressed and thereby his commitment to
efficacious love.[101]

That option for the poor and, hence, efficacious love is pivotal in Segundo's
theological method is further substantiated in the emphasis he places on the
need for commitment in his analysis of the method as exemplified in the works
of four authors, viz., Harvey Cox, Karl Marx, Max Weber and James Cone. In
his view, Cone is the only one of the four who completes the circle because of
his obvious commitment to Black liberation, his interpretation of reality in
terms of racist domination, and his determination, based upon a new experience
of theology, to put the bible in "service of the Black community". This leads
Cone to take a new direction in the interpretation of scripture. Segundo admits
the risk involved in Cone's approach but maintains, "One cannot rule out a
particular theological method which is consistent just because it entails
dangers."[102]

Segundo's own interpretation of scripture evidences a willingness to take
such a risk as inherent in any option for the oppressed, in any commitment to
efficacious love. He defends this "partial" use of the Bible on the basis of the
liberative thrust of Christianity. He writes:

... the Bible is not the discourse of a universal God to a universal
man. Partiality is justified because we must find, and designate as
the word of God, that *part* of divine revelation which *today*, in the
light of our concrete historical situation, is most useful for the
liberation to which God summons us. Other passages of that same
divine revelation will help us tomorrow to complete and correct our

present course towards freedom. God will keep coming back to speak to us from the very same Bible. [103]

Segundo's primary concern is for the liberation of the oppressed, for the realization of efficacious love.

In summary, then, Segundo proposes a theological method that is sensitive to the changing historical reality to which biblical interpretation must relate. The reality must be made to reveal its present meaning. This, in his opinion, has been neglected by traditional hermeneutics with the consequent lack of authentic Christian response in efficacious love. Segundo then stresses the need for a suspicious attitude towards ideological deformation of reality and of theology in particular. Interwoven in the stages of the hermeneutic circle that he develops are, therefore, a twofold suspicion and two basic "preconditions", viz., significant questions that demand a change of attitudes towards the most essential aspects of human life in society, and reinterpretation of scripture in response to these questions. Implied in that suspicious attitude is the concern to reshape both society and theological interpretation for the benefit of the oppressed and, hence, in terms of the fundamental value of efficacious love.

For the successful completion of the circle, Segundo emphasizes, above all, commitment to the human reality to be confronted and to the theological task of liberation. He therefore, defends the "partiality" such commitment necessarily implies. In so doing, he establishes a basis in his theological method for the pivotal position that option for the oppressed and, by implication, efficacious love, assumes in his theology. Efficacious love is, then, not only the starting point and the goal of Segundo's theological method. It is also the impulse of its development in the radical commitment it expresses in the option for the poor.

3. Conclusion

In conclusion, it must be emphasized that efficacious love best describes the *theoretical* hermeneutic principle, the mass-minority tension as well as the *practical* hermeneutic base, namely, option for the oppressed. It captures, then, the unity of theory and praxis as represented in the structure of Segundo's theology. The centredness on liberative praxis as expressed in the option for the poor throws the emphasis on the "efficacy" of love and, hence, on the novelty revealed in Christ *Incarnate*. In making efficacious love the central notion in the structure of his theology, Segundo thus makes of that novelty a pivotal concern and the task to be accomplished, the humanization of the universe.

Notes

1. Gustavo Gutiérrez, *Theology of Liberation: History, Politics and Salvation* (New York: Orbis Books, 1973), p. 15. Cf. José Miguez Bonino *Doing Theology in a Revolutionary Situation* (Philadelphia: Fortress Press, 1975), pp. 61-83; Robert McAfee Brown, *Theology in a New Key* (Philadelphia: The Westminster Press, 1978).

2. Cf. Raul Vidales, "Methodological Issues in Liberation Theology", in *Frontiers of Theology in Latin America*, p. 42; Roger Haight, *An Alternative Vision*, p. 43f.

3. Cf. Gutiérrez, *Theology of Liberation*, pp. 153-68; Ignacio Ellacuria, *Freedom Made Flesh*, translated by John Drury (Maryknoll, New York: Orbis Books, 1976), pp. 3-19.

4. The unity of theory and praxis is a basic claim of Latin American liberation theology in general. See Juan Carlos Scannone, "La relación teoría-praxis en al teología de la liberación", *Christus*, XL (June 1977), 10-16.

5. Juan Luis Segundo, "Excursus: The Beginning of a Small Idea", in his *Theology and the Church*, translated by W. Diercksmeier (Minneapolis/Chicago/New York: Winston Press; London: Geoffrey Chapman, 1985), pp. 74-78. Cf. Gutiérrez, *A Theology of Liberation*, pp. 69-72.

6. Segundo, *Grace and the Human Condition*, pp. 65-70. Cf. *The Community Called Church*, pp. 16-19.

7. Juan Luis Segundo, "Excursus" in *Theology and the Church*, pp. 73-85.

8. *Ibid.*, p. 76.

9. See Karl Rahner, "Concerning the Relationship between Nature and Grace", in *Theological Investigations*, I (Baltimore: Helicon Press, 1961), pp. 297-317; "Nature and Grace", in *Theological Investigations*, VI (Baltimore: Helicon Press, 1966), pp. 231-49.

10. *Gaudium et Spes*, no. 22, in Austin Flannery, O.P., ed., *Vatican Council: The Conciliar and Post - Conciliar Documents* (New York: Costello Publishing Co., 1975), pp. 922-24. Segundo is aware of the ambiguities in the Conciliar documents relative to this assertion. Passages that support this position are present alongside others which reflect the traditional "separation of planes". Considering the implications of the two positions, Segundo accepts the former as the more "difficult", creative choice, involving more careful deliberation. Cf. Segundo, *De la sociedad a la teología*, pp. 49-61; "Hacia una exegesis dynámica", in *Víspera*, I, no. 3 (October 1967), pp. 81-84; The *Sacraments Today*, pp. 124-36.

11. Segundo, *Our Idea of God*, p. 87.

12. Segundo, argues with Bateson that analogical thinking is not to be despised as "unscientific". The claim on which Bateson bases his argument is that "the framework (el eidos) of science is the same in all fields." See G. Bateson, *Steps to an Ecology of the Mind*, (New York: Ballantine Books, 1972). p. 100, cited in *An Evolutionary Approach to Jesus of Nazareth* p. 31.

13. Segundo, *Masas y minores*, p. 110. Segundo's use of the term "dialectic"

within the evolutionary perspective is not meant to locate the source of movement in the contradiction or tension between the "mass" and "minority" as two opposing forces of equal value. It is used to indicate that "if either of the two tendencies . . . steps beyond a critical point in relation to the other, then it turns around and operates in the opposite sense." *Evolution and Guilt*, p. 130. By this Segundo draws a distinction between his use of "dialectic" and the usage commonly attributed to Hegel and Marx.

14. See Chapter II, pp. 40-43.

15. Segundo, *Faith and Ideologies*, pp. 32-40; 87-116.

16. Segundo accepts Herbert Marcuse's analysis regarding the destructive consequences of a restricted "rationality" on Western society. See Herbert Marcuse, *One Dimensional Man: Studies in the Ideology of Advanced Industrial Society* (Boston: Beacon Press, 1964).

17. Cf. Segundo, *Faith and Ideologies*, pp. 104-113; *The Liberation of Theology*, pp. 101-110.

18. *Ibid.*, p. 22. Cf. *The Liberation of Theology*, pp. 103-106.

19. *Ibid.*, pp. 5-7; 22-24.

20. *Ibid.*, p. 25.

21. *Ibid.*, pp. 4-7; 25-26.

22. *Ibid.*, p. 26.

23. *Ibid.*, pp. 7-10; 26-27. Cf. *The Liberation of Theology*, pp. 106-110.

24. Segundo, *The Liberation of Theology*, p. 102. Cf. *Faith and Ideologies*, p. 27.

25. *Ibid.*, pp. 120-34.

26. Segundo, *Masas y minores*, pp. 109-110.

27. Segundo, *Faith and Ideologies*, p. 28.

28. Cf. Gregory Bateson, *Steps to an Ecology of the Mind*.

29. Segundo, *Faith and Ideologies*, pp. 134-36.

30. *Ibid.*, p. 155.

31. *Ibid.*, p. 136.

32. Segundo, *Berdiaeff*, pp. 12-16.

33. See Chapter II, pp. 33.

34. Segundo, *Grace and the Human Condition*, p. 32.

35. *Ibid.*, p. 33.

36. *Ibid.*, p. 34.

37. V.I. Lenin, *What Is to Be Done?* Eng. trans. (New York: International Publishers, 1929) cited in *The Liberation of Theology*, pp, 216-20; *Masas y minores*, pp. 18-22.

38. Segundo, *The Liberation of Theology,*, pp. 216-17.

39. *Ibid.*, p. 218.

40. *Ibid.*

41. José Ortega y Gasset, *The Revolt of the Masses,* Eng. trans. (New York: W.W. Morton 1932), cited in Segundo, *The Liberation of Theology,* pp. 219-21; *Masas y minores,* pp. 22-24.

42. Segundo, *The Liberation of Theology,* pp. 219-21.

43. *Ibid.*, p. 221.

44. Segundo, *Evolution and Guilt,* p. 38.

45. *Ibid.*, p. 128.

46. Segundo, *The Liberation of Theology,* p. 224.

47. Segundo, *Masas y minores,* p. 29.

48. See Chapter II, pp. 40-42.

49. Segundo, The *Liberation of Theology,* pp. 222-23; *Masas y minores,* pp. 25-26.

50. *Ibid.*, pp. 223-24.

51. Segundo, *Evolution and Guilt,* pp. 21-25.

52. Segundo, *Faith and Ideologies,* pp. 306-11.

53. *Ibid.*, pp. 308-11. This is the theory of Gregory Bateson who proposes that in human beings, the mind which functions as a "homeostatic mechanism" substitutes for animal instinct. By this he means that for human progress to occur the functions which characterize such a mechanism, viz., trial, error and correction must be applied to the appropriation of hereditary conditionings. Thus this theory keeps in creative balance the thrust towards more complex, rational evaluations and the opposite tendency towards hereditary patterns of behaviour. Hence the important factor in evolution is *flexibility* which implies having energy available to invest to the best advantage in any given situation.

54. These represent, for Segundo, the two extreme positions often assumed by Latin American liberation theologians. Cf. *Masas y minores,* p. 109.

55. This is not to say that Segundo is entirely in accord with Teilhard. In adopting Bateson's theory of evolution as described above, Segundo is able to overcome Teilhard's basically developmentalist view. Segundo criticizes him for being too optimistc and not paying enough attention to the role of entropy in evolutionary progress. Cf. *An Evolutionary Approach to Jesus of Nazareth* pp. 21-24; 93-98.

56. Segundo, *Evolution and Guilt,* p. 128.

57. Cf. Luke 6:32-34; Matthew 5:47; Luke 18:24-26.

58. Segundo, *The Liberation of Theology,* p. 230. Segundo's reinterpretation of Christian morality will be discussed more fully in the following chapter.

59. See Chapter II, pp. 28-30.

60. Segundo, *The Humanist Christology of Paul,* pp. 13-41.

61. *Ibid.*, pp. 475-98.

62. Segundo, *Evolution and Guilt*, p. 27.

63. *Ibid.*, pp. 78-79. Cf. *The Humanist Christology of Paul*, pp. 76-98.

64. *Ibid.*, p. 110.

65. According to this principle nothing appears in the universe which does not have a basis in a previous cycle of evolution. See Segundo, *Evolution and Guilt*, pp. 105-107.

66. Segundo, *Evolution and Guilt.*, pp. 107-108.

67. *Ibid.*, pp. 80-83.

68. *Ibid.*, p. 130.

69. Exactly what Segundo means by a "minoritarian" Christianity is clearly stated in the following: "(1) The exigencies of the gospel message are *minority* by their very nature and definition. (2) This does not point towards the maintenance of the interest of a small, self-enclosed group but rather towards the liberation of humanity - of the masses. (3) The liberation in question does not entail destroying the quantitative proportion existing between masses and minorities, since that remains equally operative in the Christian life. Still less does it entail reducing the exigencies of the gospel message to some minimal mass level so as to win the adhesion of the masses. (4) This minority effort among the masses is not meant to impose elitist demands on the latter, nor is it meant to construct a society based on minority exigencies. The aim is to create, for oneself and others, new forms of energy that will permit lines of conduct that are necessarily mechanized to serve as the basis for new and more creative possibilities of a minority character in each and every human being." *The Liberation of Theology*, p. 231.

70. Segundo, *Evolution and Guilt.*, p. 131.

71. Cf. Haight, *An Alternative Vision*, p. 19; Sanks, "Liberation Theology and the Social Gospel", p. 682.

72. Juan Luis Segundo, *Masas y minores* p. 110.

73. Andre Myre, *Cri de Dieu. Espoir des pauvres* (Montreal: Paulines, 1977).

74. Segundo, *The Humanist Christology of Paul*, pp. 104-10.

75. Segundo, *The Historical Jesus of the Synoptics*, pp. 111-14.

76. This concurs with the general position of Latin American liberation theology. Cf. Segundo Galilea, "Liberation Theology and the New Tasks Facing Christians" in *Frontiers of Theology in Latin America* (New York: Orbis Books, 1979), p. 178.

77. This is why Segundo finds the "Q" version of Luke's first beautitude more illuminating than the Matthian parallel. Segundo also points out the moralizing tone that pervades Matthew's account of the parables in particular.

78. Cf. Mt. 25: 31-46. We have already seen that the basis of this shift is the identification of love of God and neighbour because of the very dynamic of love. See Chapter II, pp. 26-28 .

79. Segundo, *The Historical Jesus of the Synoptics*, p. 130.

80. *Ibid.,* pp. 114-18.

81. *Ibid.,* pp. 120-31.

82. *Ibid.,* pp. 134-39.

83. Segundo suggests that the "messianic secret" which has been attributed to Jesus could refer to his occasional withdrawal from the multitudes in order to preserve the sign value of his miracles. Cf. *Ibid.,* pp. 139-47.

84. It should be noted here that Segundo does not intend to glamorize the poor. He admits that they are sinners. He is turning the focus away from personal moral guilt to sinful social structures. Cf. *The Historical Jesus of the Synoptics,* p. 122.

85. Segundo's option for Socialism over Capitalism seems grounded in this conviction. Cf. "Capitalism vs Socialism: Crux Theólogica", *Concilium* X, no. 96 (June 1974), pp. 105-23; in *Frontiers of Theology in Latin America,* pp. 240-59.

86. In this claim, Segundo differs from certain Latin American theologians who see such power in the "people", and from Marx who attributes transforming power to the proletariat. Segundo claims that the "real danger of Marxism" is in its "simplistic eschatology" which leads to "false hope." Cf. *The Liberation of Theology,* pp. 183-205; *The Humanist Christology of Paul,* pp. 173-79.

87. Cf. Segundo, *The Historical Jesus of the Synoptics,* pp. 139-41.

88. Cf. Segundo *The Liberation of Theology,* pp. 154-182; E. Schillebeeckx, "Liberation Theology Between Medellín and Puebla", *Theology Digest,* XXVIII (Spring, 1980), p. 6.

89. See Segundo, *The Liberation of Theology,* pp. 90-101; *Masas y minores,* pp. 74-90.

90. Segundo, *Masas y minores,* p. 93.

91. See above, pp. 67f.

92. Segundo, *Masas y minores,* p. 94.

93. See Chapter I, pp. 14f.

94. Segundo, *The Liberation of Theology,* p. 8.

95. *Ibid.*

96. *Ibid.*

97. *Ibid.,* p. 9.

98. *Ibid.*

99. *Ibid.*

100. See above, pp. 69-71.

101. See Chapter II, pp. 26-28 .

102. Segundo, *The Liberation of Theology,* p. 32.

103. *Ibid.,* p. 33.

Chapter Four

Efficacious Love and Personal Salvation

From one anthropological point of view, the question of personal salvation centres upon the identification of the proper access road to God. It supposes a specific understanding of the human person in relationship to God, which would indicate the appropriateness of certain means of access and the adequacy of their interpretation. Before entering into the main discussion of this chapter, viz., the thesis that efficacious love is the criterion or decisive factor of personal salvation in the theology of Juan Luis Segundo, a brief clarification of his understanding of the human person will, therefore, be attempted. Following that there will be an examination of Segundo's interpretation of the existential realities most commonly associated with the question of personal salvation in the Christian tradition. These are: grace, freedom, faith, cultic worship, human action and Christ as personal Saviour.

It will be shown that efficacious love is the fundamental value that underlies Segundo's interpretation of all of these Christian symbols. Efficacious love is the effect of that Transcendent Love which lies at the depth of human existence. It is the authentic exercise of the freedom to create and transform personal existence. Efficacious love signifies the personal response of love and commitment to the prior love of God. It celebrates and verifies in deeds the gratuitous self-gift of God. Finally, it witnesses to the immersion of God in human history and his solidarity with humanity. Hence, efficacious love is the way to personal union with God, to personal salvation.

It is hoped that in the development of the thesis stated above, Segundo's understanding of personal salvation itself will become clear. We turn now to a consideration of his concept of the human person.

1. The Concept of Person

The human being is a centre of creativity, free, personal and unique, the only absolute in the created world in the sense of being an end, irreducible to a means, and absolute even in relationship to God. God cannot force, he can only await a response from this other absolute. Segundo has drawn this basic conception of the person from Berdyaev whose prophetic existentialist philosophy focusses on the personalization of human existence as the *raison d'être* of the entire created universe.[1]

The basis of this conception is Berdyaev's definition of God as Spirit who by nature is consequently absolute liberty. The understanding of the human person is, for Segundo, linked with the image of God as person.[2] Therefore, he can concur with Berdyaev in regarding the human person as also primarily defined by liberty. However, as we have seen before,[3] it is liberty experienced in human existence as being in tension with the alienating forces of objective reality.

The human person is, then, not primarily a given nature, a static reality, but the inner self that comes to be through a dynamic struggle against the forces of nature with its own inherent laws.[4] The resistance is to being made into an instrument, to being depersonalized through mechanistic manipulation.[5] Positively, the person directs those forces and is thus *realized* in assuming responsibility for personal destiny.[6] It is only gradually, then, that the mystery of the person unfolds and the full potential that human life conceals in its depths can be achieved.

However, this personal creation in which the person is actively involved is not to be conceived as an individualistic achievement. A person, as limited freedom, needs others for personal realization and hence is created only through interpersonal relationships and social interactions.[7] The person is social by nature.[8]

With such a view of the human person, an authentic approach to God will be eminently interpersonal and social. It will be an encounter which will evidence the infinite respect of God for the real, historical conditions of human life, and his personal, free decision to become concretely involved in the creation of that life, in the process of humanization.[9] In that process the human person will find God, will achieve salvation as co-creator with him. We will now turn to a discussion of grace as the most basic given in human existence.

2.   Grace and Efficacious Love

Personal salvation is most fundamentally determined by the presence of grace. To show how efficacious love relates to the symbol of grace is, then, to clarify the link between efficacious love and salvation itself.

For Segundo, the existential reality of grace discloses above all the utter gratuity of God's salvation located within, yet not entirely within, historical existence and specifically within the interpersonal relationship of love. Gratuity is, indeed, the sign of the genuineness of love. Thus, by its very definition the reality of grace is inextricably linked with the notion of efficacious love. Segundo's reinterpretation of the doctrine of grace is situated against the background of the traditional discussion.[10] Hence, this presentation of his position will be structured according to three aspects of that debate. These are: (a) the grace-liberty problematic and "healing grace"; (b) the natural-supernatural dichotomy and "elevating grace"; and (c) the universal presence of grace and personal salvation. These areas of that discussion will draw into focus the three basic relationships which constitute personal existence, namely, the individual who is by nature disposed to become his/her true self; the person who is transformed in being caught up in the life of God himself; and finally, the person who realizes with others a common destiny. What will be of particular interest here are the nuances which Segundo introduces, based upon his concern for the value of efficacious love.

(a)   The grace-liberty problematic and healing grace

Segundo identifies the source of grace as the free self-gift of God. Grace is, then, love *par excellence*, the unconditional gift of God's very self to every human being. And it is "efficacious" in being *real* love, the only *true* love, creatively transformative of persons in their concrete historical circumstances. It makes of each person a new creation. It effects personal salvation.[11]

As expressive of God's absolute freedom, grace becomes synonymous with human liberation. Against the background of the traditional problematic of the conflict between God's grace and human liberty,[12] Segundo argues that rather than destroying human freedom, grace gives the power to exercise that freedom in directing the forces of nature. It is obvious that Segundo's understanding of the basic freedom-necessity tension is operative in this position.[13] According to him, then, "healing" grace is that release of liberty at work in self-determination, in self-creation. The result is the personalization of humanity as opposed to its instrumentalization. Liberty thus strengthened, is capable of breaking the enslavement of deterministic forces and, without eliminating them directs them for the realization of efficacious love.[14]

(b) The natural-supernatural dichotomy and elevating grace

Segundo's reinterpretation of the notion of grace as "elevating" presupposes the problematic of the natural-supernatural dichotomy against which he is arguing. He grounds his explication on the contrary affirmation of the unity of the human and the divine in history. This we have already seen is his most fundamental theological assumption.[15]

Segundo, then, understands human participation in the divine life of God not as a separate reality added to human nature but rather as personal existence *qualitatively* transformed.[16] It involves a whole new way of life that evidences the presence and exercise of gratuitous love. Since the basis of this new existence is the Incarnation, Segundo claims that the "breakthrough" to that new way of living happens *within*, not outside of the world of human beings.[17] Grace as "elevating" is thus oriented to the creation of persons in their concrete situations, the specific objective of efficacious love. As he puts it, "turning ourselves into *persons*, in the fullest sense of the term, was the end goal of hominization. And turning ourselves into *persons* also seems to be the end goal of our elevation, our divinization."[18] Personal salvation is, then, the absolutizing of that historical love, the power of which is proved to be definitive forever.[19]

(c) The universality of grace and personal salvation

The universal presence of grace, as God's unconditional love extended to all humanity, is a basic claim of Segundo, as we have already seen.[20] On this supposition he argues that the offer of salvation is universal, for according to him, authentic Christianity "teaches us to see humanity as a whole, a *whole* to be fashioned by love."[21] It is, then, on the basis of whether or not that love is operative that Segundo determines the presence or absence of personal salvation.

Personal salvation is not a question of orthodoxy. It is viewed rather over against what Segundo terms "idolatry". This latter occurs when relationships are falsified to the extent that what is free, personal and gratuitous, the presence of healing grace, disappears and is replaced by a turn to the prehuman, to depersonalization.[22] Because the possibility of such an idolatry is not excluded from Christianity, Segundo concludes that personal salvation poses the same challenge, and is equally accessible, to every person, Christian and non-Christian alike.

Finally, it must be noted that it is within that context of the basic tension between personalization and instrumentalization, the two poles of human existence, that Segundo also represents grace as the dynamic impulse which opens up new horizons, "the great wind that picks us up and carries us aloft."[23] As the stimulus of human progress, grace is thus identified with the Spirit who is Freedom and Love.[24]

In summary, then, we can say with Segundo:

> "grace" is nothing but God's gift *par excellence*: i.e., God himself made into our existence. Grace is the "Spirit that dwells in us", ... the irresistible force that seeks to make us free, that transforms us into free men and that turns us toward all free men so that we may collaborate in a common task. This task, which is both human and divine, is to create a history of love in all its fullness precisely by virtue of being free.[25]

It is clear, then, that efficacious love is identical with the existential reality of grace in this sense that efficacious love is the concrete effect of grace. As such it enters into all facets of Segundo's explication of grace. Indeed, efficacious love is the mark of a life transformed by the presence of God's Spirit and is, thus, the criterion, the norm whereby personal salvation is judged to be achieved.

3. Freedom and Efficacious Love

The relationship between efficacious love and personal salvation takes on an added dimension in the connection between freedom and personal salvation. For human liberation captures most adequately the reality of personal salvation.[26] The reason is that the latter, inextricably linked with grace, as seen above, can be achieved only through the exercise of freedom, according to the very dynamic of love. This intimate relationship between freedom and grace also determines the direction of Segundo's discussion of the existential reality of freedom. Just as Segundo's redefinition of grace eventually leads to a focus on praxis and the human-divine task of humanization, so his reinterpretation of liberty will be oriented towards its realization in the creation of persons.[27] And this is identical with what Segundo affirms of efficacious love.

Segundo's explication of liberty as it relates to personal salvation starts from the basic problematic as posed by existentialist literature, viz., the question of whether liberty is a creation or a test. As the only two possibilities open to human beings, the former represents liberty as capable of producing something new and original and, hence, constructive of the world; the latter depicts liberty as that which is only a useless "risk" and is merely the gap between persons and their final destiny.[28] These two possibilities represent distinct world views, the one, dynamic and open to a process of self creation through freedom, the other, static and determined by the order that already exists in nature. As to be expected, Segundo argues in favour of the more dynamic and creative. His option is based upon his focal concern for the value of efficacious love.

(a) Freedom as a test

Segundo's conviction is that the understanding of liberty as a "test" has historically dominated Christian praxis and has thus robbed Christianity of its very *raison d'être*.[29] He rejects such a distortion of Christianity as militating against the valuation of the world and in particular of historical human existence.

The understanding of liberty as a test is, in Segundo's view, the position of static classical theology. The image is that of human liberty poised in perfect equilibrium between already determined good and evil. Stoic influence is obvious to Segundo, but of greater seriousness is the fact that this interpretation is basically pre-Christian. It represents more appropriately the last stage of Old Testament revelation in which the justice of God is portrayed as being exercised beyond earthly existence in rewarding and punishing human deeds.[30] Segundo admits that there are traces of this stage of revelation in the New Testament. Indeed, it forms the background against which Jesus preached his message. But, by the same token, it sets off in relief the novelty of Jesus and the freedom of Sonship which he embodied. Henceforth, according to Paul, intimacy and maturity would characterize human relationship to God. Free response to love, not obedience to pre-established laws, would determine personal salvation.[31] Thus it is on the basis of an affirmation of the efficacy of love as the condition of access to God that Segundo concludes that Christian liberty cannot be regarded as a "test". The second alternative, that of liberty being creative, must then be accepted as the authentic Christian position.[32]

(b) Freedom as a creation

In arguing for this option, Segundo lays aside the classical distinction between liberty and free will. He defines liberty as the capacity to bestow meaning and value. It, therefore, operates primarily in the realm of truth by making clear the distinction between what truly comes from within a person, from a personal decision, and what results from the determinism of an external force. Free will is the human "faculty", the capacity to choose in the light of reason. Because there is, in Segundo's view, a basic continuity between the exercise of free will and the liberty which consequently characterizes a person, the distinction between the two terms loses importance for him. Liberty itself, he maintains, must be freely chosen, and chosen repeatedly.[33] Therefore, he focusses instead upon the basic tension between freedom and nature to explain what it means for liberty to be creative. Again it will be obvious that the notion of efficacious love is the controlling factor, as it was in his explication of that tension.

As explained above, in the context of the freedom-nature tension, liberty is conditioned by the determinisms of human nature and external realities. Liberty, then, cannot be imagined as being equally poised between good and evil. The odds are weighed in the direction of the mechanical forces towards easy, simple solutions. Yet true liberty counters that tendency by directing those forces while simultaneously using them in the service of efficacious love. By a slow, painful process liberty is constructed through its exercise.[34]

To speak of liberty as defining persons, therefore, entails the struggle to ensure that whatever results from a person is truly a personal response and not a semblance of that. As he puts it, in agreement with Paul, "the primary victory of liberty will be to separate what is ours from that which lodges in us."[35] In this way persons are created in the face of depersonalizing forces. That, we have already seen, is the very task of efficacious love.

As thus creative of persons, liberty is then a value to be sought at whatever risk it inevitably involves. In Segundo's view, it is the unwillingness to allow for this risk which accounts for the virtual denial of liberty in order to safeguard some "preconceived perfect nature", the common concern of traditional pastoral activity. This he rejects as rooted in a slavish fear which Christianity has, in principle, overcome.[36] Risk is then inherent in the exercise of liberty. But risk is also the very condition of self-gift, of efficacious love, and is, therefore, justified for that very reason. He writes:

> Every person is worth the trouble of being loved, because in every person treated as such there is an absolute value. And this absolute is not subject to any provisos. Self-giving is *always* constructive and constructive *forever*. From this viewpoint, there is no greater sin than not accepting this trouble which is real, and this risk, which is only seeming risk from the viewpoint of faith and its certainty.[37]

The reason that Segundo gives for the necessity of that risk is related to the limitations of human freedom. It is the impossibility of knowing experientially beforehand the path that needs to be followed.[38] Consequently, specific options must be made regarding the means to be used. These comprise the partial, incomplete, inadequate choices which, nevertheless, determine personal salvation.

Segundo's conclusion understandably echoes what we have noted above relative to grace since the effects of grace and liberty are, indeed, synonymous. It is the fact that human existence is situated between two poles, the one representing the absolutizing of all that liberty constructs in deeds of efficacious love, the other, the loss of personhood in egoistic acts and a return to the pre-human determinism of natural forces. Because redemption is given to human beings in their condition of being enslaved by such forces, Segundo maintains that personal salvation, Eternal Life, is what lies ahead to be constructed in time through the exercise of liberty. As he puts it:

In making us free through love, grace leads us towards the pole which, in its full totality, is God himself. In freely rejecting this dynamism and denying liberty through egotism, man moves in the opposite direction . . . These two poles, and only they, give meaning and sense to Christian existence. But they only give meaning and sense to an existence endowed with liberty.[39]

In summary, then, Segundo maintains that personal salvation is most adequately represented in human liberation. Because of an intimate link between grace and liberty, Segundo's reinterpretation focusses upon the creative act *par excellence*, that of the creation of persons through the efficacy of love.

Segundo, therefore, argues against the interpretation of liberty as a "test", as destructive of Christianity which is founded on the very freedom introduced by the Son of God. He argues for an understanding of freedom as creatively utilizing the forces of depersonalization inherent in human existence, while being opposed to them. Thus limited by the conditions of historical existence, liberty is constructed gradually in the specific, unfinished deeds of efficacious love which ultimately are revealed to be of eternal worth. The value of efficacious love is thus seen to be the centering concern in Segundo's understanding of personal salvation, interpreted as primarily human liberation.

4. Faith and Efficacious Love

Faith is, perhaps, the most fundamental symbol of personal salvation viewed in terms of the human response. The explication of faith's relationship to efficacious love will, then, necessarily draw out the link between efficacious love and personal salvation itself, as we shall see.

The problematic which forms the backdrop of Segundo's reinterpretation of the existential reality of religious faith in relationship to personal salvation, has its roots in the sacred-profane dichotomy which, as we have already seen, is the basis of the historical tension between faith and reason.[40] The problematic is twofold: (1) secularization and the absence of faith; and (2) absolute faith and historical relativity. Since the question of secularization and its supposed threat to religious faith is directly related to the sacralization of the means of access to God, it will be more properly dealt with in the following section which will discuss cultic worship and its relationship to personal salvation. Here, we will focus on the second formulation of the problematic, viz., that of the relationship between religious faith as belief in an *Absolute* Being, and the *relativity* of historical existence. This takes us immediately into the faith-ideology tension, discussed above, as the immediate context of Segundo's interpretation.

Again, the notion of efficacious love suggests by its very dynamic and the aspects highlighted by Segundo, a possible way of proceeding with this explanation of faith as related to efficacious love. Efficacious love specifies the object of religious faith by defining the authentic image of God. It also verifies the reality of faith in deeds that are concretely in tune with the demands of a historical existence. Finally, the effects of faith are to be seen in the transformation of a personal life through efficacious love. Hence, this discussion will focus on religious faith as being: (a) in continuity with anthropological faith; (b) the concrete embodiment of love and (c) creative and transformative of persons. We will begin with the first point.

(a) Religious faith in continuity with anthropological faith

Segundo claims that religious faith is in continuity with anthropological faith. Therefore, religious faith must also be understood as an orientation of personal life according to a system of values ordered towards one value considered as absolute. It is, then, a specific type of anthropological faith in which the absolute is identified with God and acknowledged as such.

Just as is the case with anthropological faith, religious faith also requires referential witnesses to communicate the system of values that is judged to be directed towards the Absolute. Because values can only be communicated by concrete embodiment, Segundo does not relate the question of the authenticity of Christian faith to the matter of whether or not such a God exists, as traditionally debated. Rather he shifts the discussion to ascertaining whether the values lived are, indeed, in line with the values lived by Jesus of Nazareth and thus revealed to be of ultimate worth. Segundo's concern is that an operative atheism, the identification of God with a false system of values, can be and is, in fact, present among many professing the Christian faith.[41] Thus Segundo's most basic understanding of Christian faith is developed according to the only image of God that he accepts as genuine, that revealed by Jesus of Nazareth, the image of God as Love.

(b) Faith as the concrete embodiment of love

Love given freely on the part of God becomes faith on the part of the human person who receives and incarnates that love. Thus faith is the self-gift, the total surrender of the person to God, the response to the prior self-gift of God. It is in faith, then, that personal contact with God is experienced, that personal salvation is realized.

What Segundo emphasizes in his reinterpretation of the Christian faith is the *conscious* awareness with which a person receives and in turn acknowledges the source and goal of all genuine love to be God. The fact of God's loving action in human life thus becomes the "good news" to be communicated by Christians. But this can only be done when, in fact, that love is visibly operative in such a way as to make that "good news" credible. In short, the realization of efficacious love must be the "preparation" for an acceptance of Christian faith.[42]

As we have already seen, however, love's efficacy demands an embodiment according to the conditions of human life in any given cultural and historical situation. In accordance with his evolutionary perspective, therefore, Segundo places the emphasis on the pedagogical process which has marked the history of God's self-communication to humanity. Thus he stresses that faith is a maturation process whereby the Christian learns how to judge historical events according to the values of Jesus of Nazareth.[43]

Faith is then a judgment of value, not an assent to pre-established truths. The latter would be equivalent to the amassing of information on the level of the abstract and impersonal. It would be a confusion of faith with the means used to embody faith.[44] Thus, any interpretation of Christian dogmas as perennial truths to be preserved and handed down is a misunderstanding of the Christian faith. Rather, Segundo claims, dogmas are religious symbols, the tentative attempts to capture at specific historical moments as authentic an expression of Christian experience as possible. Reformulations of such Christian affirmations are, therefore, in keeping with the maturation process of faith. He writes:

> Therefore this faith does not consist in intellectual adherence to a certain body of revealed content as the definitive solution to theoretical or practical problems. Nor does it consist in having confidence in one's own salvation, thanks to the merits of Christ. Instead it entails the freedom to accept an educational process that comes to maturity and abandons its teachers to launch out into the provisional and relative depths of history.[45]

The criterion of the judgment of value that faith is remains for Segundo, "efficacious love". For efficacious love characterizes the style of life that bears witness to the fact that the values chosen are, indeed, the values lived by Jesus of Nazareth.

(c) Faith as creative and transformative of persons

The level on which Christian faith operates is, pre-eminently *personal* vis-à-vis the impersonal forces of nature. The maturity of persons that faith gradually achieves is, then, related to effective use of appropriate means, of "ideologies". Thus Segundo can also speak of faith as a "liberative process" which is "converted into freedom for history."[46] He insists, however, that the choice of means must be made according to the criterion of efficacious love.[47]

Segundo, therefore, stresses personal attitudes, a whole style of life as reflective of faith, rather than individual acts. He insists:

> ...faith is something very different from a specific act, accessible to human beings specifically situated in history. We see it as a way of being human, as something that moves the human being from timidity to maturity, from action based on petty calculations to action performed in a gratuitous and creative manner.[48]

This type of attitude marks the shift from fear which seeks security in contractual negotiations with God to the mature creation of a "love that is truly inventive and efficacious in history."[49]

It is clear that this understanding of faith as personal cannot imply an individualistic concept of personal salvation. Rather, it shifts the focus to the interpersonal and social dimensions of human existence. This makes of Christian living a full engagement with others in the task of incarnating love. This we shall develop more fully in the following chapter.

In placing religious faith on a distinct level from that of the law, Segundo is also able to maintain the primacy and absolute value of faith for personal salvation while admitting at the same time the necessity and value of the relative expression of the "works of law". He does not then compromise the absolute claims of faith when he insists that it does not provide universal solutions for concrete, historical problems. Rather, his reinterpretation of faith gives priority to the personal realm of values and commitment as the access road to God, while acknowledging the necessary complementarity of concretization in the law.[50] Both faith and law are thus held together in creative tension. This, tension, captured as it is in the notion of efficacious love, makes of that reality the most adequate expression of authentic, salvific faith.

In summary, Segundo claims that religious faith is a particular instance of anthropological faith and is, therefore, in basic continuity with the system of values which the latter affirms. An authentic interpretation of Christian faith must, then, be concerned with the values embodied in concrete historical situations rather than with the conceptual problem of God's existence. As such, faith expresses commitment to the prior unconditional love of God and incarnates that love according to the conditions of historical existence. Therefore, salvific faith is essentially a maturation process whereby the Christian assumes the mentality of Jesus of Nazareth. It subordinates and directs the necessary use of means according to his values. Hence, it is most adequately expressed in the only absolute value which is efficacious love.

5. Cultic Worship and Efficacious Love

Cultic worship has been commonly understood as the primary act of "religion". As such, it is directly and explicitly related to the question of personal salvation. Hence, to explain the meaning of ritual activity in its relationship to efficacious love will disclose more fully the way in which personal salvation is related to efficacious love.

Segundo's reinterpretation of cultic worship or ritual activity confronts directly the problematic of secularization and the absence of faith in Latin America. The basic issue relates to the separation of the sacred and profane. We have already indicated that the unity in distinction of these two aspects of historical existence is the most basic assumption of Segundo's theology. Hence, his discussion of the existential reality of cultic worship will again explicitly uncover elements that are, indeed, operative and fundamental throughout his entire theological enterprise. We will proceed by examining four aspects of the issue: (a) secularization and the presence of faith; (b) ritual activities as instruments of faith; (c) Christian sacraments vs magical rites; and (d) Christian sacraments as liberative and transformative "signs" of faith.

The point of focus will be the function and place of the notion of efficacious love in Segundo's explanation. Faith embodied in efficacious love gives witness to the immanence of God in creation. Ritual activities are, then, to be understood as means of incarnating faith in history through efficacious love. The real efficacy of Christian sacraments, therefore, is to be found in the efficacy of the ordinary events of history. For faith active in creative, transformative, efficacious love is, indeed, the human commitment that is symbolized in the salvific reception of the Christian sacraments.

(a) Secularization and the presence of faith

It is not surprising to find that in explaining the relationship between ritual activity and personal salvation, Segundo shifts the emphasis from the realm of the sacred to that of the secular. This is what the process of secularization means. It reflects a core postulate of Christianity which has placed everything at the service of humanity and humanity itself under Christ (cf. 1 Cor. 3:22-23). Segundo writes, "Secularization, far from signifying an abandonment of the profane to its profaneness, is a recognition of the sacred that it contains within its very dynamism. It is the *consecration* of the profane."[51] Thus secularization indicates, for Segundo, that humanity as recapitulated in Christ, has become the privileged access road to God. Far from destroying faith, secularization reveals that an authentic understanding of personal salvation must entail the achievement of human maturity in Christ.[52] Ritual activity to be effective for that salvation must then be directly related to the process of humanization, and hence to the exercise of efficacious love.

(b) Ritual activities as instruments of faith

Segundo emphasizes that ritual activities which are common to all "religions" belong to the plane of objective instruments *vis-à-vis* faith which structures personal values. Hence, ritual activity is subordinated to the personal commitment that faith implies and is meaningful only in terms of that faith. If, then, faith is verified in efficacious deeds of love, ritual activity must likewise be validated by such concrete expressions of love.

As all instruments which have their own internal dynamisms, however, rites tend to be separated from the intentions of persons using them. Thus Segundo notes Jesus' condemnation of empty Pharasaic worship in the tradition of the prophets of Israel who rejected worship that co-existed with injustice and oppression of the poor. Jesus' turn away from emphasis on ritual activity to service of those in need is the fundamental Christian revolution and accounts for the resistance of early Christianity to being another "religion".[53] If Christianity is to be termed a "religion", it is, indeed, the "religion of true love." As we have already seen, Segundo then casts the emphasis on love of God and concomitantly of neighbour, as the verification of personal approach to God. Thus the question of the authenticity of specific forms of cultic worship becomes, for him, that of ascertaining what, in fact, comprises the true efficacy of love in history.

(c) Christian sacraments vs magical rites

Segundo sets up a sharp distinction between "magic" and the truly efficacious signs that sacraments, the Christian rites *par excellence*, purport to be. The former, he defines as actions which have no natural connection with that which causes them. They presuppose a realm of "extraordinary causality" which is separated from the ordinary events of human life. The magical mentality, therefore, is one marked by the expectation of such an extraordinary intervention.[54]

Segundo argues against the use of the sacraments as "sacred magic". This has happened when they have been placed in the realm of the sacred and given an absolute, extraordinary efficacy apart from secular, historical existence. The result has been the communication of an assurance of personal salvation and a sense of security beyond the vicissitudes of human life. The Christianity that has fostered this type of attitude towards the sacraments has, therefore, vitiated the Christian message in confusing faith with religious practices. In so doing, it has been able to maintain the masses in dependent security, rather than summon them to respond to the Christian call to the insecurity of historical engagement and the minority challenge of efficacious love.[55]

(d) The sacraments as liberative and transformative signs of faith

For Segundo, then, the sacraments are not so much rites as "signs" which are efficacious in making *real* what they signify. He writes:

> Under specific circumstances the sign possesses an efficacy that takes it out of the realm of mere knowledge and plants it in the realm of *reality*. In other words, what is signified is also realized, the sign *attracts* grace - even though this realization is invisible in most cases and hence affirmed with the help of faith.[56]

In this understanding of the sacraments as basically "efficacious signs" of grace, Segundo is one with traditional Catholic teaching. Where he is placing the emphasis, however, is on the concrete, historical *reality* rather than on the abstract realm of thought and intentions. Hence the novel insight that he offers in his reinterpretation of the Christian sacraments centres upon their function in challenging and fashioning a community of faith.

The creation of a transformed reality becomes, for Segundo, the basis and object of sacramental celebration. That it is a transformation through love and efficaciously creative of love is obvious from Segundo's understanding of the seven sacraments as key moments in human life when the life and love that is revealed in the total self-donation of Jesus, i.e., in his death, is made available to persons within the Christian community.[57] His insistence upon the celebration of the sacraments in community, emphasizes their social character and function. Indeed, the presence of these sacraments in the Christian community as consciously pointing to and making real the transformative power of the Death-Resurrection mystery of Christ is constitutive of the community of faith. This we shall see more clearly in the next chapter.

Closely linked to this transformative function of the sacraments is a critical function whereby the Christian community is challenged to live authentically the love that is symbolized. This is according to the human requirement of love to be efficacious in its use and direction of the instruments of nature and of culture. Critical consciousness must ensure that the determinism of nature does not dominate human response. Thus the moments of a creative and liberative directing of natural dynamisms break into what could otherwise be vitiated by routine and mechanistic manipulation.

These moments are expressed in "gestures" which are not bound by the natural efficacy ordinarily attached to human actions. Hence, they are "incidental" and "non-essential". Their sole purpose is to recall creative moments when it is clear that human intentions, not the natural dynamism of an action provided the stimulus for performing certain deeds. The gesture is, then, more capable of cutting through the ambiguity that is ordinarily inherent in human actions. It points clearly to the presence of the original intentions that purport to inform those deeds. The gesture can, therefore, call into question the natural efficacy of actions that are, in fact separated from their initial intentions. In this way, the sacraments, as gestures and words that are "incidental" and "non-essential", can challenge a community of faith to act creatively according to human intentions, rather than through mechanistic routine and by following the line of least resistance.[58]

Thus the sacraments imply commitment and responsibility to fashion a community marked by the liberative presence of grace and its effects in efficacious love.[59] This significant insight into the meaning of the Christian sacraments counters the static, "bank-deposit" approach which had made Christians "receivers" of the sacraments rather than creative agents of transformation.

In summary, Segundo regards the process of secularization as a positive shifting of the focus away from the sacred realm and ritual activities as the privileged access road to God to that of the historical embodiment of faith in deeds of efficacious love. Segundo thus regards ritual actions as instruments that are necessary to incarnate the meaning and structure of values that faith represents.

As efficacious signs of grace, the Christian sacraments are to be distinguished from magical rites which bear no connection between action and result and thus place the emphasis on extraordinary intervention. In rejecting the "magical" attitude towards the sacraments, Segundo argues for a reinterpretation of the Christian sacraments that stresses their function in creating, transforming and challenging a community of faith. In likewise highlighting their social character, Segundo makes it clear that the concern for the value of efficacious love is basic to his understanding of cultic worship in relationship to personal salvation.

5. Human Action and Efficacious Love

Focus on Christian praxis as one of the most distinguishing marks of Segundo's theology, as of the Latin American liberation theological movement in general, makes the significance of human action and hence the question of morality a central concern relative to personal salvation. It is then of extreme importance that Segundo identifies a unique contribution of Christianity in its shift from a law morality to one based on love, one having as its only criterion the law of efficacious love. Segundo's reinterpretation of Christian morality can then be examined according to three aspects of this basic shift as derived from his understanding of efficacious love. These aspects mark the shift from: (a) abstract nature/law to the creative liberty of persons in history; (b) individualistic morality of the licit-illicit to the social morality of the "advantageous" for the other; and (c) static, absolute norms to progressive, relative evaluations of the "signs of the times".

The basic terms of these shifts, namely, from the abstract to the concrete, from the individual to the social and from the static to the dynamic, recur throughout Segundo's writings. Here, in his interpretation of Christian morality in relationship to efficacious love, they enable Segundo to throw the emphasis on the concrete fashioning of history through efficacious love; on the social responsibility of meeting the needs of the other in efficacious deeds of love; and finally, on the dynamic, ongoing Christian task of inserting love efficaciously in history in accord with the demands of God's project of humanization. We will proceed by examining each of these three aspects of Christian morality in turn.

(a) Shift from abstract nature/law to creative liberty

This shift is, perhaps, the most significant move that Segundo makes in his reinterpretation of Christian morality. In it is reflected the tension of the creative "minority" thrust of efficacious love *vis-`a-vis* the easy submission to the manipulation of natural determinism, as described above.[60] The specific application here is opposed to the traditional emphasis on legalism as basically pre-Christian and indicative of the stage of slavish submission to the law (cf. Gal. 4:1-6). With Paul, Segundo claims that in Christ all things have been placed under human beings and henceforth the mature creativity of sons and daughters is the only adequate measure of Christian action (cf. 1 Cor. 3: 22-23). According to Segundo, then, this "creative" morality that Paul advocates does not draw its precepts from the world of nature but from the "project" in which the liberty of human beings will fashion a humanized world. This project is the realization of efficacious love. He writes:

> In effect what the Christian is asked to construct involves a gift of
> self to the other. To love, to love efficaciously, is the only law of the
> Christian. It is not the law which distributes among actions formulas
> of what is "permitted" or "prohibited", independent of each person;
> but the law which indicates the only true path of personal liberty: to
> create, in circumstances that are always personal and unique, a
> historical love that is also irreplaceable and unique.[61]

Christian morality must then reflect the mature and creative use of liberty in the use and direction of the resources of humanity and of the universe. It is the fashioning of a historical project of efficacious love.

(b) Shift from individualistic to social morality

The exigencies of efficacious love also demand that Christian morality be pre-eminently social. For Segundo, the emphasis on love immediately moves the question from the individualistic concern for what is "licit" to what is "advantageous" or not for the other. Segundo argues this point on the basis of Paul's assertion (cf. 1 Cor. 10: 23-24) and on the fact that the love of God necessarily includes love of neighbour. He clearly states:

> If one must construct within history which is never eternally repeated, an efficacious love of the other, Christian morality is not a morality of the "licit" or the "illicit", but a morality of what is convenient or not for the construction of love, for the efficacious gift of self...[62]

However, it is not to be concluded from this that Segundo is advocating an antinomian rejection of all laws. With Paul, he admits that not all actions are "advantageous". The use of means that negate love must then be rejected. Hence, what Segundo is claiming is that love provides a different perspective and the liberty with which to approach the demands of the law.[63]

The morality of the "advantageous" is specifically marked by interest in the other. This makes Paul's assertion to that effect (1 Cor. 10: 24-29) another important scriptural basis for Segundo's understanding of Christian morality. Preoccupation with one's personal judgment thus yields to the concern for constructing a better world for others. The concrete needs of the neighbour become the criterion or norm of salvific human action (cf. Mt. 25:31-46).

This makes of Christian morality a specifically *social* reality which is based upon the efficacious love of neighbour as the mark of genuine approach to God.

(c) Shift from static, absolute norms to progressive, relative judgments

For Segundo, love as the fundamental value affirmed by Christian morality, also makes the latter a dynamic process in tune with the concrete, historical circumstances in which love progresses. This dynamism relates not only to the fact that it is a step by step progress but also to the need for a gradual discovery of what serves love best. What the latter implies, besides, is not a movement from uncertainty to certainty, but rather one from certain convictions to others that are more open, more genuine and more fruitful. In short, Segundo is claiming that a Christian moral life parallels the life of faith which, for him, is dynamic and progressive, a gradual assuming of the mentality of Christ.[64]

Far from being an easy relativism, this kind of "progressive" morality indicates what, Segundo claims, is a "profound relativity" that "takes into account the progressive maturity of persons and the variety of human situations." He continues, "it indicates the conditions of a real progress of creative, moral conscience, which to the measure that it loves, discovers more and more the deep universal and objective dimensions of love."[65]

Christian morality must, then, be attuned to the signs of the times, must be "significative" of the historical presence of God's love at work in human life. Hence, it fosters specific ways of living and dialogic relationships whereby the authentic message of efficacious love can be inserted into the world.

The value of efficacious love as realized in the progress of humanization thus specifies the goal of Christian morality. Because, for Segundo, this implies the necessary and appropriate use of concrete means, he argues for the indissoluble link between means and ends and the continual purification of the means used to realize human projects. The danger, according to him, is not the justification of the means by the end, the traditional moral problematic, but rather the uncritical use of means that cannot in fact realize the end intended. Thus, the morality of means is determined by whether or not the means, indeed, promote concrete expressions of love in given situations.[67] Segundo further claims that the Christian message, with love at its very core, is best able to affect the purification of means. He writes:

> From the very beginning it sheds light on the relationship of love to hope: i.e., to the long range goal. It sheds light on the relationship of love to humanity as a whole, on the relationship to the power of man's heart when we do not have the means to physically carry out our love.[68]

In all of the above, it is, therefore, obvious that efficacious love is the controlling factor in Segundo's reinterpretation of Christian morality and the norm by which one judges what comprises genuine and salvific human action.

In summary, then, Segundo's reinterpretation of Christian morality is marked by a decided shift from a morality based upon obedience to the law to one based upon love. The latter implies, for him, the challenge of mature filial relationship as the basis of the new morality. It demands the free and creative determination of human projects, in lieu of passive obedience to pre-determined laws. It promotes concern with what is "advantageous" for others rather than with what an individual may or may not do. It decides within the context of concrete, historical situations what means best realize the specific project of love instead of applying absolute principles of good and evil. Thus Christian morality is finally a sign of the love of God incarnated in human life. Efficacious love is its basis and its goal as well as the verification of its authentic, salvific expression.

7. Jesus Christ as Personal Saviour and Efficacious Love

Personal salvation in Jesus Christ is, for Segundo, a question of religious faith. As such, it can have relevance only in terms of an already established anthropological faith, that ordered system of values which attests to the meaningfulness of a specific style of life.[69] Segundo's reinterpretation of Jesus Christ as personal Saviour will, therefore, evidence the decided shift to the human that marks his entire theological enterprise and, indeed, will also reveal the source of its justification. To consider, then, the relationship of efficacious love to the style of human life that Jesus exemplifies is to show how efficacious love is related to personal salvation.

Segundo begins his Christological discussion not with the question of the divine, and abstract speculations about the characteristics and implications of such a nature, but with that of the historical Jesus of Nazareth and the meaning he has for the person of today.[70] On that level of concrete human existence, Jesus Christ as Saviour is the primary witness of a human style of life that is of ultimate value because it reveals nothing less than the historical embodiment of God himself. Jesus of Nazareth reveals at once the authentic image of God and of humanity. The discussion in this section will develop each of those aspects of Jesus as Revealer and then the implications for a genuine acceptance of the salvation offered in him. The relationship between Segundo's reinterpretation and efficacious love will again be the point of focus.

It will be of interest to note the implications of the historical revelation of a God defined by love and the challenge to a humanity structured by love and for love. Nevertheless, this love which is efficaciously realized in time finds its fulfilment beyond time in the very presence of Love itself.

(a) Jesus of Nazareth as Revealer of God

The Christian God is, for Segundo, a Trinity of Persons turned towards humanity: the Father, Creator, God-before-us; the Son, God-with-us; and the Spirit, God-within-us.[71] The true image of such a God, Segundo claims, can only be revealed by him who came from within that Trinity, viz., Jesus of Nazareth, the Son who entered into human existence to reveal God's solidarity with humanity. This is the supreme gift of free, creative love through which something new and definitive enters human history. Segundo writes:

> It is precisely when this interiorization within human history reaches its acme in total self-giving even unto death (Jn. 13:1; Mt. 27: 50-51), that the veil of the temple is rent in a symbolic way. That which seemed to separate the sacred from history disappears; all that remains is history, which is simultaneously human history and divine history.[72]

Such an entrance into human history reflects the only image of God which does not devalue and alienate the human person (cf. Rom. 8:32). In accord with the dynamics of love, it does not take possession of humanity but rather places God at the disposal of every person who is then respected as an absolute.[73] Thus Segundo insists that John's definition of God as Love is the only genuine image of the Christian God.

The sources and implications of the meaning of this definition we have already discussed.[74] What is of additional interest here is Segundo's claim that the message of Jesus is focussed upon the coming "reign of God" as the inauguration of the ultimate in history through a creative project of efficacious love. Jesus' historical participation in that project thus reveals the vision of God and the system of values that orders human life in accord with its deepest and ultimate possibilities. It is only on that level of lived values that God's revelation can occur. As Segundo expresses it:

God can only be revealed in connection with values that are humanly meaningful, and those values must be manifested historically on one or more of the planes where the human being stakes the meaning of its life and the possibilities for happiness. Strictly speaking, then, we can say that there is no divine revelation that does not take its course through preferences and concrete realizations on the plane of interpersonal relations, education, economics, politics, and societal life. The revelation of Jesus does not, could not, constitute an exception.[75]

Hence, Segundo also insists upon the revelation in Jesus of God's socio-political involvement in his preferential love of the poor and marginated, as we have already seen.[76] It is the most radical expression of that gratuitous love which reveals God as totally focussed on the creation of human subjects in history and needing human collaboration to realize that project of humanization. Personal access to that God consists in that very collaboration. On the contrary, refusal to be thus engaged is indicative of that hardness of heart which expects to encounter God in "signs from heaven" and not where he reveals himself to be present, viz., in concrete historical projects of efficacious love.[77]

Segundo is arguing against the traditional Christologies "from above" which attempt to interpret the human existence of Jesus of Nazareth according to pre-established knowledge of the divine in him.[78] For him, only a Christology that is truly "from below", that represents God as bearing the consequences of the freely assumed limits of human existence, that encounters the divine in Jesus' way of being human, can adequately capture the novel revelation in Jesus of Nazareth. The latter alone presents the true image of God as the source and goal of love in human life.[79] Thus, the question of personal salvation is not a matter of belief or unbelief in just any interpretation of the Christian God. Rather it is directly related to the *identification* of that God as Love.

(b) Jesus of Nazareth as Revealer of authentic human life

Jesus of Nazareth is the primary witness of a style of life entirely dominated by the Spirit and hence incarnating the vision and values of God himself. In his manner of being human the ultimate meaning of human existence is realized in the closest possible union with the divine, viz., in the shared intimacy of Father and Son. In this twofold aspect of his human life is revealed the authentic core of human existence. This we will now consider in its relationship to efficacious love.

In Jesus of Nazareth something new and definitive has happened in human life. It is not only the revelation of the abiding presence of God's unconditional love but more significantly the new possibility of living according to the vision and values structured by that love, albeit within the limits of historical human existence. Thus gratuitous self-gift, true and concretely transformative love of others, is revealed as the absolute criterion of authentic human existence.

Therefore, Segundo stresses Jesus' engagement in the religio-political struggle on behalf of the poor and oppressed of Israel as the embodiment of God's own preferential, compassionate love. Authentic human existence in accord with the mentality of Jesus of Nazareth requires, then, a similar option. It opens human existence to conflict and to the supreme sacrifice of love unto death as it did in Jesus.[80]

That such a love is definitive and triumphs over death is what Segundo stresses in his reinterpretation of Jesus' Resurrection. For him, the latter is not so much the divine verification of the life and message of Jesus of Nazareth as the revelation of the ultimate value of his style of life.[81] Thus, Segundo claims, Jesus gives meaning to the dying and rising that is necessarily part of all human living. He testifies to the definitive power of efficacious love, to the fact that "no love is lost" in history.

It is the paradigm of sonship, however, that best defines the style of life that Jesus exemplifies. It is significant that at its basis is the shared intimacy of Father and Son which, Segundo maintains, is the novel revelation of Jesus of Nazareth. Hence, following Paul, Segundo draws out of this love relationship what is perhaps his most basic theological insight, viz., that in Christ the human person has attained the maturity of sonship beyond childish subjection to nature and its mechanisms. Creative liberty and responsible direction of the available instruments henceforth characterize human collaboration with God in the continued creation of a humanized world. This demands the exercise of love that is open to risk and is efficacious in transforming reality in lieu of the fear that seeks security in what is controllable. He writes:

> The gift that God gives to human beings in Jesus Christ is the possibility of a coherent maturity, of complete fulfillment as human beings; and this presupposes replacing the mechanisms of the Flesh with those of the Spirit... So there is no question of associating us with some unmerited justice, thanks to the merits of Jesus Christ. Faith is something very different. In Faith, the Spirit for the first time lays down the initial foundation for a completely new existence, one opposed to the mechanisms of the Flesh. Only this new life is capable of the creative boldness proper to children of God, of achieving something new in the history of the universe, which is the Creator's heritage.[82]

This, as we have been seeing, subsequently grounds the novel turn in his reinterpretation of Christianity and its doctrinal symbols. In line with this, it becomes clearer why Segundo insists with Lehmann that personal salvation in Christ is, indeed, "maturity".[83]

It is in drawing out the implications of sonship as lived by the historical Jesus that Segundo also points to the faith *of* Jesus as an important fact alongside the traditional emphasis on faith *in* Jesus. The former reveals what comprises authentic human faith in direct continuity with Abraham, the old Testament paradigm of the person of faith. This faith is characterized by the total surrender in love of Son to Father, and confidence in that love rather than in the instruments required to express that love.[84] In thus drawing attention to the faith *of* Jesus, Segundo can then argue for the priority of faith over the accumulation of merit without losing his stress on efficacious deeds of love as the norm of personal salvation.

(c) Acceptance of Jesus Christ as personal Saviour

What Segundo means by faith *in* Jesus leads us to a consideration of what personal acceptance of the revelation in Jesus of Nazareth entails. Faith in Jesus, Segundo claims, is belief in him as the ultimate meaning of human existence, the acceptance of the transcendent data witnessed to in his way of being human.[85] Because this relates primarily to a system of values, it can only be communicated through personal appropriation. Faith in Jesus can, therefore be verified only through a style of life that in turn is ordered by the values lived by Jesus of Nazareth. Thus authentic response to Jesus as personal Saviour entails a concrete following of his way of life. He writes:

> It is obvious that a value-world cannot be communicated effectively in a linear, expository way. Communication comes from the repetition of the living image of that world in our activity. That is how the *thus* of Jesus' way of acting is turned into a theme with variations on Boff's gospel as well as in the other Gospels. And each variation points up a different facet of the same meaning-structure, one which says: it is worth joining in solidarity with the crucified of this world as Jesus did, even to the point of enduring the same cross, on the proviso that this will put an end to the crucifixion of some human beings by other human beings.[86]

Thus it is clear why, for Segundo, discipleship cannot be a matter of the traditional "imitation of Christ" which relegates personal salvation to the life beyond.[87] Rather it is primarily an engagement with Jesus of Nazareth in God's own project.[88] This refers to the creation of persons in history, the project of efficacious love. In this lies personal salvation.

In sum, Jesus Christ as personal Saviour is, for Segundo, primarily witness of the authentic image of God as well as that of humanity. The image of God he reveals is that of one defined by love, the source and goal of all love experienced in human life. Jesus of Nazareth, as the embodiment of that love thus reveals divinity in the structure of values that he embraced, in his way of being human.

Likewise, Jesus of Nazareth reveals that the love experienced in historical existence is of ultimate value. This love, which is given most intimately in the relationship of Son to Father is the foundation of Christian maturity. This maturity, which is, indeed, salvation, is exemplified in his creative engagement in the project of God which he announces, i.e., the creation of subjects in history *vis-`a-vis* the mechanistic forces of nature. To appropriate the faith *of* Jesus and to believe *in* him, therefore, entails involvement with him in his humanizing task. It challenges to the ultimate self-gift and promises only that in the end it will be eternally worthwhile to have lived as Jesus did - empowered by the efficacious love of the Spirit and surrendered to that love. Therein lies the assurance of personal salvation.

8. Conclusion

It is clear from all of the above that efficacious love is the controlling notion in Segundo's understanding of personal salvation. His reinterpretation of that existential reality evidences the various facets of the meaning he gives to efficacious love. It is, first of all, the gratuitous gift of God's love which liberates the person for a creative self-determination. It transforms the person, making possible reciprocal commitment to God expressed in love of others. It celebrates the efficacious presence of that love which triumphs over death eternally and transforms and challenges the community of faith. The criterion of judgment which determines personal salvation is, then, the concrete love of neighbour according to the exigencies of specific contexts. Finally, the paradigm of a style of life which witnesses to the salvific presence of that love is that of Jesus of Nazareth who reveals ultimate meaning within, yet not totally within, historical existence. Personal salvation is, therefore, primarily achieved in the mature exercise of liberty which, in collaboration with the Spirit, directs the universe in the service of humanity, the specific project of efficacious love.

Notes

1. Cf. Segundo, *Berdiaeff*, pp. 64, 78, 120, 128, 159.

2. Segundo, *Our Idea of God*, p. 111.

3. Cf. Chapter III, pp. 55-58.

4. To explain this, Segundo draws upon Freud's description of the authentic person as being realized through the inner self or "ego" defining itself in terms of external reality. This is done in tension with the unconscious control of the "id" (the basic human drives), and the "superego" (the tendencies imposed by culture). Segundo sees a correlation between Freud's portrayal and Paul's image of the "inner and outer" human being. Although Paul's "inner" being is distinct from Freud's "ego" which is authentic only when it is in accord with external reality, still Paul's concept of personal authenticity also demands that "inner" intention be verified and made real by deeds. Cf. Segundo *Grace and the Human Condition*, pp. 35-37.

5. Segundo, *Grace and the Human Condition*, pp. 24, 160.

6. Segundo is in accord with Rahner's explanation of personal growth through the free disposition of the self. He differs from Rahner in paying more explicit regard to the tendency inherent in external nature towards entropy and the contrary struggle and impotence of persons to act entirely according to human will and decision.

7. See Chapter II, pp. 31f.

8. Segundo understands society not as an aggregate of individuals already formed but as a system of human interaction and relationships that are constitutive of the person. Cf. *Grace and the Human Condition*, p. 38.

9. Cf. Segundo, *Our Idea of God*, p. 16. Cf. "Padre, Hijo, Espíritu: Una libertad II", *Perspectivas de Dialogo*, III, no. 26 (August 1968), 183-86.

10. See Roger Haight, *Experience and the Language of Grace* (New York:

Paulist, 1978) for a concise and insightful interpretation of the historical development of the doctrine of grace.

11. Segundo, *Grace and the Human Condition,* pp. 3-11.

12. See *Ibid.,* pp. 46-50 for Segundo's discussion of the Pelagian controversy which was centred on this problematic.

13. See Chapter III, pp. 56-58.

14. Segundo, *Grace and the Human Condition,* pp. 58-73.

15. Cf. Chapter III, p. 50.

16. Segundo is rejecting here the reification of grace and a concept of salvation based upon a quantitative increase of merits. Cf. *Grace and the Human Condition,* pp. 82-96.

17. Segundo, *Grace and the Human condition,* pp. 62-74.

18. *Ibid.,* p. 70

19. *Ibid.,* pp. 139-150. Cf. Juan Luis Segundo, "La vida eterna", *Perspectivas de Dialogo,* II, no. 14 (June 1967), 83-89; no. 15 (July 1967), 109-118.

20. Cf. Chapter III, pp. 62-65.

21. Segundo, *Grace and the Human Condition,* p. 113.

22. *Ibid.,* pp. 108-115.

23. *Ibid.,* p. 163.

24. See especially Segundo, *Our Idea of God,* pp. 28-31 for Segundo's basic understanding of the Spirit.

25. Segundo *Grace and the Human Condition,* p. 169.

26. See Gutiérrez, *A Theology of Liberation,* pp. 149-87 for a discussion of salvation as liberation.

27. Segundo's emphasis on the creative aspect of liberty is influenced by Berdyaev who defines liberty as "the capacity to create . . . because the creative act always supposes the autonomy, independence and the liberty of the person." *Le Sens de la Creation,* p. 175. Cited in *Berdiaeff,* p. 44.

28. Segundo, *Grace and the Human Condition,* pp. 39-43. Cf. *Our Idea of God,* pp. 106-108.

29. Segundo uses more than once the image of Dostoievski's "Grand Inquisitor" to emphasize this point. Cf. *The Liberation of Theology,* p. 204; *A Comunity Called Church,* pp. 87-88.

30. See Segundo, *Etapes precristianas de la fe,* pp. 71-80, esp. p. 80; *De la sociedad a la teología,* pp. 81-93.

31. Cf. Segundo, *De la sociedad a la teología,* pp. 81-104. The implications of a filial relationship for Christian morality and personal salvation in Christ will be discussed more fully further on. See Chapter IV, pp. 93-96.

32. In this, Segundo is also in agreement with Berdyaev but he does not share the inconsistencies that mark the latter's formulation. Segundo has demonstrated that Berdyaev affirms two positions regarding the relationship between liberty and being. One is that liberty and being are "co-principles" of creation; the other, that being is diminished in the exercise of freedom. Cf. *Berdiaeff,* pp. 51-52.

33. Segundo, *Grace and the Human Condition,* pp. 32-34.

34. *Ibid.,* p. 146.

35. *Ibid.,* p. 32. Because of this, Segundo sees here the relevance of insights

drawn from Marxist ideological critique, Freudian depth analysis and phenomenology for the true exercise of liberty.

36. Cf. Segundo, *The Hidden Motives of Pastoral Action,* pp. 83-107.

37. Segundo, *Grace and the Human Condition,* p. 45.

38. This is the argument that Segundo uses to affirm the anthropological dimension of faith. Hence, faith, for him, as for Berdyaev, is the risk *par excellence.* Cf. *Berdiaeff,* p. 75.

39. Segundo, *Grace and the Human Conditon,* p. 46.

40. Cf. Chapter III, p. 52.

41. Cf. Segundo, *The Sacraments Today,* p. 64.

42. See Segundo, *A Community Called Church,* pp. 10-11.

43. Cf. Segundo, *The Liberation of Theology,* pp. 110-118. Cf. *Faith and Ideologies,* pp. 121-126.

44. Cf. Segundo, *Grace and the Human Condition,* pp. 108-120; *The Liberation of Theology,* pp. 97-110.

45. Segundo, *The Liberation of Theology,* p. 122.

46. *Ibid.,* p. 110.

47. *Ibid.,* pp. 110, 167.

48. Segundo, *The Humanist Christology of Paul,* p. 69.

49. *Ibid.,* p. 57.

50. Cf. Segundo, *Faith and Ideologies,* pp. 119-144.

51. Segundo, *Our Idea of God,* p. 75. Cf. "Desarrollo y subdesarrollo: Polos teológicos", *Perspectivas de Dialogo,* V, no. 43 (May 1970), 76-80.

52. *Ibid.,* p. 74.

53. See especially Segundo, *Faith and Ideologies,* pp. 40-50.

54. Segundo, *The Sacraments Today,* pp. 6, 29-32.

55. Cf. *Ibid.,* pp. 12-20; *The Liberation of Theology,* pp. 183-192; *The Hidden Motives of Pastoral Aciton,* pp. 25-44; *The Sacraments Today,* pp. 12-20.

56. Segundo, *The Sacraments Today,* p. 21.

57. *Ibid.,* pp. 68-75.

58. This is Segundo's elaboration beyond an initial insight taken from Rahner. The latter holds that the superfluous gestures of love, even more than actions that are necessarily required by love, demand the *reality* of love in order to be genuine. See *The Sacraments Today,* p. 94.

59. Segundo, *The Sacraments Today,* p. 96. Cf. Gutiérrez, *A Theology of Liberation,* pp. 262-65.

60. Cf. Chapter III, esp. pp. 51f.

61. Segundo, *De la sociedad a la teología,* pp. 97-98.

62. *Ibid.,* p. 98. Cf. *A Community Called Church,* pp. 104-110.

63. *Ibid.,* p. 98.

64. *Ibid.*

65. *Ibid.,* p. 100.

66. *Ibid.,* p. 104.

67. Segundo, *The Liberation of Theology*, pp. 170-173.

68. Segundo, *A Community Called Church*, p. 109.

69. See Chapter III, pp. 52-54, esp. p. 53.

70. Cf. Segundo, *Our Idea of God*, pp. 102-106; *The Historical Jesus of the Synoptics*, pp. 13-21. This is consistent with the shift from nature to the liberty of persons, which forms the philosophical underpinning for Segundo's theology, as we have seen. Cf. Chapter III, pp. 56-58. This emphasis on the historical Jesus is characteristic of Latin American liberation theology in general. See Jon Sobrino, *Christology at the Crossroads*, translated by John Drury (Maryknoll, New York: Orbis Books, 1978); Leonardo Boff, *Jesus Christ Liberator*, translated by Patrick Hughes (Maryknoll, New York: Orbis Books, 1978). See Roger Haight, *An Alternative Vision*, pp. 121-39 for an analysis of liberation Christology and its implications for contemporary Christology.

71. Segundo, *Our Idea of God*, pp. 20-33.

72. *Ibid.*, p. 26. Here we see the basis for Segundo's most fundamental theological supposition.

73. Cf. *Ibid.*, p. 27.

74. See Chapter II.

75. Segundo, *The Historical Jesus of the Synoptics*, p. 85.

76. Cf. See Chapter III, pp. 67-71.

77. Segundo, *The Historical Jesus of the Synoptics*, p. 132.

78. Cf. Segundo, *Our Idea of God*, pp. 102-106.

79. Segundo, *The Christ of the Ignatian Exercises*, pp. 24-39.

80. Cf. Segundo, *The Historical Jesus of the Synoptics*, pp. 71-85. Segundo holds that the "political key" is the most appropriate for understanding the mission and death of Jesus. Cf. pp. 178-88.

81. Segundo, *The Historical Jesus of the Synoptics*, pp. 166-177.

82. Segundo, *The Humanist Christology of Paul*, p. 56.

83. Segundo, *Our Idea of God*, p. 27; *De la sociedad a la teología*, p. 103.

84. Cf. Segundo, *The Humanist Christology of Paul*, pp. 48-51; 60-75. This emphasis on the faith *of* Jesus as a complement of faith *in* Jesus is part of liberation theology's shift from focus on the abstract divinity of Jesus Christ to his historical solidarity with humanity. Cf. Sobrino, *Christology at the Crossroads*, chapter IV. Sobrino attempts to retrieve the history of Jesus through a history of his faith. Ultimately, however, his concern with discipleship underlies and guides his interpretation as he moves from a consideration of the relationship between Jesus' faith and Christology to end his discussion on the relevance of Jesus' faith to Christian action.

85. Segundo, *The Christ of the Ignatian Exercises*, pp. 26-39.

86. Segundo, *The Historical Jesus of the Synoptics*, p. 9.

87. Cf. Segundo, *The Christ of the Ignatian Exercises*, pp.1-89. Segundo blames this aberration on what he calls a "Christological vacuum", the disregard of the real significance and implications of the Incarnation for the transformation of the universe. This, he claims, has often resulted in the living of Christianity as another "religion", as, indeed, the "opium" of the people that fosters passive acceptance of the *status quo*.

88. Cf. Segundo, *The Christ of the Ignatian Exercises*, pp. 90-103.

Chapter Five

Efficacious Love and Corporate Social Existence in History

This chapter on corporate social existence in history can be viewed as the necessary objective complement to the preceding one on personal, subjective salvation. But, more significantly, it brings into direct focus the shift towards the social implications of the Christian message, which has consistently marked Segundo's theological reflections. It is a shift that has become imperative in accord with his understanding of human existence as inherently social, and his consequent rejection of the traditional emphasis on individual salvation.

It is significant for us to keep in mind here how the notion of efficacious love functions in drawing out the implications of salvation as a corporate reality. Segundo grounds the possibility of that salvation in the meaning revealed in Jesus of Nazareth for all of human history. It is significant that his interpretation is again located within a dynamic, evolutionary perspective and focusses upon the love revealed in Jesus of Nazareth as the impulse of evolution from the very beginning. Based upon this revelation of the universal offer of salvation in Jesus Christ, Segundo can then proceed to reinterpret the Church as the historical embodiment and continuation of that offer of salvation to all humanity. Hence, his understanding of the Church is specifically marked by its outward thrust. In effect, he redefines the Church in terms of its mission to the rest of humanity. Its *raison d'être* is the service of true and efficacious love. Finally, Segundo discloses the type of transformation of the world that is the goal of human endeavour. It is the vision of a universe in dynamic and creative equilibrium through the mutual collaboration of all for the benefit of all. Indeed, it is the vision of a universe that is being built by efficacious love and is destined for the fulfilment of that love in Christ *Omega*.

The following discussion will, therefore, focus upon the way in which efficacious love is fundamental to Segundo's explanation of Jesus Christ as revealing the ultimate meaning of human existence. We will begin this discussion with his understanding of Christ as universal Saviour. From this most central point of Christianity, we will move to his interpretation of the Church as primarily "sign" of universal salvation. Finally, his vision of a humanized world will be explored. We turn now to a consideration of the first point, viz., Christ as universal Saviour.

1.   Christ as Universal Saviour

The question of Jesus Christ as universal Saviour is primarily that of his possible meaning for all of humanity. Segundo's discussion moves from the personal, existential question of the meaning of Jesus of Nazareth for the person of today, as presented above,[1] to explore the objective basis for the reasonableness of the question itself in the very structure of the universe and of human existence. In this is evident a continued concern with making Jesus of Nazareth credible to the contemporary scientific mentality, another reflection of the problematic of the tension between faith and reason that Segundo has persistently addressed throughout his writings. Hence, his explication is understandably an attempt to make clear the meaning of Jesus Christ within and in terms of an evolutionary perspective.

Three aspects of his interpretation will be discussed in order to bring out how the notion of efficacious love is again the basis of what is, indeed, the divine ground of the objective, social sphere of human existence. The notion will, then, be seen to unfold, in an evolutionary context, the meaning inserted into the entire length and breadth of history by the divine love revealed in Jesus of Nazareth. It will also disclose how the power of that love is truly *efficacious* in history and is, finally, intended to draw the entire humanity into a community of persons whose ultimate destiny is incorporation into the one Body of Christ.

These three aspects of Segundo's explanation of Jesus Christ as universal Saviour will, then, be presented as follows: (a) the evolutionary context; (b) Jesus Christ and the meaning of history; and (c) Jesus Christ and the reconciliation of humanity. The point of focus will be the relationship of efficacious love to Segundo's interpretation.

(a) The evolutionary context

The basic elements of the evolutionary theory of Teilhard de Chardin in particular have already been presented as a major influence on Segundo's theological reflections.[2] Here, it is necessary to focus more specifically on Segundo's understanding of the "evolutionary context" in which he proposes to reinterpret the meaning of Jesus of Nazareth for humanity as a whole.

Segundo regards as one of the most important challenges of contemporary theories of evolution the fashioning of a "new context" according to an "epistemology", or way of interpreting reality, that is evolutionary not only in theory but more significantly *in fact*.[3] By this he means that a shift to an evolutionary perspective necessarily alters the method that one employs in the search for truth. Hence, he endeavours to justify the use of "analogy",[4] as the most basic principle of evolutionary thought, for any adequate interpretation of reality. He does this in order to eventually apply that principle to his interpretation of Jesus of Nazareth.

Following Bateson, Segundo claims that the source of analogy is to be sought in the human mind, not in things themselves. He writes:

> Perhaps the human mind has no other key to apply to the universe
> except that of its own fundamental laws. Perhaps here lies the origin
> of the "analogy" we believe we perceive in things themselves. In any
> case, it seems that we must agree with Bateson's conclusion: since
> the mind is the only means of information about that reality we
> possess, "analogy" is our heuristic instrument *par excellence*, the one
> that enables us to know the rest."5

Segundo, therefore, views analogical thinking as introducing a specifically
"human" dimension into the mechanism of the universe. This makes the
questions of finality, values and humanism pertinent on all levels of enquiry.6
Hence, Segundo does not accept the position that science must be "value-free"
in order to be valid. Such a position fails to distinguish between the "formal"
(i.e., relational) likeness which analogy recognizes on various levels of human
existence, and the "material" (i.e. content) differences that exist and are
empirically verifiable through appropriate techniques.7

An adequate understanding of the evolutionary perspective thus suggests a
necessary complementarity of analogical thinking and the strict, verifiable data
of scientific analysis.8 This, we observe, parallels Segundo's discussion of the
iconic-digital tension presented above.9 In view of the link which we perceived
then between the "iconic" and "efficacious love", it is significant to note that
here Segundo argues that it is analogical thinking that offers "those premises
that seem to be necessary if we are to construct an epistemology capable of both
explaining evolution and taking over its reins."10 What he is envisioning is a
humanized world which is, indeed, the final objective of efficacious love. For
he writes of the use of analogy:

> A world populated with analogies is a world of anthropomorphisms
> and anthropocentrisms. Only in such a world can human beings feel
> respect for processes, seeing them as similar to those they respect in
> themselves and in human relations.11

It is not surprising, then, that it is is on the basis of this principle of analogy that
Segundo offers his reinterpretation of the meaning of Jesus of Nazareth within
the totality of human history. To this we now turn.

(b) Jesus Christ and the meaning of history

To present the meaning of Jesus Christ in an evolutionary context is in
accord with Segundo's fundamental shift from a static to a dynamic model of
interpretation and, more significantly, of an authentic appropriation of the
Christian message. His objective is to demonstrate that the universal reach of
salvation in Christ is not to be sought in an idealistic, immobile absolutization
of a person existing beyond all historical conflict.12 Rather, it must be grasped
in the meaning of the project which he launched within the entire movement of
history.

As we have already seen,13 Segundo sees human existence as pervaded in
all areas by a tension of opposite yet complementary forces. His interpretation
of Jesus Christ as universal Saviour according to the scientific terms of the
"entropy-negentropy " tension is, then, consistent with his thought. Here he

deals specifically with the way in which these forces operate in the movement of evolution.

Consonant with his affirmation of a "humanized" universe, Segundo argues, with Bateson, that a "mental" process of ordering is to be posited in all organisims, and in nature as a whole.[14] On the basis of this, Segundo rejects the theory that all novelty is to be attributed to "pure chance". He maintains that the latter position is in contradiction to the method of science itself which presumes a consistent pattern (a "redundancy" in Bateson's language) of specific factors.[15]

According to Segundo, new breakthroughs are to be attributed to agents of negentropy, the force which works against the degeneration of energy on all levels of existence. On the level of the human, it takes the form of the use and direction of energy towards "its maximum potential of concentration, efficacy and meaningfulness."[16] By analogy, Segundo then interprets Jesus of Nazareth as the highest form of negentropy that has appeared in history.

What he means by this is to be seen according to the evolutionary theory that he finally adopts. This, we recall,[17] is not the Darwinian "survival of the fittest", but rather that of "a homeostatic circuit in which all the elements must be integrated in dynamic equilibrium." Hence, as he continues:

> ... evolution cannot help but consist in a progressive enrichment of the system. *More elements* must be integrated into it in the process, and those elements must become more *integrated*. As they are integrated, more freedom must be left to their creative centers, with all their chances to be right or wrong.[18]

The line of "progress, of order, of meaning, of negentropy" is, in reference to this model, a "synthesis of persons." And this, we know, is the goal of efficacious love.

This understanding of evolution makes clear the basis of Segundo's interpretation of Jesus in terms of that love which appears more and more fully and obviously the higher the form of negentropy. That love thus "constitutes the qualitative vector of survival that is present in universal evolution (from beginning to end)."[19]

In light of the above Segundo can, therefore, explain the significance of Jesus of Nazareth in history in terms of the project of love, "the Kingdom of God" which he launched in history. We recall that Segundo understands that Kingdom to be specifically related to God's plan to restore full humanity to the poor and oppressed.[20] Here, it is significant to note that he interprets Jesus' action on behalf of the Kingdom as his effort to integrate the marginated into the society of Israel. For this, the gratuitous gift of self becomes necessary, as Jesus proposes in several instances (cf. Lk. 6:29; Mt. 5:40f.). "Is it not obvious", Segundo asks, "that these guidelines, at the very least, point the way to the creation of the highest negentrophy in the most difficult human relationships, the ones most tending toward entropy?"[21] He can then conclude that Jesus of Nazareth is, indeed, the foremost agent of negentropy.

However, in interpreting the historical project of Jesus of Nazareth as the highest instance of negentropy, Segundo does not intend an idealistic exclusion of entropy. Rather, in accord with the evolutionary perspective which he adopts, he recognizes that the same force of "disorder, disintegration and death" that has been evidenced throughout Biblical experience, though variously interpreted, must still be integrated, as though into a "circuit", together with what is constructive.[22]

Thus, the consistent tendency to reject what Segundo calls the "efficacy of the circuit" in the search for a "straight line" movement of "negentropy" against "entropy" leads to a distortion of the image of Jesus of Nazareth. Historically, it has resulted in the false, idealistic figure of a divine, transcendent being, capable of being co-opted as a dehumanizing factor.[23]

On the contrary, Segundo argues that the Jesus preached by Paul integrated death in such a way that it is seen to be the result of the life of love and concern that he lived. And since sin is the cause of death, sin itself can be said to enter into Jesus' life, not formally through moral guilt but, at least, materially by the fact of his solidarity with the human condition. Drawing on incidents in the life of Jesus, Segundo, therefore, argues that Jesus himself, on occasions, diverged from the ideal of gratuitous love which he proposed (cf. Mk. 7:6, 27; 11:15). For Jesus, too, must contend with the limitations of energy, of entropy, of "sin", that necessarily enters into all human projects. Thus he concludes:

> Jesus' overcoming of Sin is as invisible as his victory over Death will be: an object of faith rather than of verifiable experience. Only when the ultimate reality is presented to faith with the resurrection, will the whole transcendent datum of Jesus' victory over Sin fit into it. Not to deny history but to make it clear that he overcomes Sin insofar as his freedom never agrees, in bad faith, to be in complicity with an entropy greater than that required for the efficacy of his history project.[24]

Jesus of Nazareth, far from being the idealized, static perfection of a God become man, defines the meaning of history by being immersed in its rhythm and reality from its very beginning. In this he evidences the evolutionary quality *par excellence*, viz., "flexibility."[25] Flexibility, we recall, refers to having the right amount of energy at all times for adequate response to whatever circumstances are encountered. This represents, in evolutionary terms, the liberty that achieves its fullest expression in love that is truly and efficaciously immersed *in* history.

In sum, by applying the principle of analogy, Segundo interprets the meaning of Jesus Nazareth for all of humanity in terms of the tension of opposite yet complementary forces that pervade all of reality. In the evolutionary perspective, Jesus embodies the positive thrust of evolution as the foremost agent of negentropy. As such, he is to be understood in reference to the project of love that he released in history.

According to the evolutionary theory which Segundo endorses, this project involves the integration of the marginated into a circuit that is efficaciously creative of their persons. It also involves recognizing Jesus' universal meaning, not in terms of an idealistic exclusion of the negative forces endemic to human existence. Rather it includes these forces in such a way that they contribute to the realization of love.

It is clear that central to Segundo's understanding of the meaning of Jesus Christ for all of humanity is the concern that the love he reveals be efficaciously incarnated. This interpretation is basically, then, nothing more than the explication in scientific terms of the fact of the Incarnation. By this mystery Jesus Christ has become "the heart of the world from the start of history to its finish."[26]

(c) Jesus Christ and the recapitulation of the universe

If Jesus Christ is to have meaning for all of history, his relationship to the final goal of history is as important as his link to its beginning. That is, in New Testament language, he is both *Alpha* and *Omega*. We have seen Segundo's attempt to interpret Jesus' historical project in continuity with the creative thrust of a negentropy that is held in tension with the forces of entropy. The question here is whether or not the claim can be made that in Jesus Christ there is also present the *ultimate* victory of negentropy and, hence, of meaning in the universe.

Basic to Segundo's argument for a positive response to the question is the distinction that he makes between the empirical data available to strict scientific enquiry and "transcendent data" that are unverifiable, yet operative in all interpretations of reality. The latter, as we have already seen,[27] allow the world of meaning and values to have an impact upon one's understanding of the universe. It comprises what Bateson calls "epistemological premises" which not only suggest a new way of viewing reality but, simultaneously, a way of transforming that reality.[28]

Segundo examines this question of ultimate meaning, as symbolized in the victory of life over death in Jesus Christ, in terms of (1) the coherence of such an affirmation with the "analogical" structure of the universe; and (2) the form that it takes in the definitive future.

(1) We recall that Segundo accepts Bateson's image of the universe as analogically structured by a "mind" which is responsible for the ordering of the evolutionary process and, hence, for whatever meaning there is in the world.[29] This "mind" gradually awakens to "consciousness" on the threshold of the human. On that level, there is a virtual "explosion" of minds due to the redundancy of nature. Human beings appear as so many "centres" of consciousness with no inbuilt instinct for promoting the good of the species. If, then, meaning is to be achieved in the responsible directing of the entire evolutionary process, it can only happen through a collaboration of these centres in such a way that individual persons, as well as as the totality, are developed in the process. Allowing for the unpredictability, the "liberty", of these centres, thus makes of the process of human development a slow and painful one. But this is the necessary condition for the ordering of the universe by a mind which operates effectively only as it maintains a necessary equilibrium between "project" and available "energy", between "meaning and

realism", between "entropy and negentropy." Yet, the fact remains that human minds, as included in the "global mind" which orders the process of evolution, cannot revert to disorder and death without inherent contradiction.[30] Hence, Segundo concludes:

> . . . the transcendent datum regarding the victory of meaning over Death, the latter being the symbol and sign of definitive unfulfillment - is not illusion or the product of a credulous mind. Instead it flows from something that is thoroughly and profoundly consistent with basic human dimensions. As such, it is a reasonable wager to which Jesus is a privileged witness.[31]

(2) Segundo explains the "content" of the definitive future in terms of the eschatological data of the Resurrection and its synonyms in Paul, viz., "regeneration, restoration and recapitulation." Following Paul, then, he seeks the meaning of the Resurrection, the symbol of the victory of life over death, beyond the individual experience of "another life".

The Biblical notions of "regeneration" and "restoration", he contends, suggest the the reality of an unfinished world, consistently in need of being created anew. Hence, the image of the "new earth" in Apocalypse underlines another type of terrestrial existence in which all that indicates the failure to incarnate values in the world will disappear. What is even more important in this image, however, is the suggestion that in the creation of this new earth, God becomes personally involved. He does this in such a way that his new and definitive abode is, indeed, wherever human values flourish. Thus, it is human history that will be absolutized in the "new and definitive creation". Hence, Segundo claims, God is revealed as being identified with the culmination of history.[32]

The term "recapitulation" (cf. especially Eph. 1:3-14) captures the above, for Segundo. Etymologically, it means giving a "head", that is, a "meaning", to creation. This implies that diverse beings are meant to be united in terms of their "culmination", of their fulfilment in a totality. Thus, in view of the progress of evolution according to the law of negentropy, Paul can rightly speak of the mechanisms of the entire universe as aspiring towards nothing else except love of one another, for the commandments "are summed up in this sentence, you shall love your neighbour as yourself" (Rom. 13:8-10).[33]

However, Paul also indicates that if human history appears to be the reverse of that movement, that does not represent the entire reality. For the plan of God consists in the "recapitulating" of everything. But it is incumbent on human beings to freely introduce the definitive in history in making real the aspirations of love.[34]

For Paul, then, the meaning of the Resurrection shifts from being the revivifying of the individual to being the "manifestation" and the "glory" of the "liberty of the sons of God" (Rom. 8:19, 21). Thus, according to Segundo, the Resurrection suggests, even more than a "second creation", ". . . an opening up to the true vision, an *epistemological conversion*. We gain access to a vision liberated from time, entropy, and the deceiving impact of 'big numbers'. We come to discover the true ties of causality that were built up in the order of meaning."[36] However, the full achievement of this vision remains a future possibility because of the necessity of continuous "deactivations" in the "circuit" of human existence. For in the course of human life, periods of inactivity and passivity allow the time necessary to gather again the energy that is dissipated in moments of intense engagement. Human existence is, then, a rhythm of activity and inactivity that is meant to maintain a functional balance.

The evolutionary view, therefore, reveals the Resurrection as the definitive meaning inserted into the world. But it is a world that is being constructed in time through human effort. Hence, the meaning given in Jesus Christ discloses the divine source of historical human action itself. In this way, human beings are drawn into conscious collaboration with the divine-human project of Jesus of Nazareth.

In this perspective, Segundo concludes, *Omega* point is not the universal "phenomenon" of the conversion of all energies in Christ, as Teilhard seems to have claimed, but rather "a *transcendent datum that is grounded in faith*, be it religious or anthropological, and that in turn grounds the reasonableness of that faith."[37]

In light of the above, it is just as much a wager to hold that there is no meaning in the universe as to conceive that it is "guided by a love that cannot fail toward the new earth, one which will have room only for the negentropy that has been slowly and painfully elaborated by God and the human beings who are God's collaborators *(synergoi)*."[38] Segundo, therefore, opts for meaning. For him, indeed, it is efficacious love that finally determines the entire thrust of the universe.

In summary, Segundo endeavours to prove that the affirmation that the universe is ordered according to the ultimate meaning in Jesus Christ cannot be judged as mere unscientific credulity. Rather, the thrust towards meaning is grounded in the very structure of the universe which is ordered and kept in equilibrium by progressive activation and deactivation of energy. This makes of death a necessary complement to life and, indeed, the source of new life.

Segundo interprets the content of the definitive future in terms of the Biblical symbol of the Resurrection. According to its related terms, namely, regeneration and restoration, it represents the new creation that is being constructed in time through the collaboration of God and human beings. But even more, as suggested by the idea of recapitulation, it reveals essentially that under the seeming verifiable failures of humanity to incarnate its values, the plan of God is being realized and coming to its culmination in Jesus Christ. Hence, the Resurrection refers not so much to the new life that comes to be, as to the new vision of reality that it provides alongside the possibility of making that vision real. And that vision is the definitive victory of efficacious love in history. Hence, efficacious love provides the very horizon which determines Segundo's understanding of Jesus Christ as universal Saviour.

2. The Church as Sign of Universal Salvation

A critical examination of the pastoral practice current in the Rio Plata region of Latin America in the early nineteen sixties provides the starting point of Segundo's theological reflections on the Church.[39] At that time, the crisis of the Church, brought about by increasing secularization, signalled the demise of Christendom. It drew attention to the ineffectiveness of the kind of faith that could maintain the masses in passive acceptance of squalor and oppression.[40] The crisis was reflected in the resultant juxtaposition of two incompatible pastoral approaches: the one traditionally committed to the masses in order to ensure the salvation of all; the other turned in reaction to the minority, capable of heroic, personal commitment to an ideal Christianity.

Characteristically, Segundo's response to this crisis takes the form of probing the deeper question of the authentic embodiment of the Christian message. Hence, efficacious love, as the core of that message, becomes pivotal in his reinterpretation of the Church. The notion of true love and its dynamics provide the basis of his explanation of the various aspects of the Church. It accounts for the basic shifts which he introduces in his reinterpretation. It underlies his "uncentering"[41] of the Church by which he turns it away from preoccupation with its inner life towards service of society and humanity as a whole. The aspects of the Church which will, then, be presented in turn are: (a) its reality: particular and universal; (b) its essence: knowledge of the Christian mystery; (c) its function: service of true love; and (d) its mission: service of the rest of humanity.

(a) Its reality: particular and universal

The Church is, for Segundo, primarily a "sign" of the Mystery of Christ. As such, it is meant to manifest and to make real in the movement of history the salvific plan of God that is most clearly revealed in the Incarnation and the Death-Resurrection of Jesus of Nazareth. Hence, the Church reflects simultaneously the particular and universal dimensions that are inherent in these mysteries. On the one hand, there is the visible, concrete, historical life and death of Jesus, which is limited in space and time; on the other, there exists the faith affirmation of Christ's intrinsic solidarity with all of humanity and the possibility of the transformation of the whole universe in him. The particular and universal dimensions of the Church must, then, be held in constant tension in order to adequately signify the integrity of the Christ mystery.[42]

Accordingly, Segundo understands the universality of the Church in terms of the "qualitative" transformation that is made possible by the presence of grace in the universe. By making love the one criterion of salvation (cf. Mt. 25:31-46), Jesus reveals the equal availability of salvation to all of humanity. Hence, the Church, the sign of the presence of Christ's grace in history, is present wherever love effectively meets the needs of others. The Church universal thus extends to the whole of humanity and is meant to embrace all in the one Body of Christ.[43]

On the basis of this "qualitative" universality of love, Segundo rejects the "numerical" understanding that has historically dominated Christian pastoral practice. This has resulted in a compromise of the Christian message in order to ensure the salvation of the masses. Thus passivity, the need for security, easy solutions to complex problems, in short, mass attitudes, cultivated in Christian institutions employed as privileged environments in which the Christian message can be passed on to captive audiences, have made Christians virtually impotent in the face of historical problems.[44] This tendency he endeavours to reverse by reinterpreting the universality of the Church in terms of the minority attitude of efficacious love.

The "particular" Church, as Segundo interprets it, is that community of believers who witness explicitly to their faith in Jesus Christ and are challenged by, and celebrate in the sacraments, the love manifested in his dying and rising. This community is always limited in terms of numbers *vis-à-vis* the rest of humanity, and is relative in respect to its cultural and historical contexts. This is but the consequence of its incarnation. It is effective for salvation only inasmuch as it *concretely* fosters and communicates love.[45]

Segundo's insistence on love as the one criterion of salvation, even within this particular community, leads him to reject the claim that has been made historically that membership within this community is necessary for salvation.[46] Such an assertion indicates the understanding of election to this community as a privilege, and of ritual activity as *the* access road to God. On the contrary, Segundo emphasizes that there is only one pathway to salvation, the way of efficacious love. To belong to the particular community of faith is, then, not a privilege, but rather a responsibility that has become explicit for those who believe through the *knowledge* of the Mystery of Christ. This responsibility defines the very essence of the ecclesial community.

(b) Its essence: knowledge of the Christ Mystery

The Church, as a community of faith and of the sacraments is characterized by its knowledge of the Christ mystery. That Segundo can regard this "knowledge" as an adequate explanation of the essence of the Church is based upon his understanding of what comprises the content of its two essential elements, viz., faith and the sacraments, as mentioned above.

As we have already seen,[47] Segundo maintains that the core of the Christian revelation is the definition of God as Love. But this revelation, made in the concrete self-gift of God in Jesus of Nazareth, simultaneously manifests the fact that human existence itself is transformed by that love and is oriented to the concretization of love in love of others. Efficacious love, the gift of God's life, is the "power" given to human beings for the construction of self and others. Thus, it becomes the concrete offer of salvation. Following Paul, Segundo, therefore, concludes that this "plan of love", revealed in the central mysteries of Christ, operates on two levels. On one level, the Incarnation and Redemption pervade the entire history of humanity; on another level, "knowledge" of this plan is present only from the historical appearance of Jesus of Nazareth.

Segundo can then summarize the "faith of the Church" as follows:

> ... the message is not an a-historical one. It is essentially historical
> in the sense that it lets us know about God loving and operating in
> humanity and humanity acting with God though men may not know
> it. We also know the mechanism at work in God's activity with
> humanity: love. We not only know in some vague way that God has
> a salvation plan. We also know how this plan works itself out.[48]

In short, it is the *knowledge* of the efficacious love of God, as the source and
goal of all true love in human life, that specifies the essence of the ecclesial
community.

Segundo likewise argues that the sacraments, as the second element proper
to the Church as a particular group, are to be understood as essentially
signifying, letting us *know* in significant moments, that grace, which is already
present throughout human existence, is being effectively bestowed.[49] With
Rahner, he claims that the grace received in the ordinary circumstances of life is
no less effective for salvation than that received by Christians in the sacraments
themselves. To hold otherwise is to posit a quantitative notion of grace. And this
is unacceptable. Therefore, the Christian cannot claim a monopoly on grace
which is abundantly available to all, but the Christian "does come to know it
and to live it consciously."[50]

With this emphasis on "knowledge", and specifically of the "loving plan" of
God for all of humanity, Segundo re-enforces his claim that all "travel the same
road, and it leads them to salvation: it is the road of self-giving through love."[51]
This exclusive emphasis on love as the content of that knowledge leads
Segundo to reject any claim that Christian faith can provide privileged
information for the solution of human problems.[52] In the same way, he denies
that personal sanctity can be judged purely by participation in the sacraments.[53]
It is then legitimate to ask about the specific purpose of the ecclesial community
and to this we now turn.

(c) Its function: service of true love[54]

If, as Segundo emphasizes, the one criterion or norm of salvation is true
love, the question arises as to the real necessity and function of the Church as a
community of those who *know* the source and goal of that love. The question
applies not only to those within the Christian community but also to humanity
as a whole. In seeking to answer this question, Segundo shifts the focus from
the *fact* of existence to the *manner* of existence, by pointing to the decisiveness
of the latter within the evolutionary perspective. This shift will have significant
implications for his reinterpretation of the Church.

Within the evolutionary theory of Teilhard de Chardin, as we have seen,
consciousness marks the distinctive threshold of human life. The presence of
that consciousness, comparatively infinitesimal though it be, has subsequently
assumed the most substantial significance in the entire thrust of evolution.
Hence, the Church, characterized by the conscious awareness of the Christian
mystery, can likewise be envisioned as capable of being "the most decisive and

substantial factor in human history" by its way of living that love that is already at work in all human beings of good will.[55]

In reference to the ecclesial community, this means that the conscious awareness of love, as fostered by and celebrated in faith and sacraments, is necessary for salvation. Segundo argues, with Rahner, that just as "love lives by" and grows through seemingly superfluous "gestures", so the Christian community exists by its faith and the sacraments and thus becomes a "sign" of a whole new way of living within society. For those who have attained that level of existence, salvation cannot be achieved in a reversal of that. In view of the human situation, Segundo maintains:

> . . . . man cannot whimsically return to the instinctive level because the dawning of conscious awareness, explicitation, and reflection in him is not simply a higher perfection but a whole new world. It is the world of the human where man plays out what he once played out on the level of instinct; it is a system of relationships which, through their signification, affects and determines the very roots of life.[56]

The more significant question, however, is that of the necessity of the ecclesial community for humanity as a whole. Thus Segundo throws the focus on the relationship between the community of those who *know* the "mystery of love" and those who live that same mystery without awareness of its presence.[57] Segundo affirms the position of Vatican II which regards the constructive work of people of good will as a preparation for the Gospel (*Lumen Gentium*, 16). In that, he is also one with the traditional theology of grace in which, as we have seen before, acts of love can be regarded as the beginning of faith in persons of integrity.[58]

It is significant, however, that Segundo moves the discussion to the area of phenomenology in order to assert its basis in common human experience. He endeavours to show: "(1) why all authentic love is a faith-beginning; (2) that if love is to overcome its intrinsic obstacles, this beginning faith must pose questions and encounter the corresponding answers that can only come from full-fledged faith."[59]

In arguing the first point, that all genuine love is the beginning of faith, Segundo focusses upon the risk involved in the self-gift that defines love. Love, he says, is "an act of trust, an act of faith. It is an act of faith launched into the air, without any precise name or clear content. It is belief that love is worthwhile, which defies fate and blind indifference to the importance of self-giving".[60] What the Christian offers to this seemingly blind thrust is the knowledge that love is, indeed, worth the risk. With that assurance is born the *hope* that, in spite of all odds, the gift of self is never vain, that "no love is ever lost."[61]

Segundo's response to the second point regarding the need for collaboration between "beginning faith" and "full-fledged faith" for overcoming the obstacles to love, shifts the focus to the question of the "scope" of love. In calling for greater dialogue between Christians and non-Christians, it is obvious that

Segundo's objective is to open the Church to the concrete problems that indicate the widespread lack of concern for "the least" in a universe in need of a "new balance". Segundo is aware of the "profound transformation" that the ecclesial community must undergo in order to engage in such a dialogue.[62] But it is the only way for the Church to carry out its responsibility to prepare humanity for the "maturity" implied in the Christian faith. He writes:

> Herein lies the necessity of the Church. Here we see why it is so indispensable in the salvation plan for humanity. In the midst of the human race there must be people who know the mystery of love, who will meet and dialogue with those who are moving toward the gospel and confronting the questions raised by love. As humanity progresses on its journey, we have been slow to formulate the questions which, at the right time, would arouse people to the need for dialogue. And this dialogue is essential for what Teilhard called the "piloting of history."[63]

In Segundo's view, the dialogue in which the Church realizes its proper, sign-bearing function is finally oriented towards the humanization of the world. Collaboration in this task of humanization will, then, specify the mission of the Church and finally determine its very definition.

(d) Its mission: service of the rest of humanity

It is in terms of its mission that Segundo defines the Church, thus shifting the focus significantly from its inner life to its sign function within the wider human community. He writes:

> The Church is, essentially and primarily, a *sign* . . . placed here precisely and exclusively to pass on to men a certain siginification, i.e., a message, something that is to be grasped, comprehended, and incorporated to a greater or lesser degree into the fashioning of history and the world. If *the very existence* of the Church is meant to be leaven in the dough, salt in the meal, and light for all those who dwell in the human household, then the ecclesial community must accept the obligations that derive from its essential function.[64]

It is significant that this turn in service toward the rest of humanity is according to the very dynamic of efficacious love. This makes the capacity for self-giving and the assuming of responsibility for others a *sine qua non* for membership in the ecclesial community. Hence, his concept of a "minority" Church which is suggested in the images of "leaven" and "salt" is seen to be grounded on efficacious love, the minority attitude *par excellence*.

As we have seen above,[65] Segundo does not intend an "elitist", idealistic understanding of the Christian message but stresses rather the realistic embodiment of that love according to the exigencies of human existence. Therefore, he is not advocating an elitist ecclesial community but one consciously equipped with the power of love to direct the determinisms of nature and of culture for the humanization of all.[66]

However, Segundo does not conceive this "piloting of history" with the same optimism as that of Teilhard de Chardin. The latter, he claims, suggests too fast a leap from the ideal to the reality.[67] This can lead erroneously to the confusion of the Church with the Kingdom of God. Rather, Segundo expects of the Church the exercise of the evolutionary factor *par excellence*, "flexibility", as evidenced in Jesus of Nazareth. The Church would then be able to advance according to a functional balance between the traditions that have historically fashioned its life, and critical judgments made in reference to present questions in the light of faith.[68] In this way, it would maintain creatively the tension of the ideal demands of the Christian message and the conditionings of concrete human existence, the tension of efficacious love.

The ultimate vision of the Church which Segundo offers, in line with the Documents of Vatican II (cf. esp. *Gaudium et Spes*, nos. 11, 40), therefore, is that of the Church transparently signifying the recapitulation of the universe in Christ.[69] Because of this, he claims that the contemporary world, with its heightened awareness of the interdependence of all peoples proposes a distinct challenge to the Church. To meet this challenge, the Church must engage in dialogue and collaborate with the rest of humanity. But in doing this, it also realizes its proper destiny. He writes:

> A Church which dialogues and works with the rest of mankind is a
> Church that knows she is part of humanity; a Church that knows she
> is the conscious portion of the deeper mystery that is being worked
> out in every human life, and in all of humanity taken together in its
> process of historical becoming. A Church that dialogues is a Church
> that knows she is, by definition, in the service of humanity.[70]

In sum, Segundo conceives the Church as a "sign" of the mystery of Christ. As such, it is a reality at once particular in the concreteness and limitation of its historical embodiment, and universal in the qualitative, transformative power of the love that it affirms to be present in all of humanity. Knowledge of the mystery of that love specifically characterizes the ecclesial community. Hence, the Church is placed at the service of true love to prepare those who already realize that love in their actions to arrive at the full awareness of the mystery of that love. To do this, the Church must engage in dialogue and thus realize its being and its mission in the service of the rest of humanity. In this way, the Church functions as a decisive factor in the humanization of persons within the entire universe.

Segundo's understanding of the Church is, therefore, in every respect based upon the notion of efficacious love as central to the Christian message and, hence, to be necessarily signified in the historical embodiment of that mystery.

3. The Humanization of the World

Segundo's entire theological enterprise has been directed towards what, he claims, is the Christian task *par excellence*, viz., the humanization of the world. Humanization specifies the "project of love", the plan of God that has been launched into history through the Incarnation of Jesus of Nazareth. We have seen how this task has defined the very nature of the ecclesial community. We will now examine the meaning and implications of this project of humanization within the world of nations and the history of humanity.

Our focus will be on the relationship of efficacious love to this process of humanization. This entails, firstly, the global extent of the process which immediately surfaces the need for an interdependence among all peoples. Only mutual collaboration can bring about the necessary ecological balance and ensure the continued creation of the universe. Secondly, the process is directed towards its ultimate realization in Christ. The meaning which Jesus Christ has inserted into history is revealed through the definitive power of love. This love which constructs persons in history achieves its fulness beyond time and thus discloses the link between history and eschatology. These two aspects of the process of humanization will now be discussed. Again it will be of interest to note how Segundo grounds his explication on the fundamental value of efficacious love.

(a) The ecological balance and the interdependence of nations

The contemporary world staggers under an explosive imbalance brought about by the politico-economic and cultural domination of the majority by a powerful minority. As we have indicated above, this is the basic formulation of the problematic from the viewpoint of the "periphery", which Segundo has consistently addressed, in line with his Latin American colleagues. They attribute the widespread poverty and oppression in Latin America to the structure of politico-economic dependence, and the exploitation of that continent by the metropolitan centres of the world economy. They envision by way of a solution, the construction of a new economic world order in which the interdependence of nations would ensure a more equitable distribution of the resources of the universe and the decentralization of decision-making power in order to make possible genuine human development and liberation through self-determination.[71]

In view of the above, Segundo rejects Capitalism as a viable economic system for Latin America, specifically because of the competition and inequality of persons and nations on which it thrives. He opts instead for the socialist vision of an economic system in which public ownership directs significant enterprises towards the common good.[72] Such a choice seems to be consistent with Segundo's concern that love efficaciously transform society into a community of persons. Hence, it is reasonable that Segundo does not expect the alternative vision of Socialism to be spelt out in all its details. As we have seen repeatedly, efficacious love is a dynamic process that creates and transforms according to the conditioning and rhythms of history.

Further reflection on subsequent developments in Latin America during the entire period from 1950-1975 has led Segundo to emphasize deeper levels of the problematic beyond the economic. His present analysis identifies the root cause of the increasing dehumanization of persons in Latin America to a "growing *emotional dissociation of means and ends*" which, he claims, is evidenced in the entire Western culture. In the more developed countries, it is expressed in the phenomenon being discussed as the "death of ideologies."[73] What Segundo is indicating by this is the growing distrust of reason's ability to assess the appropriateness of means to be used to achieve desired ends. In Latin America, it has resulted in the contradictions of a politics devoid of human values and the disappearance of the hope of building anything of worth. This signals what he calls the "destruction of the *social ecology*", that complex of interpersonal connections that makes a society functionally viable.[74]

The destruction of this social ecology, Segundo argues, was intensified with the rise of guerrilla movements in Latin America. By its very nature, that kind of warfare involves many, not directly participating in the resistance, in unforseen and even unconscious complicity. Hence, basic social relationships are often disrupted. But even more disruptive of the social ecology is the breakdown of trust within the closest of interpersonal bonds. This often occurred under the repressive governments that arose to counter rebellious activities. Added to that was the destruction of the culture itself through the withdrawal and emigration of many who were capable of contributing to the cultural life of the nations.[75]

It is significant to note here that this emphasis on the destruction of the social ecology has become specifically Segundo's interpretation of the Latin American situation. This can be viewed, it seems, in terms of his emphasis on a humanization process that involves the construction of total persons starting from their relational base. And, as we have also seen, this creation of persons is the object of efficacious love.

Segundo, therefore, views the task of humanization in Latin America as that of restructuring an entire culture. That this will mean a long, tedious process, Segundo does not doubt. The present structure of the world does not promise otherwise. Yet, even limited achievement has value, in Segundo's estimation. He writes:

> We are in the same position as prisoners in jail. Like them, we must work within our limited living space to survive as human beings, and to help others do the same. We can do much more than we think. But for that to be really possible, we must recover a hope, a "premise", about all our successful little efforts to remain human in a dehumanizing world. We must see and feel them, to be important contributions to the future society that will one day rise on the ashes of the present. We must stop viewing those little efforts and achievements as failures simply because at present they cannot be politically implemented as structural changes. In short, we must work to reform things without turning into mere reformers.[76]

Segundo can sustain this position without compromising his conviction that the destiny of the entire universe remains in the hands of all of humanity working together and maintaining an ecological balance. This is so because the evolutionary perspective which he holds allows for the incorporation of destruction and death into the movement of humanization. But even more significant is Segundo's conviction that love has definitively triumphed in the universe. This is his option of faith. This we shall see more clearly from a consideration of his understanding of the relationship between history and eschatology.

(b) History and eschatology

For Segundo, history is to be understood not as a recounting of events that accumulate, but rather as the progressive interpretation of those events in changing contexts. History is, therefore, directly related to the evolution of human consciousness within a universe in which the same basic elements are to be ordered more and more strategically for the benefit of humanity.[77]

This understanding of history Segundo shares with Berdyaev who, under the influence of Hegel and Marx, envisions history as a dynamic force which orients the present towards the future. Hence, historical truth, for Berdyaev, is "not adequate knowledge of past fact, but the evolution of it in relationship to the dynamism which leads our present towards the future."[78] Berdyaev also insists that it is the person who determines the course of history, not *vice-versa.*

From this perspective, Segundo considers history as it is illumined by the Christian message. He shifts the focus from the narration of salvific events, that is, salvation history, to the "salvation of history", or the "build-up of history" by human beings as "prepared and commissioned" by God for this task.[79]

The question of what exactly is constructed in history is a significant one, for Segundo. He contends that it is not a matter of the accumulation of human goodness or evil. Instead, human beings have the possibility and the obligation to hand on "the conditioning factors that will allow love, which will ever continue to be the object of free choice and intense struggle, to unfold in all its possible dimensions."[80] Hence, a clear distinction must be made between what does accumulate and what cannot accumulate in an evolutionary history, subject as it is to the risk of personal liberty. Because of this liberty, Segundo sees humanity as entrusted with an awesome responsibility. Human beings hold in their own hands their future as well as that of the entire universe. He writes:

> I have suggested that in its ultimate stage evolution becomes a task
> for the human being — meaning the human species. It will depend
> on all human beings as a group whether the evolutionary process
> continues to go forward on the wings of flexibility, or becomes
> increasingly inflexible and ends up in a catastrophe engulfing all.[81]

Nevertheless, even in the face of that possibility, on the basis of the revelation of the appearance in Jesus Christ of the ultimate in human history, Segundo still claims that the Kingdom of God is continuous with history and is present *in* history though it does not arise *from* history. Thus he affirms a *causal* link between history and the Kingdom of God.[82]

Segundo's understanding of the Kingdom of God, as we have noted,[83] derives essentially from his interpretation of Paul. It is the "project of love", embodied and inaugurated in history in Jesus of Nazareth. As such, the Kingdom is a dynamic reality that is being fashioned wherever and whenever the love of God is being concretely and efficaciously creative of life.

This interpretation of the Kingdom, Segundo grounds on a basic difference to be found in the Synoptics between John the Baptist's proclamation of the coming Kingdom and Jesus'. Segundo argues that John preaches an imminent coming of the Kingdom that is marked by urgency and, hence, immediate response. John thus uses the Apocalyptic images of judgment to elicit conversion from sin in preparation for the "day of wrath." This he also symbolized in his entire style of life.[84]

On the contrary, Segundo points out, Jesus depicts the coming Kingdom in images of joy and consolation, specifically for those most concretely in need of such support. His lifestyle, too, signifies a different reality from that announced by John. For Jesus, the Kingdom is not the imminent breaking in of God's judgement. Therefore, it allows for the use of more long-range and complex strategies in a gradual construction of it. In this light, Jesus' miracles are specifically "signs" of the coming Kingdom. Indeed, his entire programme of love and service to the poor, the oppressed, and finally his ultimate self-donation must be interpreted as the Kingdom being inaugurated in him.[85] As we have seen before, this is the project in which Jesus has engaged his followers. Hence, the Kingdom continues in time but with a dimension that exceeds time, because efficacious deeds of love are manifested in Jesus' Resurrection to be of eternal worth.

The humanization of the world, the "project of love" thus remains a continuing task, a future challenge. The universe remains subject to the forces that resist that love, yet offers to love the means necessary for it to be efficaciously realized. But this paradoxical state of the world, Segundo claims, is the very condition for human liberty, for a human existence that is worthwhile. He writes:

> We need a world in which creation, love, and life triumph qualitatively, transforming reality irreversibly without ever escaping the quantitative victory of Sin. Only such a world can make human existence worthwhile, can put Faith in the human heart as energy concentrated on its committed involvement in history, and all the power of God in its inner creativity as child of God.[86]

To summarize, the process of humanization towards which the entire universe is directed, demands the mutual collaboration of all nations. Segundo views the present situation as one of socio-economic and political dependence of the majority of humanity on a dominating minority. That situation, coupled with the widespread destruction of the bases of socio-cultural equilibrium in Latin America, in particular, signal a dangerous ecological imbalance in the global community. Yet the present state of the world engenders not despair but is the impetus for the hope of the realization of God's love in history.

This history is, for Segundo, a dynamic process in which humanity consciously directs the resources of nature towards the personalization of the universe. As such, history is continuous with the establishment of the Kingdom of God. This Kingdom, as revealed in the life and mission of Jesus of Nazareth, is a "project of love", intended to efficaciously transform the condition of the dehumanized of society. Hence, human collaboration with God in deeds of efficacious love continues the creation of persons as subjects of their own history. In this process of humanization of the universe the Kingdom is being fashioned towards its future fulfilment in Christ *Omega*.

4.   Summary and Conclusion

Jesus of Nazareth defines the meaning of history from its beginning to its end. He is the manifestation and concretization of the Love of God that is universally present in all of humanity. In scientific terms, he is the primary agent of "negentropy", the positive thrust of evolution towards the personalization of the universe.

The Church continues in history the embodiment of the Christ Mystery. Hence, it is a reality both particular and universal. It is, in essence, characterized by its *knowledge* of the Christ Mystery as the *consciously* "Christified portion of humanity". In function, it is engaged in communicating to non-Christians knowledge of the Divine source and goal of true love; and in mission, it is sent to dialogue with the rest of humanity about the questions which point the way to the realization of a fuller humanity, a humanity entrusted with the divine-human task of co-creating the universe with God.

But the world in the process of being created is presently marked by a dangerous imbalance in the use and control of resources, and an accompanying destruction of the social ecology. Yet the Christian does not confront this world with despair but rather with hope for a more unified humanity. The Christian lives out of the assurance of faith that whatever is constructed in love, no matter how minimal, is destined to last forever.

History, as the progress of human consciousness, has a causal connection with the Kingdom of God, for the Ultimate has been revealed in history. The power of love, manifested as definitively triumphant over death in Jesus Christ, offers to humanity a new vision. It is a vision that is both dynamic and transformative and, hence, capable of effecting a new creation.

In all of the above, efficacious love has been seen to direct Segundo's reflections. Hence, efficacious love is, for him, the criterion or norm of what comprises salvific corporate, social existence in history. It is the fundamental value, the "centering focus" to which he consistently returns.

Notes

1. See Chapter IV, pp. 96-100.

2. See Chapter II, pp. 38-43.

3. Cf. Juan Luis Segundo, *An Evolutionary Approach to Jesus of Nazareth,* translated by John Drury (New York: Orbis Books, 1988), pp. 22-27.

4. Segundo uses the term "analogy" according to its Scholastic meaning, i.e., the simultaneous affirmation of likeness and difference among things being compared (cf. *De la sociedad a la teología,* p. 155). As an evolutionary principle, "analogy" refers to the presence in "primordial form" of what will appear more explicitly on higher levels of the evolutionary process (cf. *Evolution and Guilt,* p. 25).

5. Segundo, *An Evolutionary Approach to Jesus of Nazareth,* p. 34.

6. *Ibid.,* pp. 34-36. Cf. Segundo's concern that Marxian humanism be not disregarded in Marxist thought. See Chapter II, pp. 34-37, esp. p. 35.

7. *Ibid.,* pp. 37f. Cf. *The Liberation of Theology* pp. 39-68.

8. *Ibid.,* pp. 38-41.

9. See Chapter III, pp. 55f.

10. Segundo, *An Evolutionary Approach to Jesus of Nazareth,* p. 35.

11. *Ibid.,* pp. 40.

12. This is fundamental to Segundo's effort to shift Christianity's focus from the abstract and theoretical to concrete praxis.

13. See Chapter III, pp. 51-66.

14. Segundo, *An Evolutionary Approach to Jesus of Nazareth,* p. 53. Bateson uses the term "mind" to signify "a system which receives and processes information in function of the totality of the organism" *Ibid.,* p. 34. Hence, he applies the term "mental" to all the ordered processes of nature in reference to the acme of its development in the human mind.

15. *Ibid.,* pp. 43-48. Segundo is not concerned here with proving the existence of God from this structure of the universe. However, he does admit the possibility of linking the concept of God with the "mind" that orders all.

16. *Ibid.,* p. 53.

17. See Chapter III, p. 62.

18. Segundo, *An Evolutionary Approach to Jesus of Nazareth,* p. 62.

19. *Ibid.,* p. 61.

20. See Chapter III, pp. 67-72.

21. Segundo, *An Evolutionary Approach to Jesus of Nazareth,* p. 64.

22. *Ibid.,* pp. 67-74.

23. *Ibid.,* pp. 87-92.

24. *Ibid.,* p. 91. Cf. *The Liberation of Theology,* pp. 162-65.

25. Segundo, *Faith and Ideologies,* p. 309. Cf. *An Evolutionary Approach to Jesus of Nazareth,* p. 107.

26. Segundo, *A Community Called Church,* p. 14.

27. See Chapter III, pp. 53, 55.

28. Segundo holds that Teilhard's reference to the "within" of things is such an "epistemological premise." However, Teilhard does not take cognizance of that fact and continues to regard that "transcendent datum" as a "phenomenon" capable of being grasped by observation (cf. *An Evolutionary Approach to Jesus of Nazareth,* pp. 93-98).

29. See above, pp. 106-108.

30. Segundo *An Evolutionary Approach to Jesus of Nazareth,* pp. 101f.

31. *Ibid.,* p. 102.

32. *Ibid.,* pp. 103f.

33. *Ibid.,* p. 104.

34. *Ibid.,* pp. 104f.

35. Segundo also explains this in terms of the confidence and liberty that are necessary for experiencing events as directed towards life, not death. See *The Humanist Christology of Paul,* pp. 91-98.

36. Segundo *An Evolutionary Approach to Jesus of Nazareth,* p. 105.

37. *Ibid.,* p. 106.

38. *Ibid.*

39. See Segundo, *Función de la Iglesia,* pp. 5-25.

40. See Segundo, *The Hidden Motives of Pastoral Action,* pp. 3-63.

41. Cf. Gutiérrez, *A Theology of Liberation,* pp. 256-262; José Comblin, *The Meaning of Mission: Jesus, Christians, and the Wayfaring Church,* translated by John Drury (Maryknoll, New York: Orbis Books, 1977), pp. 1-25.

42. Segundo, *A Community Called Church,* pp. 13-16. Cf. Persha, "Juan Luis Segundo", for a thorough study of this issue.

43. *Ibid.,* pp. 9-10. Cf. *Función de la Iglesia,* p. 47; *Grace and the Human Condition,* p. 127.

44. Cf. Segundo, *The Hidden Motives of Pastoral Action,* pp. 26-45; *La cristiandad, ¿una utopia?* I, *passim; A Community Callled Church,* pp. 44-49.

45. Segundo, *A Community Called Church,* pp. 3-6. Cf. *Función de la Iglesia,* p. 46.

46. *Ibid.,* pp. 73-76.

47. See esp. Chapter II, pp. 26-28.

48. Segundo, *A Community Called Church,* p. 29.

49. See Chapter IV, pp. 90-93 for a fuller explanation of the Christian sacraments.

50. Segundo, *A Community Called Church,* p. 32.

51. *Ibid.*

52. *Ibid.,* pp. 34-37.

53. Cf. Chapter IV, pp. 91f for Segundo's critique of ritual activities.

54. Segundo, highlights this by making it the title of the third chapter of *Función de la Iglesia.*

55. Segundo, *A Community Called Church,* pp. 52f. Segundo thus adopts Teilhard's vision of the Church: "At the core of the social phenomenon there is coming to a head a form of ultra-socialization. Through it, the Church is gradually

taking shape vivifying all the spiritual energies of the noosphere under her influence and fashioning them into their sublimest form. The Church is the reflectively Christified portion of the world, the principal focal point of interhuman affinities for super-charity, the central axis of universal convergence" (Rideau, *The Thought of Teilhard de Chardin*, p. 498, cited in *A Community Called Church*, p. 121). However, Segundo voices reservations re Teilhard's "prematurely" divinizing the "Church together with Jesus" by positing a "lineal" continuity of "pure negentropy" towards Omega point (cf. *An Evolutionary Approach to Jesus of Nazareth*, p. 106).

56. Segundo, *A Communtiy Called Church*, p. 54.

57. *Ibid.*, p. 55.

58. See chapter III, p. 50.

59. Segundo, *A Community Called Church*, p. 56.

60. *Ibid.*, p. 57.

61. *Ibid.*, p. 58.

62. Segundo, *The Hidden Motives of Pastoral Action*, pp. 65-82.

63. Segundo, *A Community Called Church*, p. 60.

64. *Ibid.*, p. 81.

65. See Chapter II, pp. 28-30, 40-43.

66. Segundo, *A Community Called Church*, pp. 84-97. Hence, Segundo interprets the "need" expressed by Paul VI (cf. *Octogesima Adveniens*, 40) for "inner conversion" and "structural change" in terms of the necessary "complementarity" in the "mass-minority" tension. He writes: "The most favourable interpretation of the 'start' here would seem to entail the following affirmations: (a) interior conversion, the liberation of minorities, is the theoretical starting point for structural liberative praxis; (b) interior conversion is not the cause of structural change, it simply collaborates in a movement where mass lines of conduct are indispensable for achieving change; (c) if mass lines of conduct are not to oversimplify the new structures and turn them into new enslaving molds with new masters, they must always be complemented by minorities that are interiorly converted and hence more liberated from mass mechanisms; (d) assuming that a deeply lived Christianity is this latter element involved in structural change, its efficacy- which is always a requirement- will vary with the *phases* of the liberative process, and it will have to accept these variations as conditions surrounding a realistic liberation." *Evolution and Guilt*, p. 69.

67. Segundo, *An Evolutionary Approach to Jesus of Nazareth*, pp. 97f.

68. *Ibid.*, pp. 106f. Cf. *Faith and Ideologies*, pp. 308-311.

69. Segundo, *Grace and the Human Condition*, p. 127. Cf. *De la sociedad a la teología*, p. 53; *Función de la Iglesia*, pp. 67-69; *La cristiandad, ¿una utopia?* II, p. 12.

70. Segundo, *A Community Called Church*, p. 131.

71. Juan Luis Segundo, "Education, Communication, and Liberation: a Christian Vision", *International Documentation of the Contemporary Church*, North American Edition (Nov. 13, 1971); "Has Latin America a Choice?", *America*, CXX, no. 8 (Feb. 22, 1969), pp. 213-16; "Wealth and Poverty as Obstacles to Development" in *Human Rights and the Liberation of Man in the Americas*, edited by Louis Colonnesse (Notre Dame: Notre Dame University Press, 1971), pp. 23-31; *Our Idea of God*, pp. 35f; *De la sociedad a la teología*, pp. 107-39; Gutiérrez, *A Theology of Liberation*, pp. 81-88; José Bonino, *Doing Theology in a*

Revolutionary Situation (Philadelphia: Fortress Press, 1975), pp. 21-37.

72. Juan Luis Segundo, "Capitalism versus Socialism" in *Frontiers of Theology in Latin America,* p. 249. Cf. "¿Hacia una iglesia de la izquierda?", *Perspectivas de Dialogo,* IV, no. 32 (April 1969), 35-39: "La iglesia chilena ante el socialismo I", *Marcha,* no. 1558 (August 27, 1971), pp. 12-14; "La iglesia chilena ante el socialismo II", *Marcha,* no. 1559 (September 4, 1971), p. 15; "La iglesia chilena ante el socialismo III", *Marcha,* no. 1560 (September 11, 1971), pp. 19, 24; "Social Justice and Revolution", *America,* CXVIII, no. 17 (April 27, 1968), 574-77.

73. Cf. Segundo, *Faith and Ideologies,* pp. 250-60. This discussion centres on the view that there is basically no difference between the humanist values that underlie both Capitalism and Socialism. Besides, the dehumanizing results of both systems are comparable. Hence, the resultant disillusionment with efforts to radically transform society indicates the impotence of pure rationality.

74. *Ibid.,* pp. 282; 285f.

75. *Ibid.,* pp. 286-301.

76. *Ibid.,* p. 306.

77. Segundo, *Our Idea of God,* pp. 39f.

78. Segundo, *Berdiaeff,* p. 62.

79. Segundo, *Our Idea of God,* p. 37.

80. Segundo, *Grace and the Human Condition,* p. 125.

81. Segundo, *An Evolutionary Approach to Jesus of Nazareth,* p. 99. Here again, we note Segundo's recurrent use of the term "flexibility". It points up the decisive importance that he places on the realism needed for adequate human response according to available energy. Wisdom lies in making sure that energy is concentrated in the right direction, that is, in the direction of incarnating love in history.

82. Segundo, *The Historical Jesus of the Synoptics,* p. 158. Cf. "Evangelización y humanización: ¿Progreso del reino y progreso temporal?", *Perspectivas de Dialogo,* V, no. 41 (March 1970), 7-17; "Reconciliación y conflicto", *Perspectivas de Dialogo,* IX, no. 86 (December 1974), 172-78, esp. p. 175.

83. See above, pp. 111f.

84. Segundo, *The Historical Jesus of the Synoptics,* pp. 152f.

85. *Ibid.,* pp. 153-161.

86. Segundo, *The Humanist Christology of Paul,* p. 160. Cf. "La profundidad de la gracia", *Perspectivas de Dialogo,* II, no. 19 (1967), 235-40.

Chapter Six

Reflections and Conclusion

Our study of the works of Juan Luis Segundo confirms that the notion of efficacious love has provided a methodological focus in Roger Haight's understanding of that focus as "the dominant interest, passion and concern, the unifying theme that holds the whole of it [a theology] together as a coherent vision."[1] Efficacious love has, then, emerged as the fundamental value which underlies the structure of Segundo's theology. It has also most consistently organized and unified his reinterpretation of the Christian message from the perspective of the Latin American context. Thus it has illumined the meaning of human existence in its various facets and disclosed the horizon of a more authentic understanding and living of Christianity.

This chapter will assess, then, how well the notion of efficacious love has integrated Segundo's theology into a consistent whole. It will also discuss the limits and challenges of Segundo's theological contribution and offer some suggestions regarding areas in need of further exploration.

1. The Theological Achievement of Juan Luis Segundo

As a theologian offering a distinct vision from the "periphery", Segundo has provided us with a theology marked by certain important shifts of emphasis. These are the shifts from theory to praxis, from the sacred to the profane, from the static to the dynamic and from the individual to the social.[2] We have seen how these shifts have been established under the major influences of Segundo's early years and have been consistently operative in his subsequent theological works.[3] The notion of efficacious love captures these shifts. Besides, as the most fundamental value that undergirds Segundo's theological reflections, efficacious love is at the same time the only constant in human existence. It underlies and sustains those shifts in creative tension. How this is brought out in Segundo's theology we will now consider.

(a) **Efficacious love as the fundamental value and only constant of human existence**

The notion of efficacious love uncovers, for Segundo, the authentic core of the Christian message. It most adequately affirms the total self-gift of God, the Love of God revealed in Jesus of Nazareth, as the most adequate definition of the Christian God. This love of God is thus established as the source and origin of all love in human life. The human response to God's love, as concretized in love of neighbour, then becomes the verification of a life rooted in that divine love of God, the abiding, absolute ground of human existence.[4] However, this love is efficaciously incarnated in human life. Hence, its concrete expressions are according to the exigencies of specific historical moments in a universe that is being fashioned in time and bears within itself its own inherent laws.[5]

The notion of efficacious love in Segundo's theology is expanded in meaning to incorporate the existentialist concern of free, self-creation as the personal realization of love; the transformation of social structures as the social embodiment of love; and, finally, the assuming of a dynamic and transforming perspective as the effects of love in an evolving universe.[6] In all of this, what it means for love to be efficacious is made more explicit.

In sum, efficacious love can be regarded as the fundamental value that undergirds human existence. As such, it is the only absolute value, the one given that remains constant beneath the changes of historical existence. This is not to say, however, that efficacious love is a rigid absolute because it also reveals a love that is incarnated according to the rhythm of history and the conditionings of concrete human life.

(b) Shift from theory to praxis

The notion of efficacious love explains most consistently the inner logic and coherence of Segundo's entire theological enterprise as a praxis-centred model of theology. This exemplifies most clearly his shift from theory to praxis. Efficacious love, as epitomized in "option for.the poor", thus provides not only the starting point of his theological reflections, but also the goal of restructuring reality and theology itself for the benefit of the poor and marginated.[7]

Segundo thus constructs his theological method according to a "hermeneutic circle" which applies hermeneutical suspicion to uncover the reality of oppression hidden beneath societal structures. Hence, the method begins with examining concrete human experience from which the most crucial and pertinent questions are posed to the Christian message. In turn, this same hermeneutic of suspicion is applied to theology in order to disclose and subsequently free it of its unconscious complicity with maintaining dehumanizing situations. Eventually, this leads to a retrieving from scripture of the elements necessary for a more authentic reading of the Christian message. What becomes obvious in Segundo's development of this method is that the fundamental value that underlies it is efficacious love as most radically exemplified in option for the poor. Segundo's use of Marxist social analysis uncovers the structures that dehumanize the poor. His exegesis of scripture centres on God's own option for the poor as revealed in the mission of Jesus of Nazareth.[8]

God's preference for the poor is not a compromise of his universal love. Segundo defends the possibility and necessity of such an option in an incarnated love. He is primarily drawing attention to the oppressive situation of the poor, a dehumanizing condition that is repugnant to a compassionate and loving God. Hence, without denying the importance of personal responsibility for moral choices, he throws the emphasis on the need for the actual transformation of structures on behalf of the poor. Personal conversion, therefore, entails a change of mentality, a sharing in God's sensitivity to the sufferings of the poor.

Discipleship then becomes an engagement with him in making that option concretely effective through self-sacrificing love.[9]

Efficacious love is also the fundamental value that undergirds Segundo's anthropological interpretation of the categories of thought that he draws from various disciplines. Thus he is able to include the social sciences as interpretative tools in his doing of theology. He employs them to mediate the truth of concrete human experiences, just as he uses philosophical and traditional theological insights to mediate the more general and past truths of Christian experience. In doing this, Segundo makes clear the real possibility and necessity of the attempt of liberation theology to extend the theological enterprise beyond traditional confines in order to root it in concrete liberation praxis.[10]

Thus Segundo argues from the point of view of epistemology that faith, understood as an orientation of values towards a designated absolute is "dead" if it is not concretized in an ideology or system of means and ends and specifically in efficacious deeds of love. He takes from the philosophy of Nicolas Berdyaev the understanding of freedom as defining both God and the human person. And he stresses, with Berdyaev, that human freedom is creative, though limited by the objective conditions of human existence. Love that creates persons according to the exigencies of human life, efficacious love is, then, the genuine exercise of freedom. Language analysis provides Segundo with the terms "iconic-digital". Applied to human existence, these terms disclose that "iconic", subjective values that are embodied in a specific style of life need the verification of deeds that express "digitally" the logic of that life. Efficacious love expresses this iconic-digital tension. From the social sciences Segundo draws the terms "mass-minority". His anthropological use of these terms uncovers the tension that exists between attitudes of passivity, simplicity and immediacy and those of activity, creativity, mediacy and complexity. They are attitudes present in every person. Efficacious love holds in tension the "minoritarian" ideal of gratuitous self-gift and the demand of that love to effectively transform persons and structures of society in accord with the "mass" mechanisms of concrete reality. The terms "entropy-negentropy" identify the presence of that tension in the physical universe. It denotes the tendency of energy to dissipate and the counterforce towards evolutionary progress. Segundo applies these terms to a parallel phenomenon in human life, namely, the tendency towards simple solutions, the easy way, and the thrust "against the grain" towards life. Efficacious love makes clear the cost of creative self-giving love which must necessarily be according to available energy. Finally, theology discloses that the counterforces of sin and grace lie at the deepest level where human existence opens itself to the transcendent. Efficacious love is the sign that though the gratuitous love of God has, indeed, triumphed in human life, the concrete conditions of human existence witness to the incompleteness of that victory. The overcoming of all that limits love remains a task to be accomplished. But it is no other task than that of humanization, God's own project of "efficacious love".[11]

Thus the value of efficacious love consistently illumines and unifies the categories of thought that Segundo uses to construct his theology. His turn towards praxis is clear here, even as it was in the structure of his hermeneutic

circle. His is, indeed, a praxis-centred model of theology and it is based upon
the value of efficacious love.

(c) Shift from the sacred to the profane

The notion of efficacious love also epitomizes the incarnational principle
which grounds the most basic supposition of Segundo's theology and of
liberation theology in general, namely, the unity of sacred and secular history.[12]
Segundo is, therefore, able to draw out the logic of God's immersion in limited,
human history, and his solidarity with humanity. Hence, a decided shift to the
human marks Segundo's reinterpretation of personal salvation. Historical
human existence is now the privileged locus for personal encounter with God,
not ritual activities as often traditionally assumed.

Consistently, then, Segundo reinterprets the traditional symbols of personal
salvation in terms of the real transformation that occurs in personal existence
through the active presence of God's efficacious love in human life. Thus, grace
is to be understood as the creative, unconditional self-gift of God himself which
effects a new existence marked by the efficacious love of others. It is not the
abstract accumulation of merit that relegates union with God to a life beyond.
Faith is the dynamic, personal commitment of love which acknowledges the
divine origin of all love that is efficaciously experienced in human existence.
As such, it is a dynamic life orientation according to the values of Jesus of
Nazareth and not a static assent to personal truth. Freedom is creative, self-
determination which is concretely realized in efficacious acts of love. Hence,
human beings do not stand equally poised to choose between good and evil.
Cultic worship is the means of celebrating and being challenged by the love of
God efficaciously transforming human existence. Thus, human life not ritual
activity as such becomes the privileged access road to God. Human action is
the mature assuming of responsibility to creatively direct the forces of nature
for the efficacious construction of humanity through love. It is not a matter,
then, of an individualistic concern with what is permissible or not according to a
predetermined, divine law. Finally, Jesus of Nazareth, as revealer and primary
witness of God's love and appropriate human response in faith, embodies love
efficaciously as the first of many brothers and sisters. Discipleship is, therefore,
a life in accordance with the mentality of Jesus of Nazareth. It is not the
imitation of the Divine Son of God as the perfect God-man and norm of human
aspiration.[13]

In all of the above, the notion of efficacious love functions as the
fundamental value which consistently grounds Segundo's explication of the
various dimensions of personal salvation. As such, it is disclosed as the sign of
the efficacious presence of God's grace and, hence, the normative way of access
to union with him, to personal salvation.

(d) Shift from the static to the dynamic

Segundo's insistence that the novelty of Christianity lies in its manifestation
of love incarnated in human existence throws the emphasis on the "efficacy" of
love as a specifically Christian concern. The challenge is to effectively embody
love according to the concrete needs of human beings, in tune with the rhythm
of history and the "signs of the times". Hence, the notion of efficacious love is

basic to Segundo's shift from the understanding of human life understood in terms of a static adaptation to a given nature, to a definition of it as a dynamic adventure of creating persons. This is seen clearly in his presentation of Jesus Christ as universal Saviour and the ultimate embodiment and Revealer of meaningful human existence. Within the evolutionary perspective, which is Segundo's "key" for understanding Christianity, he interprets Jesus Christ in terms of the negentropy-entropy tension that underlies the physical universe. This approach, though it appears contrived at times, is both novel and insightful. It moves the redemptive act of Jesus Christ from its basis in the universality of a Being, all powerful beyond the exigencies of human existence, to insert it effectively into the rhythm of limited, unfinished human history. Thus the central mysteries of Jesus' Incarnation, Death and Resurrection assume concrete significance in the actual thrust of human existence towards life, in the face of death and destruction. The meaning of Jesus Christ is, then, to be found in the affirmation that life and love are, indeed, finally victorious in spite of all indications to the contrary.[14]

The fact that historical situations change indicates that the meaning of Jesus will also vary according to the concrete reality in need of redemption. Hence, the challenge that Segundo proposes in his reinterpretation of Jesus Christ is that of continuously creating Christologies, that is, interpretations of Jesus and his mission according to the requirements of efficacious love in changing, historical circumstances. Concretely, this entails the continued realization of efficacious love in the dynamic following of Jesus of Nazareth. Discipleship is, indeed, the goal towards which Segundo's Christology eventually leads.[15] Hence, his eventual concern is that human life be a continual and dynamic process of discernment, of attentiveness to the Spirit of Love who leads into all truth.

(e) Shift from the individual to the social

The notion of efficacious love is fundamental to Segundo's shift from the individual to the social inasmuch as the very dynamic of love draws others into one's personal world. Where this shift is most clearly evident is in Segundo's reinterpretation of the Church which is, perhaps, his most significant doctrinal focus, specifically in terms of the extent and depth of his treatment of it.[16] Again the notion of efficacious love functions as the fundamental value which grounds Segundo's reflections.

Segundo redefines the Church as essentially mission, as "leaven" permeating society, as a committed "minority" in service of the rest of humanity. It makes known the source and goal of the love that is efficaciously at work in human existence. Faith and sacraments, the distinguishing features of the Church community, take on a functional role, faith orienting Christian life in service of the absolute value, love; the sacraments fashioning a community for transforming, liberative praxis. Segundo's is a Church which is by definition in dialogue with the rest of humanity. As such, it not only embodies the Christian message in history as a dynamic on-going process, but also emphasizes the concreteness of that embodiment. Thus, its specific task is precisely the divine-human task of humanization.[17]

Segundo thus offers a vision of the Church that is capable of making the

Christian message relevant in a world where a growing interdependence of nations demands a restructuring of world institutions according to a constructive and unifying collaboration of persons. Yet Segundo's almost exclusive emphasis on love and service as the *raison d'être* of the Church, unfortunately leaves out of his discussion important dimensions of traditional ecclesiology.[18]

Of significance also, is Segundo's reinterpretation of the doctrine of the Kingdom of God as primarily "a project of love"[19] launched into human history. The causal link that he proposes between history and the definitive future is a bold assertion which he shares with his Latin American colleagues in general. Segundo makes clear that the basis for this claim is the definitive power of love as revealed in the Resurrection of Jesus of Nazareth and the traditional theology of cooperative grace. It, therefore, proceeds from the strict logic of the Incarnation itself.[20]

Although we have been discussing each of these major shifts separately for the sake of clarity, it must be noted that in Segundo's theological reflections, these shifts constantly interpenetrate and consistently mark the distinctive turn of his reinterpretation of the Christian message. Since these major shifts are, indeed, characteristic of Latin American liberation theology in general, Segundo thus contributes significantly to this movement in clarifying the bases of these shifts and their application to the major doctrinal symbols of Christianity.

2. The Limits and Challenges of Segundo's Theology

As we have seen,[21] an important "hermeneutical principle" which Segundo has employed in the development of his theology is the "mass-minority dialectic", that basic tension of opposite yet complementary forces which characterizes human existence. Hence, he has drawn into his theology terms used in other disciplines to explain that same tension. Segundo's mainly anthropological application of these terms not only demonstrates how that tension pervades the various dimensions of human life, but also draws important insights from different fields of critical investigation into a unified interpretation of the meaning of human existence.[22] This has given Segundo's theology a certain complexity of structure which defies any simplistic approach to his thought. The central position of "efficacious love" which in itself embodies that tension has confirmed Segundo's intent to hold that tension together at all times.

However, most of the criticisms that have been levelled at Segundo either reductively interpret his theology in terms of a single emphasis and, hence, ignore the complexity of his thought, or fault him for unduly over-stressing one aspect of the Christian experience and thereby overlook the underlying tension and the fact that a shift in focus does not necessarily mean an exclusive rejection of the opposite pole. Thus on the one hand, Segundo's theology has been reductively interpreted in terms of one aspect of his thought, for example "Marxist social analysis",[23] or "Freud's hermeneutic of suspicion".[24] On the other hand, Segundo has been accused of being Pelagian in exalting human achievement to the point of ignoring human reliance upon the grace of God.[25] He is, perhaps, most frequently charged with "elitism" in view of his insistence that Christianity is basically "minoritarian", demanding heroic commitment and the responsibility of a mature faith.[26] That these criticisms are, to a large extent unfounded, we can see from the preceding discussion of those issues.[27] The central position of grace underlying efficacious love in his theology is not consistent with a Pelagian mentality. Besides, Segundo has been careful in repeatedly explaining that the mass-minority tension refers to attitudes present in all human beings. In Christianity, he claims, the "heroic minority" cannot move forward without the collaboration of the "masses".[28]

Nevertheless, it must be admitted that there are areas in Segundo's theology that need fuller explication in order to make more obvious the tension that he intends to maintain. One such area is that of the ritual dimension of Christianity. We single out this area in view of the fact that, as we have indicated before, [29] Segundo has been specifically influenced by the post-Enlightenment critique of religion as a useless excuse for passivity and a prop for dehumanizing structures. Hence, his strictly functional explanation of the Christian sacraments and his emphasis on their prophetic aspect as symbols are a timely and important response to that critique. But his interpretation leaves undeveloped, for the most part, the positive aspect of those symbols, namely, the fact that they also manifest a divine reality.[30] Thus, although Segundo does maintain that the sacraments are "gestures of humanity's Savior"[31] he does not attempt to explain how exactly that is so in a way, for example, that Schillebeeckx does.[32] The latter interprets the sacraments as gestures of Jesus Christ directed both towards humanity for its redemption and towards God in worship. Thus, he is able to preserve the contemplative aspect of the sacraments, which Segundo virtually ignores.

Closely connected with the above, is the "mystical" dimension of human experience which has played an important role in traditional Christian spirituality.[33] Segundo does make reference to the "night" of Christian spirituality as a necessary time of "deactivation", of "entropy" in human existence.[34] However, his allusion does not seem to go beyond a statement on the slow, painful process through which the negativities of human life are to be integrated into the evolutionary process of creating persons capable of freely directing the universe for the good of all. It is here that Segundo's reflections on personal involvement in, and experience of the negative thrust of evolution on the human level fall short of capturing the mystery that also grounds that reality and the question of human liberty that is involved. The question arises as to whether or not Segundo needs to explore somewhat this mystical dimension of human experience in order to be able to explain more adequately the redemptive value of suffering and misery, which he also intends to affirm. Other Latin American theologians are, indeed, attempting to formulate a more adequate spirituality to ground liberation theology's option for the poor.[35] There are also indications that Segundo sees the necessity of addressing that issue.[36] A fuller development of liberation spirituality by Segundo would be an asset to the entire liberation theological movement.

Further exploration by others into Segundo's theology could also yield fruitful results. One area in need of further development is Segundo's use of the various disciplines that he has incorporated into his theology. The fact that he eclectically draws insights out of their overall contexts makes it difficult to assess specific positions in terms of their coherence within their own systems. More research is needed in this area in order to evaluate the inner consistency, beyond logical coherence, of Segundo's use of these diverse disciplines in his theological reflections.[37]

Another area of Segundo's thought which could be fruitfully explored derives from the basic argument of this thesis, viz., that efficacious love is central to Segundo's theological reflections. It relates to the question of whether or not there is basis in the entire thrust of Segundo's theology for a more explicit focus on the Spirit as the definitive Power of Love, of Grace which establishes Jesus of Nazareth as the Unique Son of God and Revealer of universal salvation. Segundo's persistent concern with grace as universally available to all humanity and, even more, his emphasis on the ongoing and dynamic collaboration of God with human beings in making that grace concretely embodied in liberative, social structures, seem to move logically in that direction. Indeed, this seems to be the logical thrust of the entire Latin American theological movement.[38] The answer to that question would be of interest to the entire theological enterprise.

However, the positive contributions of Segundo's theological enterprise far outweigh the deficiencies that are present in it. First of all, Segundo's theology offers possibilities for addressing head-on two of the most universal and pressing of contemporary problematics, viz., massive poverty and pluralism in a world that is marked by diversity in all aspects of human existence.[39]

To address the issue of pluralism, Segundo offers the universal reach of his "open" theology. It is a universality of depth that penetrates human experience and eventually embraces all of it in the search for the truth which appears in limited forms in *all cultures* and in *all religions*. To confront the problematic of massive poverty and oppression, Segundo brings insights drawn from the specific Latin American context. He emphasizes "ideological critique" as a *sine qua non* for liberating society from structures of oppression and theology itself from complicity with the *status quo*. The liberation of the poor and marginated thus intended, demands nothing less than a new type of personal and social praxis that makes efficacious love the only criterion or norm of authentic Christian response. It calls for a totally new creation of persons, of social institutions, of global structures, for the benefit of those most in need.

But Segundo's realism makes it clear that the instruments that are indispensable for the realization of human projects be adequately known and respected. Hence, the realm of science and technology, of "ideologies", must be brought into dialogue with Christian faith in order that the values which give meaning to human existence may direct the forces and resources of the universe in the service of humanity.

Perhaps, it is here that Segundo's greatest challenge now lies, where the implications of his theology are most far-reaching. He challenges Christianity to recognize and to appreciate the different levels on which Faith and ideologies operate, not in order to justify and perpetuate an easy separation of a sacred and a profane sphere, but to hold in creative tension two indissoluble realities in the constant struggle towards more adequate responses to the problems of history.

Segundo's insistence on the critical use and value-centred direction of the instruments of nature and of culture is most timely in a world on the verge of ecological destruction and bent on maintaining an explosive socio-economic imbalance.

Segundo's sober realism does not minimize the slow, painful process in which the negativities of human experience are to be integrated into the evolutionary process of creating persons capable of freely directing the universe for the good of all. Nevertheless, he offers assurance that in the end love, the positive vector of evolution, will prove to be definitive forever. It has, indeed, already efficaciously triumphed in Jesus of Nazareth. This is his conviction, namely, that "all that love realizes is inscribed in the positive history of humanity." For the effects of egotism are merely "a return to the blind, pre-human force" of a passing world "without destroying with it what is constructed in love."[40]

3. Summary and Conclusion

In summary, we have observed how efficacious love functions as a focussing concern in the theology of Juan Luis Segundo. It grounds his theological reflections in the core of the Christian message of Love Incarnated in history. Through the notion of efficacious love, Segundo is able to engineer the major shifts of emphasis in Christian self-understanding that mark modern theology in general and Latin American liberation theology in particular.

Thus, it is the fundamental value that organizes his thought in terms of a praxis-centred model which holds theory and praxis in creative tension, while stressing praxis as that which primarily mediates truth. It most consistently illumines Segundo's reinterpretation of the major symbols of Christian doctrine. Subjective, personal salvation is disclosed to be not merely an other-worldly union between persons and transcendent Creator but more significantly, the Incarnation of the efficacious love of a God who is also immersed in history and is one with humanity. Objective salvation emerges as more truly the final inclusion of all into the one Body of Christ than any individualistic striving for personal union with God. It, finally, reveals the one vocation of humanity to be the efficacious construction of love in history in a dynamic and changing world. The task of humanity is, then, a specifically urgent one in the face of a dangerously unbalanced world. It demands all the concentration of energy and all the passion of the human heart to be committed to that task. What makes such a commitment possible is the Love that continues to be gratuitously given by God, Creator and Redeemer of all. "Efficacious love" is, then, the fundamental concern of Segundo's entire theological enterprise from start to finish.

Notes

1. Haight, *An Alternative Vision,* p. 53.

2. Cf. Segundo, *The Liberation of Theology,* p. 3.

3. See Chapter I, pp. 12-17.

4. See Chapter II, pp. 26-28; Chapter III, pp. 67-69.

5. See Chapter II, pp. 28-30.

6. See Chapter II, pp. 30-43.

7. See Chapter III, pp. 67-71.

8. See Chapter III, pp. 72-75.

9. See Chapter III, pp. 71f.

10. Cf. Segundo, *The Liberation of Theology,* pp. 4f; Gutiérrez, *A Theology of Liberation,* pp. 6-15.

11. See Chapter III, pp. 51-66.

12. See Chapter III, p. 50.

13. See Chapter IV.

14. See Chapter V, pp. 106-112.

15. See Chapter III, pp. 70f. Discipleship is one of the most important themes of liberation theology. It is directly related to the emphasis on praxis. Cf. *The Historical Jesus of the Synoptics* pp. 134-49. Sobrino, *Christology at the Crossroads;* Segundo Galilea, *Following Jesus,* translated by John Drury (Maryknoll, New York: Orbis Books, 1981).

16. See Persha, "Juan Luis Segundo".

17 See Chapter V, pp. 113-118.

18. These include questions of authority in the Church and the area of Ecumenism. Cf. Persha, "Juan Luis Segundo", p. 287.

19. See Chapter V, pp. 121f.

20. See Chapter IV, pp. 121-123.

21. See Chapter III, pp. 51f.

22. See Chapter III, pp. 51-66.

23. Cf. Introduction p. 3 re Anthony Tambasco's dissertation on Segundo. However, we have seen in this thesis that Marxist analysis, though a highly important tool in Segundo's theological method is but one aspect of his thought. See esp. Chapter II, pp. 34-38.

24. Cf. James G. O'Donnell, "The Influence of Freud's Hermeneutic of Suspicion on the Writings of Juan Luis Segundo", *Journal of Pyschology and Theology,* XXX (Spring 1977), 1-9. He accuses Segundo of a "psychological reduction of Christianity" in his claim that Freudian "hermeneutic of suspicion" as presented by Paul Ricoeur is the linchpin of Segundo's theological method. Again, it seems that this position cannot be substained in any absolute sense because Segundo's use of Freud, though important, is minimal in comparison with other influences. See Chapter II, pp. 30-44 .

25. Cf. David Slade's criticism of Segundo, Introduction, p. 3; Denis p. McCann, "Political Ideologies and Practical Theology: Is there a Difference?"

Union Seminary Quarterly Review, XXXVI (Summer 1981), 243-57. McCann makes this statement: "Segundo deliberately breaks the tension between Christian hope for the Kingdom of God and the "utopian" enthusiasm commonly associated with the revolutionary praxis." *Ibid.,* p. 251.

26. Segundo himself notes this criticism and attributes it to a "misunderstanding" of his position. See "Education, Communication, and Liberation", pp. 95f.

27. See Chapter IV, pp. 82-84.

28. See Chapter III, pp. 58-61, 70, note 69; Chapter V, 117f.

29. See Introduction, p. 1.

30. Cf. Haight, *An Alternative Vision,* pp. 190-205.

31. Segundo, *A Community Called Church,* p. 39.

32. Cf. E. Schillebeeckx,*Christ the Sacrament of Encounter With God,* (London/Melbourne: Sheed and Ward, 1963).

33. It is of interest that the mystical aspect of Berdyaev's thought is, perhaps, the only area that has not significantly influenced Segundo.

34. Segundo, *Grace and the Human Condition,* p. 72; *An Evolutionary Approach to Jesus of Nazareth,* pp. 78f.

35. The question of spirituality has been a special focus of libertion theology. See "Cuaderno: Espiritualidad de la liberación: Symposium", *Christus,* ILIV (December 1979- January 1980), 59-95; Gutiérrez, *A Theology of Liberation,* pp. 203-208; *We Drink From Our Own Wells: The Spiritual Journey of a People,* translated by Matthew J. O'Connell (Maryknoll, New York/Melbourne: Orbis Books/Dove Communications, 1984); Segundo Galilea, *Contemplación y apostolado* (Bogota: Indoamerican Press Service, 1973); *Following Jesus,* translated by John Drury (Maryknoll, New York: Orbis Books, 1981); "Liberation as Encounter with Politics and Contemplation", in *Concilium* 96 (New York: Herder and Herder, 1974), pp. 19-151.

36. See Segundo, *The Christ of the Ignatian Exercises.*

37. Gregory Baum argues persuasively that there needs to be a coherence between the social science theories that are brought into dialogue with theology and the specific theological positions that are being affirmed. See his "Ecumenical Theology: a New Approach", *The Ecumenist,* XIX, no. 5 (July - August, 1981), 65-78.

38. Cf. Roger Haight, *An Alternative Vision,* pp. 140-161. Haight argues that a Christology focussed upon the Spirit in Jesus as that which makes him uniquely divine would better incorporate the intent of the liberative thrust of liberation theology than the present Logos centred approach of many of the Latin American liberation theologians. I believe this is true of Segundo.

39. Cf. Edward Schillebeeckx, *The Understanding of Faith,* translated by N.D. Smith (New York: The Seabury Press, 1974), pp. 49-55 re the question of pluralism.

40. Juan Luis Segundo, "La profundidad de la gracia", *Perspectivas de Dialogo,* II, no. 20 (December 1967), 249-55, p. 254.

Bibliography

1. Primary Sources

Books written by Juan Luis Segundo

Existencialismo, filosofía: Ensayo de Síntesis. Buenos Aires: Espasa-Calpe, 1948.

Función de la Iglesia en la realidad rioplatense. Montevideo: Barreiro y Ramos, 1962.

Etapes precristianas de la fe: Evolución de la idea de Dios en el Antiguo Testamento. Montevideo: Cursos de Complementación Cristiana, 1962.

Berdiaeff: Une réflexion chrétienne sur la personne. Paris: Montaigne, 1963.

Concepción cristiana de hombre. Montevideo: Mimeográfica "Luz", 1964.

La cristiandad, ¿una utopia? I. Los hechos. Montevideo: Mimeográfica "Luz", 1964.

La cristiandad, ¿una utopia? II. Los principios. Montevideo: Mimeográfica "Luz", 1964.

Esa comunidad llamada Iglesia. Buenos Aires: Carlos Lohlé, 1968. *(The Community Called Church.* Translated by John Drury. Maryknoll, New York: Orbis Books, 1973).

Gracia y condición humana. Buenos Aires: Carlos Lohlé, 1968. *(Grace and the Human Condition.* Translated by John Drury. Maryknoll, New York: Orbis Books, 1973).

De la sociedad a la teología. Buenos Aires: Carlos Lohlé, 1970.

Nuestra idea de Dios. Buenos Aires: Carlos Lohlé, 1970 *(Our Idea of God.* Translated by John Drury. Maryknoll, New York: Orbis Books, 1973).

¿Qué es un cristiano? Montevideo: Mosca Hnos. S.A. Editores, 1971.

Los sacramentos hoy. Buenos Aires: Carlos Lohlé, 1971. *(The Sacraments Today.* Translated by John Drury. Maryknoll, New York: Orbis Books, 197).

Evolución y culpa. Buenos Aires: Carlos Lohlé, 1972. *(Evolution and Guilt.* Translated by John Drury. Maryknoll, New York: Orbis Books, 1974).

Acción pastoral latinoamericana: Sus motivos ocultos. Buenos Aires: Busqueda, 1972. *(The Hidden Motives of Pastoral Action: Latin American Reflections.* Translated by John Drury. Maryknoll, New York: Orbis Books, 1978).

Masas y minores en la dialéctica divina de la liberación. Buenos Aires: La Aurora, 1973.

Liberación de la teología. Buenos Aires: Carlos Lohlé, 1975. *(The Liberation of Theology.* Translated by John Drury. Maryknoll, New York: Orbis Books, 1976).

El hombre de hoy ante Jesus de Nazaret. 3 vols. Madrid: Cristiandad, 1982.

Volume I: *Fe e Ideología*, 413 pp. (Vol. I. *Faith and Ideologies*. Translated by John Drury. Maryknoll, New York/Melbourne/London: Orbis Books/Dove Communications/Sheed and Ward, 1984.)

Volume II/1: *Historia y Actualidad: Sinópticos y Pablo*, pp. 1-599 (Vol. II: *The Historical Jesus of the Synoptics*. Translated by John Drury. Maryknoll, New York/Melbourne/London: Orbis Books/Dove Communications/Sheed and Ward, 1985; Vol. III: *The Humanist Christology of Paul*. Translated by John Drury. Maryknoll, New York/London: Orbis Books/Sheed and Ward, 1986).

Volume II/2 *Historia y Actualidad: Las cristologías en la espiritualidad*, pp. 611-890 (Volume IV: *The Christ of the Ignatian Exercises*. Translated by John Drury. Maryknoll, New York: Orbis Books, 1987; Volume V: *An Evolutionary Approach to Jesus of Nazareth*. Translated by John Drury. Maryknoll, New York: Orbis Books, 1988).

Articles Written by Juan Luis Segundo

"Transformación Latinoamericana y conducta moral", *Cuadernos Latinoamericanos de económica humana* (Montevideo), no. 9 (1960), 252-67.

"El círculo vicioso de la miseria. El universitario latinoamericano", *Mensaje*, II (1962), 478-83.

"Diagnóstico político de América Latina", *Mensaje*, II (1962) 656-61.

"Los caminos del desarrollo político latinoamericano", *Mensaje*, II (1962), 701-707.

"La variable política", *Revista Interamericana de Ciencias Sociales* (Bogatá). no 2. (1963), 239-93.

"Síntesis en la tipología socioeconómica", *Revista Interamericana de Ciencias Sociales*. no. 2 (1963), 1-32.

"The Future of Christianity in Latin America", *Cross Currents*, XII, no. 2 (1963), 273-81.

"Pastoral latinoamericana: Hora de decisión", *Mensaje*, IV, no. 127 (March-April 1964), 74-82.

"Problemas teológicas de Latinoamerica". Paper delivered to an international conference of Latin America during Vatican Council II, Brazil, 1964.

"La función de la Iglesia", Dialogo, I, no. 1 (December 1965), 4-7.

"La función de la Iglesia", Dialogo, I, no. 2 (February 1966), 5-10.

"La función de la Iglesia", Dialogo, I, no. 3 (April 1966), 3-9.

"La Iglesia. ¿Es necesaria?" Dialogo, I, no. 6 (August 1966), 5-10.

"El dialogo, Iglesia-mundo, reflexión", *Dialogo,* I no. 6 (October 1966), 3-7.

"La Iglesia. ¿Es necesaria?" Dialogo, I, no. 7 (September 1966), 3-8.

"El dialogo, Iglesia-mundo, reflexión", *Dialogo,* I no. 8 (November 1966), 8-12.

"Lo que el concilio dice", *Dialogo*, I, no. 10 (December 1966), 3-13.

"Qué nombre dar a la existencia cristiana?" *Perspectivas de Dialogo*, II, no. 11 (January-February 1967), 3-9.

"Intellecto y salvación", in Gutiérrez, Gustavo et al. *Salvación y construcción del mundo*. Barcelona: editorial Nova terra, 1967, pp, pp. 67-90.

"The Church: A New Direction in Latin America", *Catholic Mind*, LXV, no. 1211

(March 1967), 43-47.

"La condición humana", *Perspectivas de Dialogo,* II, no. 12 (March-April 1967), 30-35.

"La condición humana", *Perspectivas de Dialogo,* II, no. 13 (May 1967), 55-61.

"Camilo Torres, sacerdocio y violencia", *Víspera,* I, no. 1 (May 1967), 71-75.

"La vida eterna", *Perspectivas de Dialogo,* II, no. 14 (June 1967), 83-89.

"La vida eterna", *Perspectivas de Dialogo,* II, no. 15 (July 1967), 109-18.

"Un nuevo comienzo," *Víspera,* I, no. 2 (August 1967), 39-43.

"America hoy", *Víspera,* I, no. 2 (October 1967), 53-57.

"La Profundidad de la gracia", *Perspectivas de Dialogo,* II, no. 19 (1967), 235-40.

"La Profundidad de la gracia", *Perspectivas de Dialogo,* II, no. 20 (December 1967), 249-55.

"Hacia una exegesis dinámica", *Vispera,* I, no. 3 (October 1967), 77-84.

"Hipótesis sobre la situación del Uruguay: Algunas posibilidades de investigación", in Juan Luis Segundo, Pedro Almos, Dionisio J. Garmandia et al., *Uruguay 67: Una interpretación.* Vol. I. Montevideo: Editorial Alfa, 1967, pp. 11-32.

"¿Dios nos interesa o no?" *Perspectivas de Dialogo,* III, no. 21 (March 1968), 13-16.

"Del ateismo a la fe", *Perspectivas de Dialogo,* III, no. 22 (April 1968), 44-47.

"Social Justice and Revolution", *America,* CXVIII, no. 17 (April 27, 1968), 574-77.

"Padre, Hijo, Espíritu: Una historia", *Perspectivas de Dialogo,* III, no. 23 (July 1968), 71-76.

"El poder del hábito", *Perspectivas de Dialogo,* III, no. 23 (July 1968), 90-92.

"Padre, Hijo, Espíritu: Una sociedad", *Perspectivas de Dialogo,* III, no. 24 (July 1968), 103-109

"Padre, Hijo, Espíritu: Una libertad I", *Perspectivas de Dialogo,* III, no. 25 (July 1968), 142-48.

"Padre, Hijo, Espíritu: Una libertad II", *Perspectivas de Dialogo,* III, no. 26 (August 1968), 183-86.

"Has Latin America a Choice?" *America,* CXX, no. 8 (February 22, 1969), 213-16.

"¿Un Dios a nuestra imagen?" *Perspectivas de Dialogo,* IV, no. 32 (March 1969), 14-18.

"¿Hacia una Iglesia de izquierda?" *Perspectivas de Dialogo,* IV, no. 32 (April 1969), 35-39.

"Riqueza y probreza como obstáculos al desarrollo", *Perspectivas de Dialogo,* IV, no. 32 (April 1969), 54-56.

"Ritmos de cambio y pastoral de conjunto", *Perspectivas de Dialogo,* IV, no. 35, (July 1969), 131-37.

"¿Autoridad o que?" *Perspectivas de Dialogo,* IV, no. 39-40 (December 1969), 270-72.

"Fundamental Theology and Dialogue", in *Concilium 46: The Development of Fundamental Theology,* ed., Johannes B. Metz. New York/Paramus/New Jersey: Paulist Press, 1969, pp. 69-79.

"Introduction", *Iglesia latinoamericana, ¿protesta o profecía?* Buenos Aires: Busqueda, 1969, pp. 8-17.

"Evangelización y humanización: ¿Progreso del reino y progreso temporal?" *Perspectivas de Dialogo*, V, no. 41 (March 1970), 9-17.

"Desarrollo y subdesarrollo: Polos teológicos", *Perspectivas de Dialogo*, V, no. 43 (May 1970), 76-80.

"El posible aporte de la teología protestante para el cristianismo latinoamericano en el futuro", *Cristianismo y Sociedad*, VIII, no, 22 (1970), 41-49.

"Possible Contribution of Protestant Theology to Latin American Christianity in the Future", *Lutheran Quarterly*, XXII (Fall 1970), 60-68.

"Wealth and Poverty as Obstacles to Development", in *Human Rights and the Liberation of Man in the Americas*. Edited by Louis Colonnesse. Notre Dame: Notre Dame University Press, 1971, pp. 23-31.

"La Iglesia chilena ante el socialismo I", *Marcha*, no. 1558 (August 27, 1971), pp. 12-14.

"La Iglesia chilena ante el socialismo II", *Marcha*, no. 1559 (September 4, 1971), p. 15.

"La Iglesia chilena ante el socialismo III", *Marcha*, no. 1560 (September 11, 1971), pp. 19, 24.

"Education , Communication and Liberation: A Christian Vision", *IDOC International — North Américan Edition* (November 13, 1971), 63-96.

"Liberación; Fe e ideología", *Mensaje* (July 1972), 248-54.

"Las elites latinoamericanas: Problemática humana y cristiana ante el cambio social", in *Fe cristiana y cambio social en América Latina: Encuentro de El Escorial*, Salamanca: Sígueme, 1973, pp. 203-12.

"Teología y ciencias sociales", in *Fe cristiana y cambio social en América Latina: Encuentro de El Escorial, 1972*. Salamanca: Sígueme, 1973, pp. 285-95.

"On a Missionary Awareness of One's Own Culture", *Jesuit Missions Newsletter*, no. 33 (May 1974), 1-6.

"Reconciliación y conflicto", *Perspectivas de Dialogo*, IX, no. 86 (September 1974), 172-78.

"Fe y ideologiá", *Perspectivas de Dialogo*, IX no. 89-90 (December 1974), 172-82.

"Theological Response to a Talk on Evangelization and Development", *Studies in the International Apostolate of Jesuits* (November 1974), 79-82.

"Teología: Mensaje y proceso", *Perspectivas de Dialogo*, IX, no. 89-90 (December 1974), 259-70.

"Capitalism vs Socialism: Crux Theológica", *Concilium*, X, no. 96 (June 1974), 105-23, in *Frontiers of Theology in Latin America*. Edited by R. Gibellini. New York: Orbis Books, 1979, pp. 240-59.

"Perspectivas para una teología latinoamericana", *Perspectivas de Dialogo*, IX, no. 207 (1975), 24-30.

"Conversión y reconciliación en la perspectiva de la moderna teología de la liberación", *Cristianismo y Sociedad*, XIII (1975), 17-25.

"Teilhard de Chardin". Conference, Montevideo, 1975.

"Condicionamientos actuales de la reflexión teológica en Latinoamérica", in *Liberación y cautiverio: Debates en torno al método de la teología en América Latina*. Mexico City: Comité Organizador, 1975, pp. 91-101; 561-63.

"Condicionmientos actuales sociopolíticos, ecclesiales, e ideólogicos para la reflexión teológica en América Latina: Condensación", *Christus*, XL (October 1975), 23-25.

"Statement by Juan Luis Segundo", in *Theology in the Americas*. Edited by Sergio Torres and John Eagleson. Maryknoll, New York: Orbis Books, 1976, pp. 280-83.

"Liberation et Evangile", *Relations* (Montreal), XXXVI (1976), 151-55.

"Comment l'Eglise este-elle universelle c'est dire catholique?" *Eglise et Mission,* no. 207 (1977), 24-30.

"Derechos humanos, evangelización e idelogía," *Christus* (November 1978), 29-35.

"The Shift Within Latin American Theology". Lecture given at Regis College, Toronto School of Theology. March 22, 1983. Toronto: Regis College Press, 1983.

"Excursus: The Beginning of a Small Idea", in *Theology and the Church*. Translated by John W. Diercksmeier. Minneapolis/Chicago/New York: Winston Press; London: Geoffrey Chapman, 1985, pp. 73-85.

II. Selected Secondary Sourcs

A. The Theology of Juan Luis Segundo

Baum, Gregory. "The Theological Method of Segundo's *The Liberation of Theology"*, *Catholic Theological Society of America Proceedings*. XXXII (1977), 120-24.

Cabestro, Teofilo, ed. "A Conversation with Juan Luis Segundo", in *Faith: Conversations with Contemporary Theologians*. New York: Orbis Books, 1980, pp. 172-80.

Cook, Michael L. "Jesus from the Other Side of History: Christology in Latin America, *Theological Studies*, XLIV (June 1983), 258-87.

Ferm, Deane W. "South American Liberation Theology", *Religion in Life*, XLVIII (Winter 1978), 474-91.

Haight, Roger. "Book Reviews ... Juan Luis Segundo's *Liberation of Theology"*, *Emmanuel*, LXXXIII no. 12, pp. 605-10.

_____ "Books Reviews ... Juan Luis Segundo's *Faith and Ideologies"*, *Cross Currents*, XXXIV (Spring 1984), 106-109.

Hennelly, Alfred T. "The Challenge of Juan Luis Segundo", *Theological Studies,* XXXVIII (March 1977), 125-35.

_____. "Theological Method: The Southern Experience", *Theological Studies,* XXXVIII (December 1977), 709-35.

_____. *"Theologies in Conflict: The Challenge of Juan Luis Segundo.* Maryknoll, New York: Orbis Books, 1979.

Kondrath, William Michael. "The Theology of Juan Luis Segundo and Its Significance for the Understanding of Christian Identity and Mission". M.A. Thesis, Institute of Christian Thought, University of St. Michael's College, 1977.

Lakeland, P. "Responding to Liberation Theology: Interaction of Faith and Social Commitment", *Month* XIII (Janauary 1980), 12-15.

Leech, Kenneth. "Liberating Theology: The Thought of Juan Luis Segundo", *Theology*, 84 (July 1981), 258-66.

McCann, Dennis P. "Political Ideologies and Practical Theology: IsThere a Difference?" *Union Seminary Quarterly Review*, XXXVI (Summer 1981), 243-57.

Merkle, Judith A. "The Fundamental Ethics of Juan Luis Segundo". Ph.D. Dissertation, University of St. Michael's College, Toronto, 1985.

deMuth, T. "Segundo: Latin American Church Irreversibly Altered", *National Catholic Reporter*, XV (February 16, 1979), 5.

Niemeyer, Gerhert. "Structure, Revolution and Christianity", *Center Journal*, I (Winter 1981), 79-99.

O'Donnell, James G. "The Influence of Freud's Hermeneutic of Suspicion on the Writings of Juan Luis Segundo", *Journal of Psychology and Theology*, XXX (Spring 1977), 1-9.

Peel, David. "Juan Luis Segundo's 'A Theology for Artisans of a New Humanity': A Latin American Contribution to Contemporary Theological Understanding", *The Perkins School of Theology Journal*, XXX (Spring, 1977), 1-9.

Persha, Gerald Justin. "Juan Luis Segundo: A Study Concerning the Relationship Between the Particularity of the Church and the Universality of Her Mission". Ph. D. Dissertation, University of Ottawa, 1979.

Riddell, Roger. "Part I: The Liberation of Theology", *Month*, CCXXXVIII (May 1977), 149-53.

Roach, Richard R. "A new Sense of Faith", *Journal of Religious Ethics*, V (Spring 1977), 135-54.

Sanks, T. & B. Smith. "Liberation Ecclesiology: Praxis, Theory, Praxis", *Theological Studies*, XXXVIII (March 1977), 3-38.

Sanks, T. Howland. "Liberation Theology and the Social Gospel: Variations on a Theme", *Theological Studies*, XLI (December 1980), 668-82.

Slade, Stanley David. "The Theological Method of Juan Luis Segundo", Ph.D. Dissertation, Fuller Theological Seminary, 1979.

_____. "Liberation Anthropology: Segundo's Use of Teilhard de Chardin", *Studia Biblica et Theólogica*, IX (1979), 61-80.

Sweeney, John. "For the Builders of a New Ireland: The Theology of Juan Luis Segundo", *Furrow*, XXXI (December 1980), 738-9.

Tambasco, Anthony Joseph. "The Contribution of Juan Luis Segundo to the Hermeneutical Question of the Relationship of the Bible to Christian Ethics". Ph.D. Dissertation, Union Theological Seminary in the City of New York, 1981. Published under the title, *The Bible for Ethics: Juan Luis Segundo and First World Ethics*. Washington D.C: University Press of America, 1981.

Tripole, Martin. "Segundo's Liberation Theology vs Eschatological Ecclesiology of the Kingdom", *Thomist*, XLV (June 1981), 1-25.

Weir, J. Emmette. "The Bible and Marx: A Discussion of the Hermeneutics of Liberation Theology", *Scottish Journal of Theology*, no. 4 (1982), 337-50.

B. Other Sources Relevant to the Theology of Juan Luis Segundo

Books

Alves , Rubem. *A Theology of Human Hope.* Washington/Cleveland: Corpus Books, 1969.

Assmann, Hugo. *Opresión-Liberación: Desafío a los cristianos.* Montevideo: Tierra Nueva, 1971. Reprinted under the title, *Teología desde la praxis de liberación.* Madrid, 1973. English translation. *Practical Theology of Liberation.* Translated by Paul Burns. London: Search Press, 1975.

_____. *Theology for a Nomad Church.* Translated by Paul Burns. Maryknoll, New York: Orbis Books, 1976.

Bateson, Gregory. *Steps to an Ecology of Mind.* New York: Ballantine Books, 1972.

Baum, Gregory. *Religion and Alienation: A Theological Reading of Sociology.* New York/Paramus/Toronto: Paulist Press, 1975.

Berdyaev, Nicolas. *Freedom and Spirit.* Translated by George Reavey. London: The Centenary Press, 1935.

_____. *Slavery and Freedom.* Translated by George Reavey. London: The Centenary Press, 1943.

Berger, Peter and Thomas Luckmann. *The Social Construction of Reality.* New York: The Penguin Press, 1966.

Boff, Leonardo. *Jesus Christ Liberator.* Translated by Patrick Hughes. Maryknoll, New York: Orbis Books, 1978.

_____. *Liberating Grace.* Translated by John Drury. Maryknoll, New York: Orbis Books, 1979.

_____. *Teología desde el cautiverio.* Bogatá: Indoamerican Press Service, 1975.

Bonino, José Miguez. *Christians and Marxists: The Mutual Challenge to Revolution.* Grand Rapids, Michigan: Eerdmans, 1976.

_____. *Doing Theology in a Revolutionary Situation.* Philadelphia: Fortress Press, 1975.

Brown, Robert McAfee. *Theology in a New Key.* Philadelphia: The Westminster Press, 1978.

Bultmann, Rudolf. *Faith and Understanding.* Translated by Louise Pettibone Smith. London: S.C.M. Press, 1969, pp. 53-65.

_____. *Jesus Christ and Mythology.* New York: Charles Scribner's Sons, 1958.

de Chardin, Pierre Teilhard. *The Divine Milieu.* Translated by Bernard Wall. New York: Harper and Row, 1965.

_____. *The Future of Man.* Translated by Norman Denny. New York: Harper and Row, 1964.

_____. *The Phenomenon of Man.* Translated by Bernard Wall. London: Wm. Collins and Co., 1959.

Comblin, José. *The Meaning of Mission: Jesus, Christians, and the Wayfaring Church.* Translated by John Drury. Maryknoll, Nw York: Orbis Books, 1977.

Documents of the Medellín Conference. *The Church in the Present-day Transformation of Latin America in the Light of the Council.* 2 vols. English translation. Washington, D.C: Latin American Division, United States Catholic Conference, 1970.

Dussell, Enrique. *A History of the Church in Latin America.* Translated by Alan Neely. Grand Rapids, Michigan: Wm. B. Eerdmans, 1981.

_____. *History and the Theology of Liberation: A Latin American Perspective.* Translated by John Drury. Maryknoll, New York: Orbis Books, 1976.

Ellacuria, Ignacio. *Freedom Made Flesh.* Translated by John Drury. Maryknoll, New York: Orbis Books, 1976.

Fe cristiana y cambio social en América Latina. Edited by Alfonso Bolado. Salamanca: Sígueme, 1973.

Gadamer, Hans-Georg. *Truth and Method.* New York: Crossroad, 1982.

Galilea, Segundo. *A los pobres se les anuncia el evangelio?* Bogotá: Paulinas, 1975.

_____. *Contemplación y apostolado* Bogotá: Indoamerican Press Service, 1973.

_____. *Following Jesus.* Translated by Sister Helen Phillips. Maryknoll, New York: Orbis Books, 1981.

Gibellini, Rosino, ed. *Frontiers of Theology in Latin America.* Translated by John Drury. Maryknoll, New York: Orbis Books, 1979.

Gutiérrez, Gustavo. *A Theology of Liberation: History, Politics, and Salvation.* Translated by Sister Caridad Inda and John Eagleson. Maryknoll, New York: Orbis Books, 1973.

_____. *La fuerza histórica de los pobres: Selección de trabajos.* Lima Peru: Centro de Estudios y Publicaciones, 1979. English translation. *The Power of the Poor in History: Selected Writings.* Translated by Robert R. Barr. Maryknoll, New York: Orbis Books, 1983.

_____. *Lineas pastorales de la Iglesia en América Latina.* Lima, Peru: Centro de Estudios y Publicaciones, 1976.

_____. *Praxis of Liberation and Christian Faith.* Texas: Mexican American Cultural Center, 1974.

_____. *We Drink From Our Own Wells: The Spiritual Journey of a People.* Translated by Matthew J. O'Connell. New York/Melbourne: Orbis Books/Dove Communications, 1984.

Haight, Roger, S.J. *An Alternative Vision: An Interpretation of Liberation Theology.* New York/Mahwah: Paulist Press, 1985.

_____. *The Experience and Language of Grace.* New York: Paulist, 1978.

Lamb, Matthew. *Solidarity with Victims: Toward a Theology of Social Transformation.* New York: Crossroad, 1982.

Liberación y cautiverio: Debates en torno al método de la teología en America Latina. Mexico City: Comité Organizador, 1976.

Lonergan, Bernard. *Method in Theology.* New York: Herder and Herder, 1972.

Machovec, Milan. *A Marxist Looks at Jesus.* English translation. Philadelphia: Fortress Press, 1976.

Mecham, J. Lloyd. *Church and States in Latin America.* Chapel Hill: The University of North Carolina Press, 1934, 1966.

Metz, Johannes. *Faith and History in Society.* Translated by David Smith. New

York: The Seabury Press, 1980.

Miranda, José. *Marx Against the Marxists: The Christian Humanism of Karl Marx.* Transated by John Drury. Maryknoll, New York: Orbis Books, 1980.

_____. *Marx and the Bible: A Critique of the Philosophy of Oppression.* Translated by John Eagleson. Maryknoll, New York: Orbis Books, 1976.

Moltmann, Jurgen. *The Crucified God.* London: S.C.M. Press,, 1974.

_____. *Theology of Hope.* New York: Harper and Row, 1967.

Nucho, Fuad. *Berdyaev's Philosophy: The Existential Paradox of Freedom and Necessity.* Garden City, New York: Anchor books, 1966.

Oliveros, Roberto. *Liberación y teología: Génesis y crecimiento de una reflexión 1966-1977.* Lima Peru: centro de Estudios y Publicaciones, 1977.

Puebla and Beyond. Eds. Eagleson, John and Philip Scharper. Translated by John Drury. Maryknoll, New York: Orbis Books, 1980.

Rahner, Karl. *The Shape of the Church to Come.* Translated by Edward Quinn. New York: The Seabury Press, 1974.

Rideau, Emile. *The Thought of Teilhard de Chardin.* Translated by Rene Hague. New York/Evanston: Harper and Row, 1967.

Scannone, Juan Carlos. *Teología de la liberación y praxis popular: Aportes críticos para una teología de la liberación.* Salamaca: Sígueme, 1976.

Schillebeeckx, Edward. *Christ the Sacrament of Encounter With God.* London/Melbourne: Sheed and Ward, 1963.

_____. *The Understanding of Faith.* Translated by N.D. Smith. New York: The Seabury Press, 1974.

Sobrino, Jon. *Christology at the Crossroads.* Translated by John Drury. Maryknoll, New York: Orbis Books, 1978.

Soelle, Dorothee. *Political Theology.* Translated by John Shelley. Philadelphia: Fortress Press, 1974.

Tillich, Paul. *Dynamics of Faith.* New York: Harper and Row, 1957.

Torres, Sergio and John Eagleson, eds. *The Challenge of Basic Christian Communities.* Translated by John Drury. Maryknoll, New York: Orbis Books, 1981.

Tracy, David. *Blessed Rage for Order: The New Pluralism in Theology.* New York: Seabury Press, 1975.

Vidales, Raul. *Cuestiones en torno al método en la teología de la liberación.* Lima: Secretariado Latinoamericano, 1974.

Articles and Parts of Books

Alves, Rubem. "Christian Realism: Ideology of the Establishment", *Christianity and Crisis* (September 17, 1973), 173-76.

_____. "Theology and the Liberation of Man", in *New Theology* No. 9. New York: MacMillan, 1972, pp. 230-50.

Assmann, Hugo. "EL aporte cristiano al proceso de la liberación de América Latina", *Perspectivas de Dialogo* (June 1971), 95-105.

_____. "El pasado y presente de la praxis liberadora en América Latina", in

Liberacion y cautiverio: Debates en torno al método de la teología en América Latina. Mexico City: Comité Organizador, 1976, pp. 293-96.

_____. "Fe y promoción humana", *Perspectivas de Dialogo* (August 1969), 177-85.

Baum, Gregory. "Ecumenical Theology: A New Approach", *The Ecumenist,* XIX, no. 5 (July - August 1981), 65-78.

_____. "Liberation Theology and the Supernatural", *The Ecumenist,* XIX (September - October 1981), 81-87.

Berryman, Phillip E. "Latin American Liberation Theology", *Theological Studies,* XXXIV (1974), 357-95.

_____. "Doing Theology in a (Counter -) Revolutionary Situation: Latin American Liberation Theology in the Mid-Seventies", in *Theologies in the Americas.* Edited by Sergio Torres and John Eagleson. Maryknoll, New York: Orbis Books, 1976, pp. 54-83.

Boff, Leonardo. "Salvation in Jesus Christ and the Process of Liberation", in *Concilium 96: The Mystical and Political Dimension of the Christian Faith.* Edited by Geffre, Claude and Gustavo Gutiérrez. New York: Herder and Herder, 1974, pp. 78-91.

_____. "Qué hacer teología desde América Latina?", in *Liberación y cautiverio: Debates en torno al método de la teología en América Latina.* Mexico City: Comité Organizador, 1976, pp. 129-54.

Bonino, José Miguez. "Visión del cambio social y sus tareas desde las Iglesias cristianas no-católicas", in *Fe cristiana y cambio social en América Latina.* Edited by Alfonso Bolado. Salamanca: Sígueme, 1973, pp. 179-202.

Comblin, José. "Movimientos e ideologías", in *Fe cristiana y cambio social en América Latina.* Edited by Alfonso Bolado. Salamanca: Sígueme, 1973, pp. 101-27.

Cormie, Lee. "The Hermeneutical Privilege of the Oppressed: Liberation Theologies, Biblical Faith, and Marxist Sociology of Knowledge", *Catholic Theological Society of America Proceedings,* XXXIII (1978), 155-81.

Cuaderno: "Espiritualidad de la liberación: Symposium", *Christus,* 44 (December 1979- January 1980), 59-95.

Cuaderno: "Iglesia y Puebla: Symposium", *Christus,* 42, (December 1977), 21-51.

Cuaderno: "Pecado y gracia en la liberación Latinoamericana: Symposium", *Christus,* 43 (May 1978), 27-55.

Davis, Charles. "Theology and Praxis", *Cross Currents* (Summer 1973), 154-68.

Dussell, Enrique. "Discernment: A Question of Orthodoxy or Orthopraxis?", in *Concilium 119: Discernment of Spirit and of Spirits.* Edited by Floristan, S.C. & Christian Duquoc. New York: The Seabury Press, 1979, 47-60.

_____. "Historia de la fe cristiana y cambio en América Latina", in *Fe cristiana y cambio social en América Latina.* Edited by Alfonso Bolado. Salamanca: Sígueme, 1973, pp. 65-99.

_____. "Para una fundamentación dialéctica de la liberación latinoamericana", in *Método para una filosofía de la liberación.* Salamanca: Sígueme, 1974, pp. 259-88.

_____. "Sobre la historia de la teología en América Latina", in *Liberación y cautiverio: Debates en torno al método de la teología en América Latina.* Mexico City: Comité Organizador, 1976, pp. 19-68.

Ellacuria, Ignacio, "Fe y justicia: I", *Christus* (August 1977), 26-33.

_____. "Fe y justicia: II & III", *Christus* (October 1977),19-34.

Galilea, Segundo. "Between Medellín and Puebla", *Cross Currents,* XXVIII, no. 1 (1978), 71-78.

_____. "Evangelización de la religiosidad popular: dialéctica de dos modelos pastorales", *Sal Terrae,* LXIV, no. 10 (1976), 724-30.

_____. "Evangelization of the Poor", *Ladoc,* VII, no. 5 (May-June 1977), 46-54.

_____. La fe como principio crítico de promoción de la religiosidad popular", in *Fe cristiana y cambio social en America Latina.* Edited by Alfonso Bolado. Salamanca: Sígueme, 1973, pp. 151-58.

_____. "Liberation as an Encounter with Politics and Contemplation", in *Concilium* 96. New York: Herder and Herder, 1974, pp. 19-33.

Galilea, Segundo. "Liberation Theology and the New Tasks facing Christians", in Gibellini, Rosino, ed. *Frontiers of Theology in Latin America.* New York: Orbis Books, 1979, pp. 163-83.

_____. "The Theology of Liberation: A General Survey", *Lumen Vitae,* XXXIII, no. 3 (1978), 331-53.

Gutiérrez, Gustavo. "Freedom and Salvation: A Political Problem", in *Liberation and Change.* Edited by Ronald H. Stone. Atlanta: John Knox Press, 1977, pp. 1-94.

_____. "Notes on a Theology of Liberation", *Theological Studies,* XXXI (1970), 243-61.

_____. "Liberation and Development", *Cross Currents* (Summer 1971), 243-56.

_____. "Liberation Praxis and Christian Faith", in Gibellini, R., ed. *Frontiers of Theology in Latin America.* Maryknoll, New York: Orbis Books, 1979, pp. 1-33.

Haight, Roger, "Grace and Liberation: An Interpretation of History", *Thomist* (October 1978), 539-81.

_____. "Institutional Grace and Corporate Spirituality", *Spirituality Today,* XXXI (Spetember 1979), 209-20; 324-34.

_____. Mission: The Symbol of Understanding the Church Today", *Theological Studies* (December 1977), 620-49.

_____. "The Suppositions of Liberation Theology", *Thought,* LVIII, no. 299 (June 1983), 158-69.

Hennelly, A. "Courage with Primitive Weapons", *Cross Currents,* XXVIII (Spring 1978), 8-19.

_____. "Theological Method: The Southern Experience", *Theological Studies,* XXXVIII (December 1977), 709-35.

Herzog, J.A. "Liberation Hermeneutics as Ideology Critique?" *Interpretation,* XXVIII (October 1974), 387-403.

Laishley, J. "The Theology of Liberation", *The Way,* XVII (July 1977), 217-28; (October 1977), 301-11.

Lamb, Matthew. "The Theory-Praxis Relationship in Contemporary Christian Theologies", *Catholic Theological Society of America Proceedings,* XXXI (1976), 149-69.

Lonergan, Bernard. "A Transition from a Classicist World View to Historical Mindedness", in *Law for Liberty*. Edited by James E. Biechler. Baltimore: Helicon, 1967, pp. 126-33.

_____. "The On-Going Genesis of Methods", *Studies in Religion*, VI, no. 4 (1977), 341-69.

_____. "The Origins of Christian Realism", *Theology Digest*, XX (1972), 292-305.

_____. "Theory and Praxis", *Catholic Theological Society of America Proceedings*, XXXII (1977), 1-20.

Moltmann, Jurgen. "An Open Letter to José Miguez Bonino", *Christianity and Crisis*, XXVI (March 29, 1976), 57-63.

O'Conner, June. "Process Theology and Liberation Theology: Theological and Ethical Reflections", *Horizons*, VIII (Fall 1980), 231-47.

Rahner, Karl. "Concerning the Relationship Between Nature and Grace", in *Theological Investigations* I. Baltimore: Helicon Press, 1961, pp. 297-317.

_____. "Christianity and the New Man", in *Theological Investigations* V. Baltimore: Helicon Press, 1966, pp.135-53.

_____. "History of the World and Salvation History", in *Theological Investigations* V. Baltimore: Helicon Press, 1966, pp. 97-114.

_____. "Nature and Grace", in *Theological Investigations* IV. Baltimore: Helicon Press, 1966, pp. 165-88.

_____. "Reflections on the Unity of the Love of Neighbour and the Love of God", in *Theological Investigations* IV. Baltimore: Helicon Press, 1966, pp. 231-49.

_____. "The Theological Concept of 'Concupiscence'", in *Theological Investigations* I. Baltimore: Helicon Press, 1961, pp. 347-82.

_____. "Theological Reflections on the Problem of Seclurization", in *Theological Investigations* X. New York: Herder and Herder, 1973, pp. 318-48.

Ricoeur, Paul. "El conflicto: ¿Signo de contradicción y de unidad? *Selecciones de Teología*, XIII, no. 51, pp. 243-52.

Scannone, Juan Carlos. "La relación teoría-praxis en la teología de la liberación", *Christus*, XL (June 1977), 10-16.

_____. "Necesidad y posibilidades de una teología socioculturamente latinoamericana", in *Fe cristiana y cambio social en América Latina*. Edited by Alfonso Bolado. Salamanca: Sígueme, 1973, pp. 353-72.

_____. "Popular Culture: Pastoral and Theological Considerations in Latin America", *Lumen*, XXXII, no. 2 (1977), 157-74.

_____. "Theology, Popular Culture and Discernment", in Gibellini, R., ed. *Frontiers of Theology in Latin America*. Maryjnoll, New York: Orbis Books, 1979, pp. 213-39.

_____. "The Theology of Liberation - Evangelical or Ideological?", in *Concilium* 93. New York: Herder and Herder, 1974, pp 147-56.

Schillebeeckx, Edward. "Liberation Theology Between Medellín and Puebla", *Theology Digest*, XXVIII (Spring 1980), 3-7.

Sears, Robert. "Trinitarian Love as Ground of the Church", in *Why the Church?* Edited by Walter J. Burghart and William G. Thompson. New York: Paulist Press, 1977.

Sobrino, Jon. "Christian Prayer and New Testament Theology: A Basis for Social Justice and Spirituality", in Fox, Matthew, ed. *Western Spirituality: Historical Roots, Ecumenical Routes.* Norte Dame, Indiana: Fides/Claretian, 1979, pp. 76-114.

_____. "Cristología en discussión: Panel sobre la cristología desde América Latina de Jon Sobrino", *Christus,* XLIII, no 511 (1978), 23-54.

_____. "Derechos humanos, evangelización e ideológica", *Christus,* XLIII, no. 516 (1978), 19-35.

_____. "El conocimiento teológico en la teología europea y latinoamericana", in *Liberación y cautiverio: Debates en torno al método de la teología en América Latina.* Mexico City: Comité Organizador, 1976; *Estudios Centroamericanos,* XXX (1975), 426-45.

Sobrino, Jon. "El Jesus histórico: crisis y desafío para la fe" *Christus,* XL, no. 480 (1975), 6-18.

_____. "Following Jesus as Discernment", in *Concilium* 119. New York: The Seabury Press, 1979, pp. 14-24.

_____. "La conflictividad dentro de la Iglesia", *Christus,* XVII, no. 65 (1978).

Soelle, Dorothee. "Remembering Christ: Faith, Theology and Liberation", *Christianity and Crisis,* XXXVI, no. 10 (June 1976), 136-41.

Vidales, Raul. "Evangelización y liberación popular", in *Liberación y cautiverio: Debates en torno al método de la teología en América Latina.* Mexico City: Comité Organizador, 1976, pp. 209-33.

_____. "Methodological Issues in Liberation Theology", in Gibellini, R., ed. *Frontiers of Theology in Latin America.* Translated by John Drury. Maryknoll, New York: Orbis Books, 1979, pp. 34-57.

Index

155